National Bicentennial Aboriginal and
Torres Strait Islander Programme

Published for the Australian Bicentennial with special assistance from the
Aboriginal and Torres Strait Islander Programme of the
Australian Bicentennial Authority

Plate 1. *Marou Mimi, a significant Eastern Islands leader during the Second World War*

Torres Strait Islanders: custom and colonialism

JEREMY BECKETT

Department of Anthropology, University of Sydney

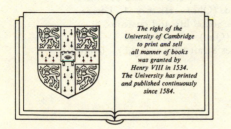

The right of the
University of Cambridge
to print and sell
all manner of books
was granted by
Henry VIII in 1534.
The University has printed
and published continuously
since 1584.

CAMBRIDGE UNIVERSITY PRESS

Cambridge

New York New Rochelle Melbourne Sydney

Published by the Press Syndicate of the University of Cambridge
The Pitt Building, Trumpington Street, Cambridge CB2 1RP
32 East 57th Street, New York, NY 10022, USA
10 Stamford Road, Oakleigh, Melbourne 3166, Australia

First published 1987

Printed in Australia

British Library cataloguing in publication data

Beckett, Jeremy.
Torres Strait Islanders: custom and colonialism
1. Ethnology – Australia – Torres
Strait Islands (Qld.)
I. Title
994.38   GN671.T6

Library of Congress cataloguing in publication data

Beckett, Jeremy.
Torres Strait Islanders: custom and colonialism
Bibliography.
1. Torres Strait Islanders – Social conditions.
2. Queensland – Native races. 3. Australia – Native
races. 4. Acculturation – Australia – Torres Strait
Islands (Qld.) I. Title.
DU125.T67B43   1987   306'.099438   87–6552

National Library of Australia cataloguing in publication data

Beckett, Jeremy.
Torres Strait Islanders: custom and colonialism
Bibliography.
1. Torres Strait Islanders – Social life and customs.
2. Torres Strait Islands (Qld.) – History. 3. Torres
Strait Islands (Qld.) – Social life and customs. 4.
Torres Strait Islands (Qld.). – Politics and
government. 5. Torres Strait Islands (Qld.) – Colonial
influence. I. Title.
994.3'8

ISBN 0 521 33361 X

BO

For Simeon and Sophy,
and in memory of Marou, Solomon, Mota,
John, Napairie, Isau and Francis

Contents

Plates

With the exception of Plates 5 and 9, all illustrations are the author's own.

Maps

Preface

Torres Strait has an established place in the history of anthropology because of its association with the Cambridge University expedition of 1898 (Gathercole 1976). Its leader, Alfred Cort Haddon, had acquired his interest in the subject while conducting research in marine zoology there in 1888 and he returned ten years later, with a team that included the anthropologist C.G. Seligman, the linguist Sidney Ray, the psychologist William McDougal and the physical anthropologist C.S. Myers. W.H. Rivers, perhaps the most distinguished of the party, 'discovered' kinship in the course of psychological investigations, and may be said to have begun his career in anthropology at this time (Langham 1981:64–9). The findings of the expedition, including ethno-musicology, dance, colour perception and ethno-astronomy, as well as material culture, social organization and religion, appeared under Haddon's editorship over the next thirty-seven years, in the six large and profusely illustrated volumes of the Cambridge Reports.

Writing in his introduction to the final volume, Haddon summed up what had been for him a lifetime's work:

> Since 1888 I have consistently tried to recover the past life of the islanders, not merely in order to give a picture of their former conditions of existence and their social and religious activities, but also to serve as a basis for an appreciation of the changes that have since taken place. It has generally been acknowledged by me that ethnologists should study the existing conditions of backward societies, but to interpret these it is first necessary to know from what they have originated and then to trace the successions of new contacts and their influences on the people. I must leave it to another to describe this metamorphosis. (Haddon 1935:xiv)

When I first went to Torres Strait in 1958, some sixty years after the Cambridge expedition and forty-five years after Haddon's last visit, it was in effect to take up the task that he had left for his successors. He had already reviewed much of the published information on the early years of contact in the final volume (1935), and included passing observations of the contemporary scene here and there through the Cambridge Reports, and in his popular account, *Headhunters, Black, White and Brown* (1901). But of course much had happened since that time. Already by 1898 the Islanders had been in contact with Europeans for more than a century, and had experienced thirty years of Anglo-Australian colonialism. They were now about to come under the more rigorous regime of Queensland's official Protectors of Aborigines. In 1958, although the island communities enjoyed a considerable degree of local autonomy, this regime was still in force. However it was on the verge of fundamental changes that were to see Islanders acquiring the rights of Australian citizens, and settling in considerable numbers on the mainland. Since the early 1970s Australia has both intensified and diversified its intervention in the affairs of Islanders and Aborigines, giving rise to conditions that I term welfare colonialism. Inevitably, with these changes the culture of the Torres Strait Islanders has also changed, to the point where much that Haddon and his colleagues recorded is forgotten. But their sense of identity is sustained by the practice of island custom which, implicitly and at times explicitly, proclaims continuity with the Torres Strait of Haddon's day and beyond.

As my sub-title indicates, this book is the work of an anthropologist with historical inclinations. However it cannot, as in earlier years, be written with only a scholarly or official readership in mind. All Islanders are in some degree literate, secondary education is general among the younger generation, and there is a small but growing number who have tertiary training. Some of these have read the Cambridge Reports, and they will no doubt see what I have written here. Since they tend to be historically minded I think that they may find some value in having information about their past brought together within the covers of one book. At the same time, they may be uneasy about having the affairs of their communities exposed to view. Except for a few leaders well known within Australia, publicity is a novel experience. Entering an island community is more like entering someone's house in Western society; simply by being there one comes to know things that would not otherwise reach the out-side world, and discretion is the duty of one who has accepted hospitality. One solution to this problem would have been to use pseudonyms, but such disguises are transparent and give the impression that the actors have something to hide. I have pre-ferred to identify the individuals and communities described in this book, while striving to achieve a balance between a faithful presentation of the facts as I understand them, and respect for the sensitivities of those concerned. I believe that the Islanders' experiences of the last hundred years and more have a universal quality that makes them worth communicating to others, not least their own descendants. However, I want to emphasize that my intention is to convey understanding of those experiences, not to pass judgement on the actors or what they did.

I went to Torres Strait at the suggestion of Mervyn Meggitt, then a lecturer in anthropology at Sydney University. As a research scholar of the Australian National University I carried out twenty-four months of field research, over the years 1958 to 1961, mainly on Murray, Badu and Saibai Islands. In 1964 I com-pleted a PhD dissertation under the supervision of Professors John Barnes and W.E.H. Stanner (Beckett 1964). Since that time I have made four return visits to Torres Strait, the most recent in 1985, and several short visits to Islander communities on the mainland, all with assistance from the University of Sydney.

The Queensland Sub-Department of Native Affairs, now called the Department of Community Services, gave me the initial permission to conduct research, allowed me to go where I wished, and assisted me with transportation and many other necessities. The Anglican Diocese of Carpentaria also helped on several occasions. On recent visits the Commonwealth Depart-ment of Aboriginal Affairs has been helpful in a number of ways. Although it is probably invidious to single out individuals, I would like to record my particular gratitude to the government teachers, the late P.R. Frith and Mrs Frith, and to Arthur and Vicky Woodward, for their friendship and hospitality. I must also acknowledge an enormous debt to John Scott, Area Officer for the DAA. Though he has been living in Torres Strait for more than twenty years, his interest in the place, the people and their history has remained fresh and lively, and I take his opinions very seriously.

To give adequate acknowledgement to the Islanders who have

helped me in my work would take many pages, and a mere listing of their names would scarcely indicate the gratitude I feel for their kindness and generosity towards a guest whom they had not invited. I must first express my thanks to the councils of Murray, Badu and Saibai, who not only allowed me to live amongst them, but assisted me far beyond the call of duty. I must also record my gratitude to those who took me into their homes, including the Reverend Asai Baruna and the late Ruth Baruna, the late Solomon Nona and Irad Nona, Pilemon Nona and his wife, Wilfred Tapou and his wife, the late Napairie Morseo and Olive Morseo, the Warusam family, and George and Jenny Mye. With George Mye I have enjoyed a friendship extending over twenty-five years, and despite his many official commitments he has not spared himself with advice and knowledge. With Sam Passi too I have passed many hours, exploring the borderlands between Meriam and European culture. Without knowing Sam Passi one cannot understand Murray Island. But I must also recall the friendship of the Mast family, the Tapous, the Isua brothers, Iopili Panuel, Luna Neliman, Joe Mairu, Marriott Mabo, Koiki Mabo, Gobeda Noah, George Passi, Emeni Mundy. Even this list is not complete, and I must ask the pardon of those whom I remember with affection but cannot find space to include.

I began writing this book in 1980, while a visiting fellow at the City University of New York's Graduate Center. The discussions that I had with colleagues there, and at the Columbia University Anthropology colloquium, were of great help in clarifying the problems that confronted me. In the later stages of writing a number of colleagues have helped with comments on chapters or sections of the book, and I must record my thanks to Brian Fegan, Maureen Fuary, Edward Hansen, Margaret Jolly, Mervyn Meggitt and Aram Yengoyan. I am particularly grateful to both Sheila Shaver who, with her understanding of the welfare state, helped me to develop my concept of welfare colonialism, and to John Scott, who has corrected at least some of my errors, and acted as a sounding board for some half-formed ideas.

Last but not least I must acknowledge my thanks to the Secretary of the Anthropology Department at Sydney University, Robyn Wood, for help in many matters, and to Lorraine Howard and Marjorie Fisher for their patience, interest and good humour in typing this manuscript.

Abbreviations

AD	Queensland Aboriginals Department
ADC	Commonwealth Aboriginal Development Commission
Age	*Age* Newspaper, Melbourne
CM	*Courier-Mail*, newspaper, Brisbane
CPA	Queensland Chief Protector of Aboriginals
DAA	Commonwealth Department of Aboriginal Affairs
DAIA	Queensland Department of Aboriginal and Islander Advancement
DCS	Queensland Department of Community Services
DNA	Queensland Sub-Department of Native Affairs
IIB	Queensland Government Island Industries Board
LMS	London Missionary Society
NAC	National Aboriginal Committee, also National Aboriginal Conference
NACC	National Aboriginal Consultative Committee
NADC	Commonwealth Government Northern Australia Development Commission
PS &	Queensland Parliament Royal Commission into the
BMC	Pearl Shell and Beche-de-Mer Industry of 1907
QYB	Queensland Year Book
SMLB	Somerset Magistrate's Letter Book
SMH	*Sydney Morning Herald*, newspaper
TSLI	Torres Strait Light Infantry Battalion
Tribune	Weekly newspaper published by the Communist Party of Australia in Sydney
TN	*Torres News*, occasional newspaper Thursday Island

I A 'tombstone opening' and the problem of island custom

In the Christmas of 1976 more than one hundred Melanesian Australians returned to their home on Murray Island, at the easternmost end of Torres Strait. They had come from the towns and cities of north Queensland, from the pearl culture stations of the Northern Territory, and from the new mining towns of Western Australia to celebrate the interment of a kinsman. Gelam had died at Rockhampton, where his children lived, but he had spent most of his life on Murray and the family wanted him to be buried there. His ashes had to wait several years until the money could be raised and his far-flung kindred assembled to accompany him on his last journey. With them they brought an inscribed tombstone, the 'opening' or unveiling of which would mark the end of mourning. It was usual for several years to elapse between the death and the opening ceremony, leaving time for grief to abate. So there was nothing unseemly about the festive character of the occasion or the feasting and dancing that would follow. The kinsfolk would give the dead man his due and, with this 'last goodbye', return with easy minds to the business of living.

The family had quietly interred the ashes some days before and, in a private ceremony, had linked hands to form a chain behind the two men who mounted the tombstone in its cement base. Along with two other tombstones that would be unveiled at the same time, it was now draped with yards of bright cotton cloth and surrounded by a fence from which hung shredded palm leaves and paper Christmas decorations. The Anglican priest, himself a Meriam (as the Murray Islanders call themselves), led the company in prayer and blessed the stone. Then two elderly relatives of the deceased began to unwind the cloth which, together with the ten dollar bills pinned to it, would be their payment for this service. While they worked, the onlookers sang an old Meriam hymn such as the dead man would have heard from childhood.

This done, a cousin who had come up from Townsville delivered a short speech in a mixture of Meriam and English. He recalled the main events of Gelam's career, giving particular importance to his service in the Torres Strait Light Infantry during the Second World War and explaining how this had won for Islanders the 'wonderful freedom' they now enjoyed on the mainland. By the time he had finished night was falling, and we made our way to the other end of the village where a feast had been prepared. On long trestle tables under the trees were bowls of turtle meat and eggs, fish stewed in coconut cream, tinned meat, rice, damper bread cooked in an earth oven, and huge pots of tea. After a brief speech of welcome, some two hundred people sat down to eat, and an hour later we were all sitting around on mats, waiting for the dancing to begin.

The visitors were to compete against a home team, and we could hear the sounds of last-minute rehearsal not far off in the darkness, punctuated by the crack of beer cans being opened. But following the 'island time' of countless jokes, it was almost midnight before the drums began to sound and fifty men trooped into the circle of light and began forming ranks on the dancing ground. Dressed alike in short red waist cloths, called *lavalavas*, and white singlets, with coloured scarves around their heads, they moved into the first set of coordinated movements that characterize 'island dance' throughout Torres Strait. After an hour or so the dancers and audience were getting into the swing of things. The stamping grew heavier and the leaps lighter. The air was full of whoops and ear-splitting whistles. In the breaks, women went round the dancers with mugs of water, shaking talcum powder over their sweating shoulders till they turned white. Old women jumped up and clowned to gales of laughter. On any big occasion the dancers 'go for daylight', and these must make the most of their time for the boat was due to return the next day.

Among the visitors were a number who had not been back to Murray for many years. Their brief visit recreated for a few days the vital community that had existed up to the early 1960s, when the sons of Gelam and many others had emigrated in search of better economic and social opportunities. What they left behind was a rump, numbering a little over three hundred, with more than its share of the very old and the very young.

Plate 2. A tombstone is blessed: Father Seriba Sagigi

A short history of island custom

These events could have taken place with only minor variations in any one of the thirteen other Torres Strait Islander communities in the Strait, in the administrative and commercial centre on Thursday Island, or in urban settings such as Townsville,where Islanders were present in force. They were manifestations of what Islanders call 'island custom'. Asked to describe it, they would probably first cite their dancing and music, and their way of celebrating important occasions such as tombstone openings or Christmas. But they would also have in mind a certain ordering of relations among themselves, usually in the idiom of kinship. Island custom stands in a contrapuntal relationship to 'white man custom', something that is appropriate for Islanders and inappropriate for Europeans, as for example dancing. Alternatively, it may be something that is appropriate only in their own domain, like the *lavalava* men wear at home, in preference to the trousers they put on for town. There has long been a protocol for receiving visiting dignitaries 'island fashion', and nowadays Islanders on the mainland display what they call their 'culture' in festivals of multi-culturalism. There are a few who make their living as dancers. But this is not yet what Blanca Muratorio has called 'alienated folkloric consciousness' (1980:51); it is rather the outward aspect of a way of life that they maintain primarily for their own satisfaction. Island custom is a lived and living culture, strong enough to survive not only a succession of changes in its original environment, but also transplanting; a culture capable of taking on new meanings and functions.

Like the *costumbre* of the Meso-American Indians[1] and much of the *kastom* of the Pacific Islands[2], island custom is traditional primarily in the sense of being distinctive to a stable, long established, closely knit and self-conscious society. Historically it is a thing of shreds and patches, many of which have come from other places over the last century or so.

This is not to suggest that nothing survives from the period before Europeans invaded Torres Strait. Judith Fitzpatrick-

---

[1]   There is a voluminous literature on the *costumbre* of the Meso-American Indians. I have found Kay Warren's *Symbolism of subordination* (1978) of particular interest.

[2]   For an overview of *kastom* in post-independence Melanesia, see Keesing and Tonkinson, 1982.

Nietschmann (1980b) has shown, for example, that the structures underlying the modern ritual of tombstone opening are those of the old mortuary rites. There is the same idea that the spirits linger about the living after death, and that their separation must be effected through ritual treatment of their remains, some time after the first disposal. The division of ritual labour is also unchanged, as are the gifts that conclude the affair. But the old mortuary rites included mummification on some islands and preservation of the skull on others, practices that were abandoned in the 1870s when the Islanders converted to Christianity. Some time later the rites were reconstituted in a form acceptable to the authorities, to be performed on consecrated ground with a priest officiating. However, the feasting, the singing and the dancing are all local adaptations of forms brought in by Polynesians and Melanesians who came to work in Torres Strait during the second half of the nineteenth century. According to Anna Shnukal,

> 'Torres Strait Broken' was brought to Torres Strait by the South Sea Islanders who spoke a pidgin that had developed in the Pacific region during last century . . . It was a lingua franca for the different language groups who worked in the marine industry in Torres Strait, but became a creole in Torres Strait around the turn of the century, first on Darnley and Stephen Islands and a little later on St. Paul's Mission, acquiring as native speakers the children of the South Sea men and their Torres Strait Island wives. (Shnukal pers. comm.; also 1983a, 1983b)

It is now the vernacular on Thursday Island and, in modified form, on the Australian mainland.

The foreign presence dates back one hundred and twenty years. Torres Strait was discovered for Europe as early as 1606, but contacts were brief and infrequent until the foundation of the Australian colony in 1788, when it became a regular seaway. Even then the passing vessels did not disrupt the established way of life, though they disturbed it violently on more than one occasion. During the 1860s, however, numbers of small vessels, owned by Europeans but manned by South Sea Islanders and Asians, came to exploit pearl shell and trepang (*beche-de-mer*). At about the same time the Queensland Government was bringing the region into its sphere of influence and under its jurisdiction. Then in 1871 the London Missionary Society began the work of conversion in this latest of unevangelized fields. By 1877 there was a small but thriving settlement on Thursday Island, with a miniature official and military establishment, and a motley assemblage of peoples and nationalities, brought thither by the developing marine industry. When the Cambridge anthropological expedition arrived in 1898 the Melanesians, whose savage civilization they had come to study, were already devout churchmen, loyal subjects of Queen Victoria and participants in the international division of labour. Today, more than half the estimated 16,000 Torres Strait Islanders live (like Gelam's kinsmen) on the Australian mainland.

Emigration to the mainland is a development of the last twenty-five years. For the preceding century, the Islanders had lingered on the periphery of the modern world, providing its garment industries with the shell for making buttons, yet still planting bananas and hunting turtle for their food. It is this latter feature that differentiates them from most mainland Aborigines. Conquest was not for them a catastrophe that left them dispossessed of their land and deprived of their traditional means of livelihood. Rather, through a coincidence of commercial and government policies, they were confined to their islands as a labour reserve, dependent on certain commodities yet able if need be to maintain themselves by subsistence activities.

The Islanders, restricted in their movements, were not left alone. First missionaries and later government officials reconstructed and managed their communities along lines deemed appropriate to their new status as Christians and British subjects. They had no option but to go along with these changes, but they were not necessarily averse to them. Longtime traders, the good things of life had always come to them from faraway places, and white people had some very good things. Accepting one thing, however, committed them unwittingly to others that they might rather have done without, in a process that got increasingly out of their control.

They nevertheless attempted to reassert control, mitigating in some degree the effects of dependence and domination. According to the old myths, their ancestors subjected the fetishes brought in from other places to a process of 'domestication', integrating them into the local structures without denying their exotic origins. In the same way, latter day Islanders domesticated not only the songs and dances they adopted from the South Sea people, but also the diving boats, the church and government, weaving them about with customary practices and organizing them along customary lines. Thus island custom became, to adapt the title of Eugene Genovese's 1974 study of slavery, *Roll, Jordan, Roll: The World the Slaves Made*.

Colonial authority made no objection to island custom. While it suppressed practices it found offensive, it did not expect Islanders to become like white people, but rather to live in a manner appropriate to their presumed stage of cultural evolution. Thus government and church saw no harm in extending their patronage to island festivals.

Islanders at first found this patronage gratifying, but later they began to wonder if it was not rather patronizing. The island custom, by which they had lived without thought for so long, now became problematical. Was it not so much a statement of difference as of inferiority? Was this, after all, a way of life appropriate to Christians and Australian citizens who wanted to be considered 'civilized'? Yet how could people reject the practices that had formed the fabric of their daily lives? Could island custom not perhaps be reconstituted in such a way as to free it of its colonial associations? This was the conclusion that Gelam's kinsfolk had reached, when they made their way back to Murray – but only after a long period of uncertainty and painful experience.

Understanding island custom

Island custom also poses a problem for the social scientist, for it is amenable to two modes of analysis, which I shall somewhat arbitrarily designate as political economy and anthropology.

Anthropology began as the study of 'primitives' through the technique of intensive fieldwork. Dedicated to the understanding of non-Western peoples, its weakness was that it disregarded external linkages to isolate a 'culture' suspended in space and time. According to Eric Wolf's critique, 'a methodological unit of enquiry was turned into a theoretical construct by assertion, a priori' (1982:14). Anthropology has nevertheless tended to carry these constructions over into the study of 'ex-primitives', conceptually isolating peoples who are indisputably part of mass industrial society.

Political economy, in any case, has little use for the anthropologist's 'local knowledge'. It assumes a capitalist world system that penetrates into the remotest places and transforms all that it touches. Institutions, however bizarre, are no longer expressions of other traditions but instruments of *force majeure.* Other cultures, however exotic, are no more than false consciousness, to be seen through but not seen.

Fieldwork does not absolve the anthropologist from considering global forces; rather should it provide a particular perspective on them, as they are experienced by a particular group of people in a particular socio-cultural setting. The task is to analyse the ways, great and small, in which this setting mediates the global forces that bear upon it, redistributing their effects and transforming their meanings – even as it is itself being transformed.

The highlands of Papua New Guinea provide a convenient illustration. During the early years of colonization, highland men were prepared to work for Europeans in return for shells, which they used in ceremonial exchange. By suddenly increasing the flow of shells, the employers created an inflation in the gift economy and so, wittingly or not, secured a continued supply of labour. Thus one might say that ceremonial exchange now had the function of reproducing labour for the capitalist system. But one cannot reduce it to this function, for it was simultaneously part of another system of values and relations, with its own 'laws of motion'.[3] This does not mean that the two systems were locked in a frozen embrace. The imposition of peace and the continuing inflation of the shell supply precipitated changes in the indigenous political system, which in turn had consequences for the conduct of colonial government (Feil 1984). Such situations are better understood in terms of what John Comaroff has called the 'dialectics of articulation', a process 'which not only constitutes and transforms all the parties to it, but also constructs the very boundaries between the "internal" and the "external" ' (1984:574).

C. A. Gregory writes of the highlands, 'The essence of the PNG economy is ambiguity. A thing is now a gift, now a

---

[3] Some Marxist scholars have attempted to analyse such problems in terms of the articulation of modes of production (c.f. Foster-Carter 1978). In an earlier article (1977; 1982), inspired by Harold Wolpe's analysis of internal colonialism in South Africa (1975), I attempted to understand Torres Strait in these terms. However, while I was able to clarify the dynamics of the island economies, the articulation model did not enable me to make sense of the government intervention, which has been the all-important factor in Torres Strait. I now consider that a direct comparison of Australia and South Africa is not useful. (For another view, see Hartwig 1978.)

commodity, depending on the social context of the transaction'
(1982:116). Indeed ambiguity is the essential quality of the
institutions and ideas that articulate systems, and it is for this
reason that they become pressure points in times of change.

While colonial Papua New Guinea is readily understood as an
articulation of pre-existing socio-cultural systems, it must also
be understood as an emerging unitary system, characterized by
economic, political and cultural inequality. Viewed in this
frame, the indigenous system takes on an oppositional character
that is at least analogous to that of subordinate groups in more
homogeneous societies. The perpetuation of traditional forms
of sociality and meaning, and the improvising of new forms can
both be understood as means by which people without power
attempt to exert some control over their lives, even if it is only to
choose to do what they have to do anyway. Thus Genovese
writes of slaves in the Caribbean:

> The ways in which slaves, and later freedmen, cooked their
> food, reinterpreted received religious doctrines, organized a
> division of labor in the home, sang songs, worked hard or
> shirked – the ways, big and small, they shaped their own
> lives – provided them with reference points of their own.
> These reference points had strong African antecedents, but
> also drew on Europe, the colonial setting, and above all on
> the immediate plantation community. The slaves ruthlessly
> appropriated to themselves everything they needed and
> could use. The world view they fashioned in consequence
> allowed them to meet the demands of the economic and
> social system without fully becoming its creatures. (1975:73)

Through this astonishing creativity the slaves achieved not just a
corpus of satisfying and meaningful activities, but a domain in
which for a brief time they could be masters of themselves. It is
in this sense that Sidney Mintz speaks of the socio-political
significance of everyday life (1974:32). But while this may have
constituted resistance for the slaves, it could only do so as long as
it constituted accommodation for the slave owners, who
tolerated and even gave it their patronage on this assumption.
Indeed, many of the things out of which the slaves made their
world still 'belonged' to their masters, mediating, in Genovese's
terms, a 'hegemonic ideology' – hegemonic because it compelled
them 'to define themselves within the ruling system even while
resisting its aggression with enormous courage and resourceful-
ness' (1975:77). But meanings are harder to police than codes, so

that it is finally impossible to stop people from reinterpreting received doctrines in the drive to make sense of their experience. Thus while the slaves could look at themselves only in the mirror that their masters gave them, what they saw was not necessarily what their masters intended.

There is, of course, a world of difference between the highlanders, who still controlled the means of the subsistence production by which they mainly lived, surrendering only a narrow segment of themselves to the plantation, and the African slaves who controlled little besides their creativity, and even that only at their masters' pleasure. What they shared was the capacity to reserve an essential part of themselves outside the relations of production and consumption, which constituted the dominant order, and to defend this domain against encroachment. From this base they could project their own meanings and values onto this order, for example by their attribution of externally caused disease to sorcerers within the group, and the consequent search for healing within the same setting.

The highlanders' domain was based in their kin-ordered mode of production; that of the slaves and other such groups is harder to define. Gerald Sider, in an article on Newfoundland fisherfolk, has argued that the capacity of a people to resist domination

> lies, in part, in their cultural unity, and this unity is not based on a common depth of oppression or impoverishment nor, perhaps, even in a shared ideological commitment to oppose oppression, nor, definitely, in shared abstract images, such as ethnic identity. The core of culture lies in how people conceptualize their relations to each other, the claims people make on each other, the deferences towards each other's claims, and the concerns and caring people have for one another. (1980:21)

These relations, Sider explains, 'can be directly stated or denied, or they can be encapsulated in the symbols and rituals of daily life, the cycle of festivals, the ceremonies of birth, initiation, marriage and death, and the symbolic panoplies through which power and domination are imposed and supported or resisted'. However, despite surface appearance that the relations thus represented are abstract and static, they are rather based on 'the actual ties people develop with one another in the course of organizing both the labour of production and daily life, and the social appropriation of the product' (*ibid.*:22). In an earlier article (1976a), Sider describes the decline of mumming in outport Newfoundland, following the replacement of the kinship based fisheries by industrialization, and offers a dismal prognosis for the revival and perpetuation of folk cultures. Persuasive as his argument is, Sider runs close to reducing representation to an epiphenomenon of daily life and so leaving it without a reason for existence.

It seems to me more useful to see the two in a dialectical relationship, allowing for the possibility that representations can, so to speak, survive uprooting, if they can be transplanted in a suitable environment. While the industrial world is littered with the remains of dead and dying folk cultures, there are also instances of traditional institutions becoming re-established in these surroundings. Roger Bastide, discussing the transportation of African slaves to Brazil, writes 'The world of values had been cut off from social reality ... but it had secreted a structure in which it could incarnate itself to make a signifying substance effective' (1978:404). Moreover, people who no longer live or work together have managed to establish new claims and deferences through participation in rituals and festivals, and on this basis mount at least a cultural resistance. The Islanders who returned home for the tombstone opening and, incidentally, resisted the prevailing consumerism to the extent of diverting their earnings to social investment, were sustained by more than simple nostalgia.

The Torres Strait Islanders are exactly comparable with neither the highlanders of Papua New Guinea nor the slaves of the New World. Like both, however, they have devised a body of practices that mediates between them and the global and national systems of which they are a part. What I have called for the sake of simplicity their custom emerged out of the articulation of their kin-ordered mode of production with the Australasian periphery of European capitalism. The articulation was such as to leave them in occupation of their ancestral homes, and to involve them in the cash economy not as individuals but as members of their communities and of an emerging indigenous minority. When the subsistence economy began to erode, the work the Islanders did together in the cash economy and the ways in which their communities were incorporated within the Australian nation state provided a continuing basis for religious observance and festivals; and these activities in turn fortified their cultural and political unity, not only in resisting what they did not want but in pursuing what they did want. Even today, with economic dependence intensified and many living in towns on the mainland, it can be advantageous for Islanders to deal with the state as members of an indigenous minority rather than as citizens, a fact of life that is not irrelevent to the continued existence of an Islander society through the practice of custom.

Colonialism and citizenship

The Torres Strait Islanders today are a self-conscious group that has official recognition as Australia's other indigenous minority. But the reasons why a people who are Australian citizens and Christians, and who live in all parts of the continent, should identify with those who inhabited Torres Strait when Europeans first came there, is by no means self-evident. Culturally, the latter day Islander has changed almost out of recognition. An immediate explanation can be sought in the historical fact that Islanders have experienced this transformation as a collectivity, and have transmitted a sense of it from generation to generation, just as they have transmitted something that, although itself changing, they have long called island custom.

This book will attempt to convey some understanding of this collective experience, but also to explain why it was collective, and how Islanders were able to form and sustain over five generations and more a sense of continuity. Such explanation must be sought in the dynamics of the global system that overtook Torres Strait in the 1860s and has carried the Islanders in its wake ever since; but it will also be sought through an understanding of the traditional communities in which the Islanders, for most of their history, have experienced the world.

The global forces affecting Torres Strait since the 1860s have been various, and have varied over time. But the Queensland Government has generally modified the impact of other forces, and in this century its influence over the Islanders' lives has been paramount. As a consequence, the political mode has been dominant, and the emergent social formation can best be described as colonial.

Colonialism, as the term is used here, refers to the political outcome of European expansion into other quarters of the globe, the process described in Wolf's epic *Europe and the People*

Without History (1982).[4] John Rex has rightly observed that the various empires of this period had their distinctive character (1982:201), but they shared certain common features and could scarcely be understood apart from one another. The motivating force of Europe's expansion was economic and, at least in its later phase, was sustained by the dynamics of capitalism, but in its local manifestations military strategy or the logistics of transportation might be the critical considerations rather than the exploitation of labour and resources or the securing of markets. A colonial order arises when the state which has annexed a territory formally and systematically discriminates between the conquering and subject groups, in such a way as to entrench the differences between them and to foster their economic, political and cultural inequality.[5] This discrimination is sustained by some form of ideology which justifies the domination of the indigenous population in terms of differences of race, mentality, moral qualities, cultural advancement or religion.

Although the term is usually applied to the overseas possessions of some metropolitan country, it has also been applied to the position of peoples brought within national boundaries, as in the case of Britain's 'Celtic fringe' (cf. Hechter 1974), and to the indigenous populations of colonies of settlement, such as Australia (Rowley 1971; Hartwig 1978) and the United States (Bee and Ginderich 1977), which subsequently became independent. But if the alternative for external colonies is sovereignty, what is the alternative for internal colonies? For Rodolfo Stavenhagen, whose writing on Meso-America has done much to establish the concept of internal colonialism[6], it is class. Emphasizing that 'the class character and colonial character of

---

[4] This definition excludes the expansion of communist or pre-capitalist systems into new territory. One would expect there to be some parallels; nevertheless, the dynamics of these systems, and their ideological formations, seem to me to justify separate treatment.

[5] By emphasizing indigenous populations I have excluded from the definition colonial transplanted groups, such as Afro-Americans, East Indians in the Caribbean, and Chicanos in the United States. There are obvious parallels, and both indigenous and immigrant groups are often included within the same system of racial classification; nevertheless, there are important differences in the formation of identity, and the structures of economic exploitation. (But c.f. Barrera 1980.)

[6] Two recent studies have made interesting use of Stavenhagen's formulation: Warren *op. cit.* and Barrera 1980, though the latter is concerned with Chicanos in the United States.

inter-ethnic relations are two intimately related aspects of the same phenomenon', he argues that 'the colonial character of inter-ethnic relations impresses particular characteristics upon class relations, tending to stop their development' (1965:76). Along similar lines, Rex suggests that colonial conditions may prevent the emergence of class struggle (*op. cit.*:200) and give rise to a stratification composed of 'estates' rather than classes (*ibid*:211). These disappear with economic development, so that the interaction of persons holding opposed economic positions becomes increasingly independent of ethnic considerations (*ibid*). Thus, as the labour market expands, the Indian who has been tied to community and kept in 'semi-feudal' dependence on some Ladino patron, becomes free to move as he pleases and sell his labour.

Whatever the situation in Meso-America, colonial relations in the liberal democracies do not stand opposed simply to class relations, but to a complex of political and ideological constructions that are supposed to transcend or compensate for their inequalities. The British sociologist T. H. Marshall grouped these constructions under the heading of citizenship, which he divided into three stages: the civil, the political and the social, the last being broadly conceived as 'the whole range from the right to a modicum of economic welfare and security to the right to share to the full in the social heritage and to live the life of a civilized being according to standards prevailing in the society' (1963:72–4). Tracing the development of citizenship in his native Britain from the eighteenth century, he located the social stage in the twentieth and particularly in the time that he was writing, when the welfare state was entering a new phase of development.

Citizenship followed a similar career in the liberal democracies of North America and Australia which, however, withheld it from their indigenous peoples until after the Second World War. Up to this time Indians and Inuit, along with Aborigines and Torres Strait Islanders, were primarily integrated through colonial structures, sometimes as the clients of employer-patrons, but more often as the wards of missions or the government agencies specially assigned to their management. The establishment of these agencies can be traced to the particular circumstances of colonization. In many instances the incorporation of indigenous population was incidental to other considerations, and the emerging economy had little use for their labour, or else preferred to bring in more tractable labour from elsewhere (cf. Bee and Ginderich 1977:74–5; Beckett 1977:34; Gartrell n.d.:20). When extermination ceased to be politically acceptable, the victims of displacement were left to linger on the margins of society, as a reserve of cheap labour or as paupers. The government agents correspondingly became recruitment agents for labour whose chief virtue was that it was cheap and easily controlled, or dispensers of relief which, like the Poor Law in nineteenth century Britain, was represented as an alternative to citizenship rather than an entitlement of it (Marshall 1963:83). Required to practice strict economy, they were often left otherwise free to follow their own notions of improvement and rehabilitation. Like the theocracies established by Christian missions, their regimes were occasionally imaginative and enlightened, but as often petty despotisms that owed more to the private obsessions of their architects than to the practicalities of adaptation.[7] Their victims, isolated in enclaves of underdevelopment, hampered by official regulations and often excluded by European workers as a threat to working conditions, had little prospect of attaining citizenship through entry into the mainstream of the work force. If citizenship was to be theirs it must come by other routes.

Citizenship first became an issue during the Pacific War, when governments sought to counter the dangers of indigenous disaffection in vulnerable areas such as Arctic North America and northern Australia. Indigenes re-emerged as a political embarrassment during the Cold War when their governments were trying to present themselves to the non-aligned new nations of the Third World as untainted by racism. The indigenous minorities which have come to be known as the Fourth World (Graburn 1981) emerged out of this nexus, with a political leverage out of all proportion to their numbers, exercised through their new-found ability to embarrass their governments before national and international opinion. In the words of Beverley Gartrell:

> What power can a tiny minority wield? Unable to exert material control over the environment of the powerful, it

---

[7] A classic example is provided by the rule of Sir Arthur Grimble in the Gilbert Islands (now called Kiribati), of which Anthony Daniels writes: 'No aspect of life was too trivial or private for Grimble's interference. His ideal was a well-ordered army – or maybe Scout-camp, where everyone obeyed and no one questioned' (Daniels 1983).

can only challenge the self concepts of both bureaucratic and political office-holders, and the citizens of the nation, and appeal to the legal rights institutionalized in an earlier phase. The resulting power is tenuous and fluctuating, for it is based on ideologies themselves changing, and it depends on the receptivity of some audience – elements in the wider society willing to listen to the message being sent by the dominated group. (Gartrell 1986:11–12)

While governments have readily committed themselves to citizenship for their indigenous minorities, the implementation of this goal, particularly in its socio-economic implications, has proved to require more than just the passing of legislation. Nor can the problems be solved simply by making them eligible for the regular benefits provided by the welfare sector to all citizens. What is required is that the state support a comprehensive programme of economic, social and cultural rehabilitation, in addition to the assistance provided through the regular channels of redistribution. As Beverley Gartrell puts it, 'Indigenes can lay claim to payments both in their newly acquired rights as citizens, and in their old status as indigenes eligible for special benefits not open to other citizens'. (*ibid.*:11)

The outcome of the drive to transform indigenous people into citizens has, by an irony, been the rehabilitation of the old colonial structures. Indigenous status takes on new ideological significances and the old administrative apparatus is retooled for new tasks. The formation which, as Gartrell notes (*ibid.*), is found only in wealthy states with very small indigenous populations, has come to be known as welfare colonialism. Robert Paine coined this term in connection with the Canadian north but recognizes that it has wider application. Continuous with classic colonialism, it is solicitous rather than exploitive, and liberal rather than repressive (1977:3). However,

> Any decision taken by the colonizers has a basic flaw: a decision made for the material benefit of the colonized at the same time can be construed as disadvantaging them; a 'generous' or 'sensible' decision can be at the same time, morally 'wrong'. This is so because it is the colonizers who make the decisions that control the future of the colonized; because the decisions are made (ambiguously) on behalf of the colonized, and yet in the name of the colonizers' culture (and of their political, administrative and economic priorities). (*ibid.*:46)

The ideological restraints under which colonialism now has to work oblige it to seek the consent of its clients, giving rise to the need for representation and a new kind of politics.

Welfare colonialism, then, is the state's attempt to manage the political problem posed by the presence of a depressed and disenfranchised indigenous population in an affluent, liberal democratic society. At the practical level it meets the problem by economic expenditure well in excess of what the minority produces. At the ideological level the 'native', who once stood in opposition to the 'settler' and outside the pale of society, undergoes an apotheosis to emerge as its original citizen.

The incorporation of the Torres Strait Islanders within Australian society can be understood in terms of the concepts of colonialism and welfare colonialism as I have set them out in the preceding discussion, but obviously we have to take account of the particular ways in which these formations manifested themselves. The colonization of the Strait was precipitated by strategic considerations as well as the discovery of resources that could be commercially exploited, whereas the labour of the indigenous population was for most of the time under-utilized. The economic penetration of the island economies was thus relatively weak, leaving land, fresh foods and handicrafts outside the domain of commodity exchange. Their further integration with the Australian economy was a consequence of state intervention, primarily through the department set up by the government of Queensland for the management of its Aboriginal and Islander peoples. This department found itself both reconciling and playing off the interests of the regional and metropolitan economies, in the process acquiring a relative autonomy that enabled it in some measure to follow its own logic. As Harvey Feit has observed of government intervention in northern Quebec: 'It is clear that in addition to economic interest, governments are motivated by a range of specifically short-term political, social, and bureaucratic interests, that often lead to policies and programmes whose impacts need to be analysed rather than assumed' (1982:389). Considerations of this kind seem to have led the department to develop a special relationship with the Islanders, administering them through a system of elected councils. This innovation was not only in striking contrast to its autocratic treatment of Aborigines, but without parallel in Australian colonial practice anywhere. From modest beginnings in local government, these councils came to act as intermediary in relations between the Islanders and the outside world, reinforcing the island community as the basic building block in the colonial order.

State intervention took on a very different form during the Pacific War, when Torres Strait came under military control and Islander men were formed into a unit of the armed forces. The issue of citizenship, posed by the wartime emergency and the experience of military service, could not be simply forgotten once the colonial regime had been restored. But it was the combination of a burgeoning Islander population, a declining regional economy, political disaffection and, most powerfully, the opening up of the mainland labour market, that brought citizenship to realization. However, from the late 1960s and particularly from the election of the Whitlam Labor Government, these developments were at least partially reversed by the emergence of welfare colonialism.

In the recent period Islanders have been subject to conflicting pressures. In the Strait their mature representative structures have enabled them to take advantage of the opportunities presented by welfare colonialism, which have been all the better because of the rivalry between the Queensland and Commonwealth governments. Islander identity thus stands vindicated. On the mainland welfare colonialism has less to offer Islanders, who are in any case virtually without representation. Citizenship would seem to provide the most viable mode of integration, were it not for the high levels of unemployment which leave Islanders without the means of supporting this status. In this predicament, the indigenous identity upheld by Islander representatives in the Strait offers at least the possibility of a solution. Reunions such as occurred at Gelam's tombstone opening are thus both symbolic and practical responses.

An anthropological history

What began for me as a conventional field study of Torres Strait quickly slipped into the historical mode. While the setting was the small, long-established island community, physical isolation was belied by profound dependence on the outside world. The forms of this dependence were changing even while the study was in progress, and they had changed repeatedly over the years, producing effects that the community might redistribute but could not deflect. So inured were the Islanders to change that they saw current events in the light of others that had gone before, to construct a seriality that was their history.

They were perhaps predisposed to a sense of history by a mythology that located events in a temporal sequence. Their early indoctrination by missionaries and government teachers with the ideals of spiritual and material progress reinforced this disposition, so that they came to view their place in Australian society and the world at large as an evolution that had begun with the coming of the Gospel and would end with their attainment of material and moral parity with white people. This perspective informed their local politics and it was the equipment their leaders brought to their first meetings with white officials and politicians. It likewise permeated the informal discussions I had with them. While they recognised their final dependence, they thought of themselves as participating in their history. The events of history were thus realized for them in the lives and adventures of themselves and their fellows, and on occasion attributed to the deeds of certain figures who were for them the movers and shakers of Torres Strait.

I might have contented myself with recording the Islanders' contemporary perception of their place in history, but the interaction between events and interpretation that I observed while I was among them impelled me to try to discover what had happened earlier. I went to the archives, first in the hope of filling in the background knowledge which they assumed in their recollections, but which I lacked, and secondly to get a sense of the economic, political and cultural forces that had determined this history. The historical documentation for Torres Strait is voluminous, though not all periods are equally well served. From the 1840s come no fewer than four journals, kept by members of naval surveying parties at a time when the Islanders were still essentially autonomous and self sufficient (Jukes 1847; MacGillivray 1852; Allen 1977; Moore 1979). The 1870s and 1880s, when Europeans were establishing their presence in the region, are also extensively reported in government and mission archives. For later periods we can draw upon government reports which, however, are for long periods taken up with information of a routine character and politically motivated apology. Newspapers yield rare reports on unusual events, but it is only over the last twenty years or so that the region has received more than passing attention. Torres Strait has also featured in occasional travelogues over the years, unfortunately of a uniformly poor and declining quality.

These sources are all primarily concerned with the activities of Europeans who had to do with Islanders, rather than with the Islanders themselves. The latter appear, typically, as either responding gratefully to official leading or as wilfully resisting it. We have some notion of what they did, but little of what they thought. As for the Islanders themselves, though literate from the 1880s, the only writings which they have left us are a few myths, some garden lore and the court books.

For the period around the turn of the century we can consult the writings of A. C. Haddon who visited Torres Strait in 1888 and 1913, as well as 1898, the year of the Cambridge Expedition. Apart from the Reverend William Mcfarlane who made amateur investigations of the traditional culture through the 1920s (Haddon 1935 *passim*) no anthropologist came to Torres Strait until my arrival in 1958.

I have attempted to weave together these sources with the oral record. This consists of much more than the responses given to direct questions. There are the reminiscences that happen to come up in the course of conversation, and these are many for the Islanders are great talkers. And there are the 'yarns' which may retail events within or beyond living memory, but which, because they are in some way interesting, acquire a set form through constant repetition. Such data must be read critically, but as Sydel Silverman has reminded us, the anthropologist's informant is not only a 'myth teller' but also a 'history teller' (1979:419). When checked against the documentary record, some yarns do indeed appear to be myths (see for example chapter IV), but others prove to be accurate, as in the case of the army strike of 1944, discussed in chapter III.

After I finished my initial field study in 1961, Torres Strait Islanders entered into a period of change more radical than anything they had experienced since the establishment of the Australian presence a century earlier. Realization of the magnitude of these changes has impelled me to keep abreast through return visits to the Strait and to the places in north Queensland where Islanders now live. In between times I get news from old friends passing through Sydney and occasional telephone calls.

Recently there has been a further round of anthropological research among Islanders. In the 1970s Bernard Nietschmann

studied dugong hunting (1981) and Judith Fitzpatrick-
Nietschmann studied funerary rites (1980a and b) on Mabuyag,
while Noni Sharp investigated aspects of Islander history (1980;
1981) and Lawrence Cromwell studied the ethnography of
speaking among Islanders in Townsville (1982). In the last few
years, Maureen Fuary has investigated the culture and history of
Yam Island while Anna Shnukal has studied Torres Strait
Broken (1983a,b). These researchers have all been generous
with their time and material, which I have drawn upon in the
final section of this book.

Although my history will survey the entire period of the
Torres Strait Islanders' involvement with the Western World,
from the middle of last century to the present, I have to admit
that my study's centre of gravity lies in the twenty-four months
of anthropological field work I carried out between 1958 and
1961. No doubt this is partly due to the freshness of my early
impressions. I found Torres Strait beautiful and its people
welcoming. I was impressed with the vitality of island custom
and captivated by the music and dancing. But, as it happened, I
had also come at a time of transition. The old colonial regime
was still entrenched, yet the tide was about to turn, and the
people were awaiting it, whether with joy or foreboding.
Queensland was still firmly in control yet, before I left, the
Commonwealth had intervened to give Islanders the vote.
Thursday Island was a town in which black and white scarcely
met outside the course of business, yet 1961 saw a government
employee marry an Island girl. Pearling, the staple industry of
almost a century, was going through an upturn in 1959, but went
into permanent decline after 1960, owing to competition from
plastics. As a direct consequence emigration increased, separating
parents from children and wives from husbands. These changes
caused endless questioning. Would the communities survive,
and if they did, would they still follow island custom? Would the
Sabbath be observed? Would wives be able to divorce their
husbands? Would the free availability of alcohol cause riot and
dislocation? In sum, should Islanders become like white people,
and could they?

These changes were evident wherever I went – and I managed
to visit all but a few very small communities, at least briefly. But
they manifested themselves in different ways from island to
island, for despite an underlying uniformity of culture, each was
caught up in its own dialectic with the world about it. The

contrast was greatest between Badu and Murray Island, and it was on this account that I devoted most of my time to them. With populations of between five and six hundred, they were in many ways the liveliest communities in the Strait, each proud of its reputation. Badu had committed itself to pearling. Murray had opted for politics. The Meriam, one official told me, were the Irish of Torres Strait: with a long tradition of resistance to colonial authority, they had never had much confidence in pearling, winning instead the right to seek work on the mainland. Those at home cultivated their gardens and pressed their representatives to 'fight the government' for more assistance, pending the abolition of the colonial order. Badu's leaders worked within the existing order and, by keeping the community under tight discipline, achieved a considerable success in pearling. They took pride in Badu being 'first' in Torres Strait, and pushed the impending changes to the corners of their minds. The custom that the two communities observed was formally almost identical, but its significance for them, and the ways they used it in their daily lives, differed markedly.

I have been able to trace back the beginnings of this divergence to the early years of the century. Following their subsequent history, I see them continuing along their chosen paths. Badu, though shaken by the collapse of pearling, is now enjoying a new time of prosperity based on cray fishing. Murray, lacking the same opportunities, and more dependent than ever on government aid, still looks for political solutions.

In the next chapter I trace the emergence of the colonial order from its beginnings in the middle of the last century, describing the interaction of government, mission and industry. In chapter III, I continue the story from the outbreak of the Pacific war, documenting the increasing strains to which the old order was subject, up to the collapse of pearling and the beginning of emigration in the 1960s. In chapter IV, Reflections in a Colonial Mirror, I discuss the ways in which Islanders thought about themselves and their situation, using the ideas and values that Europeans had given them. Chapters V and VI follow the careers of Murray Island and Badu over the first hundred years of colonization. Chapter VII describes developments of the last twenty years, the emergence of welfare colonialism in the Strait, bringing new life to its political system, and the growth of an Islander community on the mainland with rather different needs and aspirations. The final chapter describes the implications of these developments for Islanders living on Murray and Badu, as well as in Townsville, and reconsiders the role of island custom in mediating their relationship with the Australian majority and reproducing the structures of Islander society.

II   Pearlers, pastors and Protectors

Every Torres Strait schoolchild knows that history begins on
1 July 1871, with the landing of the London Missionary Society
on Darnley Island. The first landing was not, as some like to
imagine it, a first contact. The people of Darnley had been in
intermittent contact with European vessels at least since Bligh's
voyage of 1792 (Lee 1920:175–8), and they were at the time
involuntary hosts to a European trepanger and a score or so of
his Pacific Island workers, who made free with their gardens and
women (Murray and McFarlane 1871:30–5). The landing did
however inaugurate a new moral order, imposed upon the
Realpolitik of the preceding period. At first the mission also took
responsibility for law and order, since the island had not yet been
annexed. Although in later years Queensland would institute its
own rule, driving out not only trepangers but missionaries, it
would build on the foundations laid by the LMS. The Society's
achievement was to persuade the Islanders to accept not just the
Gospel but the whole colonial experience. In the short run this
meant accepting European authority, but in the long run it
meant taking responsibility for themselves as individuals and
as communities.

Any question of the Islanders taking responsibility for their
lives must be understood in the context of the radical transformation that was in train. Beginning in the mid-nineteenth century,
when Islanders still went naked and hunted for heads, European
expansion proceeded according to its own logic, without regard
for their interests. Torres Strait was never to become a place of
importance in the world, but it became very much a part of the
world. Within a few months of the discovery of pearl shell,
Sydney-based concerns were making good money in the markets
of London and New York, and as the industry prospered it
attracted labour from every quarter of the Pacific basin. The
LMS, directed and funded by British Congregationalists, used as

evangelists recent converts from the Loyalty Islands. Meanwhile the colony of Queensland was annexing the islands, subject to the approval of Her Majesty's Government in Whitehall.

At the outset the Islanders could scarcely conceive of these forces, let alone contend with them. It was a long time before they could get the measure even of their immediate surroundings, and longer still before they could begin to organize effective responses. But in 1936 they mounted a concerted protest against the regime of the Queensland government. Queensland's response was to give more responsibility to the local councils, and it was in one sense a concession (cf. Sharp 1980), but it was made in the realization that they no longer had to be coerced into meeting the basic requirements of orderly government. The way to win their cooperation was to trust them more. From the Islanders' point of view, cooperation was the price they paid for regaining a measure of control over their lives.

Before the Europeans

We do not know when the islands of Torres Strait were first settled, but the logs of the Torres expedition of 1606 report the presence of natives who were black, and who had turtle shell masks, outrigger canoes and bows (Hilder 1980:74-7). There can be little doubt that these were the ancestors of today's Torres Strait Islanders.

The strategic location of the islands between Melanesia and Aboriginal Australia has given them a particular importance for the ethnologist, as stepping stones in a two-way genetic and cultural traffic. The indigenous tradition that they were settled from Papua is supported by the Islanders' physical appearance, particularly the characteristic 'frizzy' hair. The language of eastern Torres Strait, which linguists formerly called Miriam and Islander linguists now render as Meriam Mir, is a member of the eastern Trans-Fly family. However, while the language spoken on the other islands — formerly called Mabuiag and now Kala Lagaw Ya on Mabuyag islands and Kalaw Kawaw Ya on Saibai — includes Melanesian elements, its structure is Aboriginal. This may indicate a merging of Papuan and Aboriginal peoples at some time in the past (Wurm 1972:364-9). In material culture, the Papuan influence was again dominant, though some Islanders used the mainlanders' spear thrower (Haddon 1912:196). But trade with Papua was much more important than with Australia, in particular that to secure the dugouts from which the Islanders made their canoes (Haddon 1904:295; 1908:186-7). Since there was no suitable timber on the islands, Papua may be said to have underwritten the island economy. And yet the Torres Strait Islanders had devised their own distinctive way of life. Their great oceangoing canoes, up to twenty metres in length, and equipped with double outriggers and a distinctive form of rigging (Haddon 1912; Moore 1979 *passim*), enabled them to exploit a much wider range of resources than either Papuans or Aborigines.

In all there are more than one hundred islands in the Strait. Most of them are very small and many lack drinking water, so that while they can be exploited for some resources, they can not be occupied for any length of time. The total population at contact was probably between four and five thousand, dispersed among a score of communities that ranged from above eight hundred to below one hundred.[1] Each community directly exploited a constellation of islets, reefs and sandbanks within easy reach of its home base, and a much larger region, including the two mainlands, indirectly through trade.

The Torres Strait region offers a considerable variety of resources and physical features, which need be only briefly described here. (But see Haddon 1935; Walker 1972.) The waters are a labyrinth of coral reefs, gradually increasing in depth from west to east, and subjected to alternating currents from the Coral and Arafura seas, with the annual shift from the southeast to the northwest trade winds. The islands are of four types.

1. Small, high volcanic islands with relatively fertile soil and dense vegetation. These are all located at the eastern end of the Strait within sight of the Great Barrier Reef, and include the Murray group (Mer, Dauar and Waier), Darnley and Stephens Islands.[2]

[1] Population at contact – bearing in mind that contact occurred much earlier for some islands than for others – can only be a matter of approximations. The present figure is based on a revision of my earlier estimate (Walker 1972:311) based on Harris' figures for the Western Islands (Harris 1979:87-92).

[2] Naming the islands presents a problem since all except Saibai were renamed by Europeans during the early years of exploration. But while some of the new names displaced the old (for example Prince of Wales for Muralag), others did not (for example Boigu is almost never called Talbot Island even by Europeans). As far as possible I have followed local usage. The orthography of the indigenous names has in some instances been revised but while Mabuyag seems to have replaced the standard Mabuiag, Baduans have not yet begun to render their island as Badhu. Again I have tried to follow local usage.

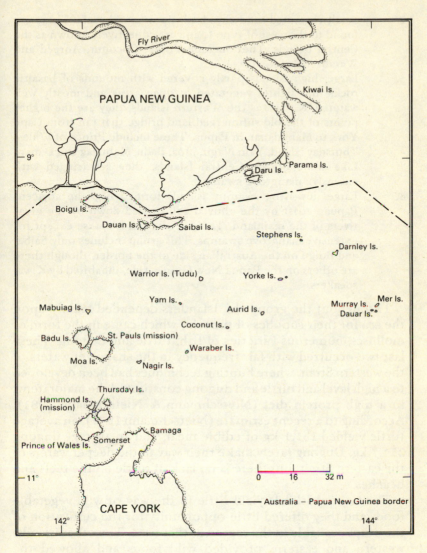

Map 1. Torres Strait

2.   Small vegetated sand cays built up on coral reefs. These are found to the west of type 1, and are collectively known as the Central Islands. They include Yorke, Coconut, Aureed and Waraber Islands.

3.   Large, high islands partly covered with mounds of basaltic rocks, but lightly vegetated in open areas and mostly well watered. Known as the Western Islands, they are the higher points of the old submerged land bridge that ran from Cape York to Mabudauan in Papua. These include Prince of Wales, Thursday Island, Yam Nagir, Moa, Badu, Mabuyag and Dauan. Like some of the Central Islands, they are fringed with extensive mangrove swamps.

4.   Large, low-lying swampy islands formed like the adjacent Papuan coast by the alluvial soil carried down by the great rivers of the mainland. Their vegetation is sparse except for extensive mangrove swamps. This group includes only Saibai and Boigu on the Australian side of the border, though there are others on the Papua New Guinea side, inhabited by Kiwai speakers.

Throughout the group the Islanders depended mainly upon the sea for their supplies of protein, which came in the form of molluscs, numerous varieties of fish, turtle and dugong. These last two occurred with fair frequency in the shallower waters of the western Strait, where hunting techniques had been developed to a high level and turtle and dugong constituted the major items in a high protein diet (Nietschmann & Nietschmann 1981). According to a recent estimate (Nietschmann 1977), an average turtle yielded 131.1 kg of edible meat, and an average dugong 254.7 kg. Dugong rarely make their way to the deeper waters of the eastern Strait, but there is no lack of turtle on the reefs and beaches.

The Central Islands yield little in the way of wild vegetable foods and they offered little opportunity for the cultivation of the crops available in the region at that time. The other islands, western and eastern, provided wild foods and allowed the cultivation of bananas and various root crops.[3] Each community worked out its own combination of hunting, fishing, gardening

---

[3]   Among cultivated crops, yams seem to have been the most important; taro could only be grown on some islands. There is some uncertainty about sweet potato, which some writers have assumed to have been long established in the Strait. However, the Islanders' use of the Polynesian name *kumala* suggests to me that it may have been introduced, as varieties of banana and yam seem to have been. Information regarding the various wild roots and aroids is incomplete, but see Harris 1977.

and foraging, partly in response to local conditions but also to other factors such as population density and the possibility of trade. The Central Islanders, having few terrestial resources, voyaged far and wide in search of things to eat and to trade. In the small, fertile, densley populated Eastern Islands, the people put their emphasis on gardening. The Westerners emphasised hunting, each using surplus produce to exchange for things that were scarce.[4] In Papua one could get a canoe hull for turtle and dugong, or alternatively, for conus armshells and human heads taken in war (Haddon 1904:295; 1908:186-7; Moore 1979:303). During the proto-colonial period, islands located along the sealanes got iron from passing vessels or from wrecks, some of which they then put into the trading networks (Moore 1979:303). Other trade items included stone for adzes and clubs – a scarce item in this region – ironwood for spears, and 'luxuries' such as drums and bird-of-paradise plumes.

Non-material items, such as songs, dances, magical spells and objects, and perhaps whole cults (c.f. Haddon 1908:42-4), were transmitted along these same routes. Occasionally women and children featured in the traffic. Women were also abducted on raids (Haddon 1904:300) and occasionally cult objects were taken, although the regular prizes were human heads, used for divination or to enhance the power of some shrine (Haddon 1935:346).

Just as the island economy depended on its trading connections, so the island culture was enriched and enlivened by these importations. Correspondingly, the Islanders regarded their overseas connections as extensions of the relations they maintained within their communities, and conducted them in the idiom of kinship, totemism and cult membership. Each community was segmented into a number of patrilineal descent groups in a manner that is broadly characteristic of southern Papua (cf. chapters V and VI). Each group had a name and was associated with a place and perhaps a shrine and, in the case of the Central and Western Islanders, with a totem. But these groups emerged only occasionally in the performance of rituals, or as the units within which marriage was prohibited. Marriage itself, and the exchanges of gifts that occurred through the lives of the couple, mobilized the respective kinsfolk of husband and

---

[4] There is a copious literature on trade in Torres Strait: for the main sources see Haddon 1904:295; 1908:186-7; McCarthy 1939; Moore 1979; Harris 1979.

Plate 3. The Malu–Bomai rites re-enacted on Murray Island

wife. Although, formally, the wife passed from her own family to
her husband's, the rules of residence left the couple to follow
their personal preferences.

The documentary sources do not allow us to form more than a
vague impression of island life in pre-colonial times, and no
doubt there were important variations, for example between the
semi-nomadic Prince of Wales Islanders and the sedentary
Meriam. However, the rich body of myths, folktales and
traditions suggests that the fear of violent death was never far
from people's minds. Warfare was a major preoccupation, while
headhunting occupied a place of central importance in their
cultural and religious life (Haddon 1904:298-319; 1908:189-91;
1935:343-7). Certain communities were hereditary enemies,
and between them there was the constant possibility of surprise

attack. Even contacts between friends were never wholly free of risk. Within the community there was perhaps more combative display than actual fighting, but there was a lively fear of sorcery. Yet despite the violence and suspicion there was a frequent coming together for trade and ritual, and also for dancing and amusement.

Underlying all this, particularly among the men, was a continuing quest for supernatural power – a concept that is articulated as *sasirim* in Meriam Mir and *parapar* in the Western language. Each individual had his own secret store of magic to help him in gardening, hunting, sailing, amorous adventures and so on. A smaller number, probably, had powers that were believed to affect the lives of others, through control of the elements or the increase of plants and animals, or through the ability to inflict sickness and death. The sorcerer who had *maid* was indeed possessed of a need to kill, even his own kin (Haddon 1904:321–3; 1908:322–6).

Of greater social significance, however, were those who had gained control over the access to some fetish, which was always of exotic origin. In a number of instances, these fetishes became the focus of major cults that provided the inspiration for headhunting raids.[5] How these cults formed we cannot tell, but as in other parts of Melanesia (Brunton 1975) they carried the custodians of the fetishes to positions of political ascendancy.

The coming of the missionaries and the imposition of the Pax Australiana put an end to warfare, the old cults and much else besides. The fighting men had to go in search of other trophies, the sorcerers had to retreat into the shadows, and the seekers after power had to find new resources to monopolize. At the same time, the establishment of new ties of economic and cultural dependence with Europeans required the learning of a new social idiom. Initially, as in other parts of Oceania, Islanders believed that the white strangers were ghosts of the dead, and individuals were sometimes claimed as returned kinsfolk (Moore 1979:143,146). But most Europeans did not understand or did not respond to such overtures. Similarly, attempts to establish ties through the giving of women were soon frustrated by official disapproval of such liaisons. Islanders had thus to divide their

[5] See for example the accounts of the Kwoiyam cult on Mabuyag (Haddon 1904:367-73), those of Sigai and Maiau on Yam (Haddon 1904:373-78), Malu-Bomai on Mer (Haddon 1908:281-313), and Adhi Buiya on Saibai (Lawrie 1970:162-3).

social world. On the one hand were relations with Islanders, including some from other parts of the Pacific, which were defined in terms of kinship and affinity and sustained by the exchange of gifts; on the other were relations with Europeans, which were defined functionally and regulated by the workings of the market and the state. Intermediate between the two relationships and articulating them was the Church.

First encounters

The history of Europeans in Torres Strait begins in 1606, when vessels of the two great maritime powers, Holland and Spain, independently discovered the Strait (Haddon 1935:3-4; Hilder 1980). These were voyages of discovery, without consequence for the Islanders beyond whatever impact the sight of strange vessels and people may have made on their consciousness. Nor does anyone seem to have followed the discoverers until Cook's voyage of 1770, but thereafter, and particularly after the foundation of the colony of New South Wales, the Strait became a regular seaway. It was a hazardous seaway, because the labyrinth of reefs was as yet uncharted, and because the survivors of a wreck were likely to be killed by the Islanders. These dangers resulted in a series of naval expeditions to search for castaways and chart the region (Haddon 1935:1-13).

We do not have full records of all contacts made during the first half of the nineteenth century, but from the accounts written during the 1840s it is evident that at least three communities, Murray, Darnley and Prince of Wales, were used to the sight of Europeans, could manage simple communication, and had realized the possibility of exchanging fresh food and curios for iron (Jukes 1847; Moore 1979). But not all encounters were peaceful. During this period Islanders learned that they could not withstand the white man's guns. The naval ships, well disciplined and under instruction to establish good relations with the natives, usually went no further than to demonstrate their fire power. But the pearlers and trepangers who came in the next decades were under no such control and were there to stay. If their men chose to make free with gardens or to abduct women, the Islanders had no way of stopping them.

As early as 1846 a naval vessel encountered a trepang boat working out of Sydney (MacGillivray 1852:1.308). It seems likely that there were others around this time, but the record is silent—

indeed it is non-existent from 1849, when the last of the naval survey vessels left, to 1863 when Queensland established a post on Somerset. By then a number of vessels were at work, and in 1868 the first pearl shell station was established on Warrior Island. When representatives of the London Missionary Society made their first tour of inspection in 1871, they found that the marine industry had made a profound impact almost everywhere. An observer of the period wrote of the pearlers and trepangers:

> There are, of course, among these men, some of excellent character and integrity of purpose, but there are others of whom . . . to say they are about as bad a lot as sail out of any port on earth is not to say too much. (Somerset Magistrate's Letter Book:13.3.1877. See also Moresby 1876: 14)

A missionary found on Darnley Island a Rotuman 'of infamous character' who

> by some means has acquired an influence both among the natives and his fellow workmen which renders him a sort of king among them and enables him to act pretty much as he pleases. He has four wives for only one of whom he is allowed provisions from the establishment to which he belongs. To provide for the other three he is accustomed to take his gun and go with them to the plantations of the natives and keep guard while they help themselves. (Murray 1872:32)

More to the point, the pearlers and trepangers were forcing men and women to work for them, withholding promised payment, and abducting women to serve the sexual needs of their foreign crews (Evans 1971:*passim*). In 1872 it was reported that 'the once confident and fearless' people of Mabuyag had become 'cowed and sullen, going bush' as soon as a sail was sighted (SMLB 1872). The inhabitants of the smaller islands were less fortunate, having no bush to flee to.

The missionaries blamed these abuses for the catastrophic decline in population, but they themselves contributed to the process by insisting on clothing the people and organizing villages. Probably, however, exotic diseases were the major lethal factor, and epidemics ravaged the Islanders until the end of the century, by which time their numbers had fallen below 3,000, perhaps half the original.[6] Even so, the pearlers and

---

[6] Queensland published no estimates of Torres Strait population until 1913 (CPA 1914). Thereafter, until the outbreak of the Second World War, estimates appeared at frequent intervals.

trepangers were wantonly wasting a local labour resource that they would later need. It remained for the mission and the government to look after their long term interests by checking abuses and regulating employment.

Buttons and aphrodisiacs

The northern coasts of Australia are rich in trepang, and its pearl shell beds are the largest in the world. Trepang, also known as *beche-de-mer*, is a species of sea slug (*holothuria*) which, when smoked, has a prized place in Chinese cuisine as a delicacy and aphrodisiac. Pearl shell, a more mundane but also more widely marketable commodity, has been principally used in the manufacture of buttons, but also for ornamentation. It comes in various forms, of which the gold-lip mother-of-pearl 'oyster' and the trochus cone have been the most marketable. Although the getting of these shells is commonly known as pearling, pearls occur only in the gold-lip. Their discovery is too unpredictable to provide anything more than a lucky bonanza to the finder.

Trepang and trochus shell are found in shallow water, where they can be gathered by what used to be called 'swimming-diving'. The organization of production is correspondingly easy, requiring a cutter or small lugger of perhaps 20 tons to carry fifteen to twenty workers to the fishing grounds, and several dinghies to take them to the shallow places. The fish are cleaned over-night, but trepang have also to be smoked, requiring trips to the shore station every few days. Gold-lip is found in a variety of conditions, from the shallow edge of the sea to a depth of forty fathoms. However the shallow beds were soon worked out, so that from as early as 1877 most commercial concerns were using diving equipment (SMLB 1877).

The level of production and income fluctuated wildly throughout the industry's hundred year history, reaching its peak in 1897.[7] In 1904, 378 boats employing 2,509 men produced 798 tons of shell worth £108,130. But in the next year, 366 boats employing only 1,321 men produced 543 tons, worth only £62,130. Although this drop was unusually sharp, it was still characteristic of an industry in which the price was fixed not by

[7] These figures were published annually by the Queensland Department of Harbour and Marine. They are conveniently brought together, along with much other statistical information, in a report of the Commonwealth Northern Australia Development Commission 1946.

the producers but by a few buyers in London and New York. Apart from actual manipulations of the market, the producers' fortunes were tied to those of the European and North American garment industries (North Australia Development Commission 1946; Bach 1961). Nor could producers control the level of production. Bad weather hindered work, whatever the price, and one season's overfishing resulted in several poor seasons to follow. Finally, though organized into a Master Pearlers' Association, the producers could never agree upon quotas (Bach 1961).

The structure of the industry varied considerably over the years, sometimes dominated by metropolitan companies such as the Sydney-based Burns Philp, at others consisting of small, locally based operators (NADC 1946; Bach 1961). But attempts at large-scale, capital intensive operations, with fleets of cutters working from a 'mother ship', simply resulted in overfishing and a transfer to other grounds for several years after. There was in any case always room for the small man to start up on his own account with little or no capital. He could lease a boat and equipment from a larger operator, even borrow the money to fit it out and victual it, paying his debts and his men's wages when the shell was sold. Such marginal operations were vulnerable to sudden drops in the price of shell, or to weather or bad luck, but the industry as a whole had some flexibility in that the same boats and workers could be used for gold-lip, trepang or – after 1916 – trochus. And if conditions proved unfavourable in Torres Strait, they could sail off to Darwin, or Western Australia or further afield. There was no further diversification of the regional economy, however, so if the owners reinvested some of their profits outside the industry it was also outside Torres Strait.[8]

The owners of the boats, who were almost all Europeans, seldom went to sea themselves. They evidently preferred the comfort of life ashore to the cramped, squalid conditions on board, the poor diet and the weeks of monotony; and they left to others the dangers and debilitating effects of deep water diving, which put an end to a man's working life by the age of forty. This

---

[8] Haddon in 1888 reported that the pearlers 'got good profits but are spendthrifts and big drinkers'. However, Burns Philp was able to draw off substantial profits, both from its pearling and trading operations (Buckley and Klugman 1982; 1983 *passim*).

was the view of Roughly (1936:225). Similarly, the Northern Australia Development Commission reported in 1946 that

> For many years, pearl shell fishing was a most hazardous occupation. One of the risks to which the whole crew was exposed was that of beri-beri, owing to the necessity for using preserved foods with no fresh fruit or vegetables; another common hazard among the divers was that of divers' paralysis, a result of too rapid changes of pressure. Many men died of these diseases. The rough and ready life also took its toll. Living quarters were cramped and uncomfortable, the life was utterly monotonous, there was little provision for living while on shore. It was taken for granted that luggers' crews spend the last days of their lives as physical wrecks.

The report added that there was now more skill in treating the 'bends', though fatalities still occurred, as they do today (1946:8). In the early years, when the price of shell was still high, whites were ready to run these risks which might bring them as much as £500 in a year (SMLB 3.4.1875). But as shell became easier to buy on the market and harder to get out of the sea, the owners began to cut wages, their major production cost. It was not hard to find Asian and Pacific Island workers who would accept lower rates, and who were more amenable to discipline and more reliable (Searcy 1907:316). There was a considerable movement of labour around the Pacific at this period, and although some of the men were unsophisticates who had been blackbirded, others were seasoned travellers who had seen Sydney, San Francisco and even London, and were well able to take command of a lugger. The first crop of skippers came from the Loyalty Islands, Rotumah, Samoa and Niue. Later the masters imported labour, often already experienced in the work, from Malaya, the Philippines and Japan. The Japanese divers, who appeared in the 1890s, undercut and outworked everyone else, requiring special legislation to stop them taking over the industry (Bach 1961).

At the turn of the century, agitation for a White Australia culminated in legislation which excluded cheap coloured labour. In 1907, following the deportation of Pacific Islanders who had worked in the Queensland sugar industry, the Royal Commission appointed to inquire into the workings of the pearl shell and *beche-de-mer* industries considered the feasibility of similar changes (1908:ix). But it concluded that no European who could earn £8 a month in coastal shipping would risk life and health for £8.17, which was the going rate for Japanese divers (*ibid.*:xiv). The masters pointed out that they were competing with producers in countries such as the Philippines where labour was cheaper, and insisted they could not pay more. (They would no doubt have been reluctant to take on inexperienced whites.) The Commission concluded that a government subsidy seemed to be the only way of attracting white divers, but this option was not taken up. The outcome was that the Pacific Islanders were repatriated, but the Japanese stayed on, with some Malays, up to the outbreak of war in the Pacific. This remission of the White Australia policy went unremarked by its supporters because it was safely confined to a marginal industry at the back of beyond.

The Commission recognized that if white men would not work as skippers or helmet divers, there was no way that they could be got to work as deck hands or skin divers at the going rate of between £1 and £2 per month. But it observed that Islanders, Aborigines and Papuans were 'tractable' and had 'natural rights to employment' (*ibid.*:xix). In fact, as we have seen, Islanders had been employed from the beginning. When shell could be got by wading, women as well as men collected it (McFarlane 12.1875–1.1876), but they were at first unwilling to work steadily or to spend long periods away from home. Though attracted by the trade goods which they were promised, they were soon repelled by dishonest employers and abusive skippers. In 1874 a missionary reported that the Mabuyag people were keeping out of the way of 'the pearl shell fishers as they are tired of working for them, and they find it difficult to keep from getting entangled with them when they are in the way' (Murray 4–5.1874:34).

Mission and government were presently to mitigate the worst abuses, letting European commodities work their magic. Iron had exerted a powerful attraction from the outset. Flour, rice and biscuit met the Central Islanders' chronic shortage of carbohydrate, the Western Islanders' 'hungry time' during the norwest monsoon (December – March), and periodic crop failures in the Eastern Islands. For some these foods were also 'softer' and so preferable to 'bush tucker'; and traded tobacco and sugar became preferable to the local products. The discovery of 'shame' created a need for clothing, while the Thursday Island stores soon came to cater for the Islanders' love of decoration and novelty. Under the impact of this transformation, regional trade declined. The Eastern Islanders, with their abundance of crops, were less susceptible to European foods than the others, but they too needed iron tools, clothing, bottles, pans and the like. Moreover, every island was affected by the incursion of foreign seamen, seeking wives and ready to offer trade goods by way of bride price. According to Haddon, parents were inclined to favour foreign sons-in-law on this account, leaving local men with the choice of matching them or missing out (1908:115).

However, what looked like a proletariat in the making remained for some time a labour reserve. The pearlers and trepangers had used indigenous labour from the beginning, but it proved less tractable and less hardy than the imported labour. Moreover, the numbers were not sufficient, becoming less so as the population succumbed to exotic diseases and conditions. At the first official count in 1913 there were a mere 2,368 Islanders (Chief Protector of Aborigines 1914) and in the same year the industry employed 1,300 men (NADC 1946). Not until the late 1930s, with a population recovery in full swing, could the Islanders come near to supplying the same number. With the addition of Aborigines and Papuans the industry could have been locally manned a good deal earlier, but the masters preferred Japanese and Malays, particularly as divers and skippers. Thus until the outbreak of the Second World War, local labour never exceeded 50% of the total work force, with Islanders providing around 20%.

We have seen that the marine industry's major cost item was labour, and that it had won exemption from the normal restrictions on the importation of cheap 'coloured' labour from overseas. It was thus in the happy situation of being able to utilize labour without having to maintain the populations from which it was drawn. The foreign workers, often from subsistence or semi-subsistence economies, came in as single men, and if they returned it was usually with very little money. The Islanders were also largely maintained by fishing and gardening. There was, however, a difference in that the foreigners, being indentured, could not be laid off before the end of their term, should there be a downturn in the market. Local workers could be laid off at any time, giving the industry a degree of flexibility that it badly needed. Moreover, according to a ranking that had become established over the years, it could pay them less:

Islanders less than foreigners and Aborigines and Papuans less than Islanders. Thus, from its point of view, the ideal labour force consisted of a mixture of local and foreign workers.

It might be said that the marine industry carried the Islanders to the threshold of the industrial world and left them there. They had become a part-time proletariat, with all the contradictions that such an idea implies. They were drawn from their subsistence activities by the lure of consumer goods, only to be forced back on these activities again. Meanwhile the mission, as the second pillar of the colonial order, was reconstructing the island communities around this contradiction.

Bringing the 'Light'

To describe the London Missionary Society as a pillar of the colonial order is not to reduce it to a mere adjunct or instrument of the economic and political interests at work. Its Torres Strait representatives were of working rather than middle class origins, and they were answerable to their directors in London, not to the pearlers on Thursday Island, with whom they were often in conflict, or to the colonial government in Brisbane, whose increasing antagonism led to their withdrawal in 1914. But what Rex has set out in general terms is applicable to their case:

> the overall impact of their preaching and their work has been to provide a long-term moral rationalization of the colonial enterprise as a whole rather than the immediate self interest of settler or planter. Obviously they have much in common with the administrators who do the same job on a legal and political level, but one must expect in colonial society to find a distinct estate of clergy at odds at one time or another with all groups, including the administrators themselves. (Rex 1982:211)

The consequence of the twenty or so years during which the LMS virtually ran the island communities was that the inhabitants were reconciled to the colonial order and kept where they belonged, on its periphery.

The 'Light' came to Torres Strait on 1 July 1871, when an LMS ship landed two Loyalty Island teachers on Darnley Island (Murray and McFarlane 1871). Two more were stationed on Dauan, and by the end of the decade the few communities that did not have teachers were begging for them. On Murray the

Papuan Institute prepared Torres Strait converts for missionary work in neighbouring Papua (McFarlane 1888). The readiness with which the Islanders received the mission and acceded to its considerable demands surprised even the white superintendents. After a few months the 'entire population' of Murray

> attached themselves to the teacher. They treat himself and his family with great kindness, supplying their wants without charge so far as they are able and seeming ready to yield themselves implicitly to his guidance. No work is done on the sabbath and the people come together from the three islands to attend the services which, except the hymns and reading of the scripture, are conducted in the native tongue. (Murray 9–12.1872:34)

The writer concluded that they were a people 'prepared of the Lord' (*ibid.*:33). Prepared they certainly were, if not quite in the sense he supposed. To begin with, they now knew better than to attempt violence against Europeans, or against those who had their protection (McFarlane 11.1875 – 1.1876). Secondly, it soon became apparent that the mission was able and ready to protect them from the 'dark deeds' and 'infamous acts' perpetrated by foreign seamen (Murray 9 – 12.1872:28; McFarlane 8.9.1876:4). Thirdly, though this is more speculative, the mission offered an end to the never-ending cycle of feuding and raiding (Murray 9–12.1872:35; McFarlane 19.1874).

It seems likely that the Islanders initially viewed the mission as simply the latest in the series of cults that came to them from time to time, albeit one that promised unprecedented power and wealth. Only later, when the missionaries desecrated their shrines and took away their sacred objects (Haddon 1904:368; 1908:289), would they have realized that this cult demanded their whole devotion. But consideration of the conditions under which conversion took place and of the probable misunderstandings should not lead us to ignore the fervour with which the new religion was practised, or the speed with which communities made it their own. The explorer, Captain Strachan, described the conduct of the Saibaians in the absence of their mission teacher in 1885.

> Alees . . . brought forth a number of paper-covered books, which I found to be copies of a native translation of the Gospel of St. John. These he handed round to a considerable number of the natives.

Annu opened the service by kneeling and praying with
apparent earnestness in the native tongue for a few moments.
The people again sat down, and opening the book, Annu
read what appeared to be the first verse of the first chapter
of St. John's Gospel and was followed in succession by the
others until the chapter was finished. A pause ensued for a
few moments and then, turning to the beginning, Annu
started to expatiate on the chapter they had just read.
When he had finished, he was followed by others, until
nearly all who had engaged in reading had made some
remarks. Then after singing a hymn, Annu closed the service
of the evening, with the benediction in the native tongue.
(Strachan 1888:136-7)

There can be no doubt that the mission had done its work well,
though this same community was to be the centre of an anti-
European cargo cult thirty years later (Haddon 1935:46-8).

If the mission filled a spiritual vacuum, it also filled a political
vacuum. Queensland had established a station at Somerset on
Cape York as early as 1863, but it had not completed annexation
of the outer islands until 1879, and even then lacked the means
of administering them. According to the LMS superintendent,
the Reverend Samuel McFarlane,

About 1878 Mr. Chester [the Government Resident] advised
the chiefs to appoint magistrates and police. In the presence
of the Rev. Mr. Chalmers and myself the laws were formally
inaugurated and the officers appointed by Mr. Chester who
publically (*sic*) requested Josiah (the pastor) to guide them
in their administration (he being accustomed to a similar
state of things in his own country) until they themselves
were capable. These laws were, on the whole, equitably
administered, Josiah being occasionally required to interfere
in the interests of mercy, the native judges being inclined
to severity. (McFarlane 17.7.1882)

McFarlane had occasion to recall these events, following a
government complaint that Josiah had flogged a Pacific Island
seaman and a Murray Island woman for adultery (*ibid.*). He
insisted that this had been the work of the chief and police; but,
bearing in mind the weakness of the chiefs, it seems likely that
they were acting as the secular arm of the mission. Throughout
the Pacific, the Society had been accustomed to running its
missions as petty theocracies, sometimes in the absence of
secular government, and such punishments as flogging, head-

shaving and the stocks were imposed indifferently for secular and religious transgressions (cf. Beaglehole 1958). The pastors and teachers the Society brought to Torres Strait were the products of such regimes, and more zealous than their European mentors. The Queensland government was eventually to break their hold, but for the moment it left them in charge, even making several European superintendents justices of the peace (Hunt 4.3.1889).

The first requirement of the new order was that the people should come together in a village, around the church, which was sited adjacent to a good anchorage. This required a considerable adaptation of the Western and Central Islanders, who had moved about a good deal in search of food, and it was effected at the cost of increasing their dependence on the marine industry. But under the eye of teacher or pastor, the people could be kept to a daily routine of religious observance and their conduct subject to close surveillance. Piety and good character were duly rewarded through admission, first to the 'seekers class', then to membership and finally to the deaconate (McFarlane 12.1884: 6,8,11). Promising young men could also train for the mission field. As Strachan's account illustrates, the congregational structure of the LMS church allowed local participation from the outset, while its overseeing of the *mamooses* (chiefs) gave a new kind of legitimacy to secular leaders (McFarlane 12.1884:8,11; Chalmers 1897:32). Its puritanical moral code, which provided a new means by which Islanders could control and judge one another's conduct, was to remain in force into the 1960s. The mission also insinuated itself into the gift economy, becoming the principal beneficiary. Not only were Islanders as individuals and as communities encouraged to give, but they were brought together for the annual *Mei* festivities under conditions which reanimated traditional rivalries to make generosity competitive. In 1911 the Protector was annoyed to discover that even the coconuts from his copra planting drive had been given to the church (CPA 1911:20). Thus it was that the mission effected the reconstruction of the indigenous communities, giving them a new focus and new ways of expressing claims and deferences.

The reports and correspondence of the Torres Strait missionaries, in which they put before the directors their aims and intentions, are couched in the high flown rhetoric of the subculture. The Islanders are 'poor benighted heathen', sunk in 'blindness and degradation', yet capable of acquiring the 'dignity of sons of God and heirs of Heaven.' This requires the overturning of their 'idol gods', suppressing 'disgusting and revolting' customs such as mummification of the dead and infanticide, and teaching them to 'know shame' (i.e. wear clothes) and give up unacceptable customs such as polygyny. With regard to less offensive practices, such as dancing, the British missionaries counselled forbearance; but their Pacific Island pastors, with all the fervour of recent converts, were less tolerant, although they were often prepared to countenance dances from their own places. Reflecting the values of the respectable working class, the LMS seemed to have in prospect model Christian communities which would produce faithful servants and put to shame the drunken and profligate Europeans of Thursday Island.

In reality the mission reproduced the economic contradiction in which the Islanders were already placed: the push-pull of an industrial system that required the continuance of subsistence production. It insisted that the 'greatest stronghold of the devil is the idleness of heathenism' (Walker 13.7.1896), and the life it urged upon its flocks, the clothing, the houses, the churches and the training of mission teachers, required a cash income. Yet work on the boats meant contact with 'a certain class of foreigner' who not only exerted a 'withering and deteriorated influence' (Murray and McFarlane 1871:48; Douglas 1899), but also undermined the authority of the mission. Near the end of the century a missionary, the Reverend F. W. Walker, would help the Islanders to operate their own boats free of such danger, but in the meantime another solution arose.

As it happened, the young men whom the employers preferred as workers were the ones whom the communities could most readily spare. Traditionally the period before marriage had left them with few economic duties and ample time for sexual adventures. With fornication declared a sin and a crime, they could be packed off to sea, while their elders stayed home to acquire merit in the church: a moral differentiation which negated the economic importance of the young men and coerced them into giving the bulk of their earnings to their parents. Since they now had to provide a bride price in cash, they could not marry without their parents' consent, with the inevitable result that the age of marriage was pushed back from late teens to mid-twenties.[9] This also meant that parents could enjoy the labour of their daughters for several more years. By making marriage an indissoluble bond, the mission also strengthened the husband's authority over his wife, who now had to play a larger part in maintaining the household. Thus through the combined influence of industry and mission, the family came to articulate the two economies.

By 1890 the Torres Strait Mission was beginning to run down (Lawes 3.10.1889; Hunt 24.10.1889). With the work of conversion completed there and vast areas of Papua waiting for the Light, it was considered not to need the attention of a full-time superintendent. The Reverend James Chalmers left the islands to the pastors he had brought with him from Samoa, making hurried tours of inspection each year from his headquarters at Saguane in Fly River. It now became the turn of the Queensland government to fill the political gap. Government Residents had periodically complained about the tyrannical regime of the pastors, but they had lacked the funds and the means to replace them. Now better provided, they sent teacher–supervisors to the larger communities, precipitating an immediate confrontation with the pastors and their church courts (Haddon 1908:178-9). In 1904 a government agent assumed comprehensive controls over the Islanders' affairs, which may have prompted the LMS to appoint once again a full time representative. But it was unwilling to confine its activities merely to spiritual matters, and when its request to have charge of education was denied, it passed its flocks over to the Anglican diocese of Carpentaria, formally withdrawing in 1914. Unlike the LMS the bishop was content to leave secular matters to the government; indeed, with meagre funds and only two priests to serve fourteen island parishes, he had little choice in the matter.

Protective segregation

When the Queensland government established its post at Somerset, on Cape York, it was mainly to provide a port of call

[9] Haddon states that before contact both men and women married soon after puberty (1908:115). However actual figures from Murray Island around the turn of the century suggest a great variation; although the sample is small, the average ages at first marriage were 20.2 years for males and 18.5 for females (1935:113-14). Figures I took from the marriage registers of Badu and Murray, running from the late 1920s to the outbreak of war, had males marrying on average at around twenty-four and females around twenty-two years of age.

for passing ships and protection for castaways. The Acts of
Annexation in 1872 of islands within sixty miles of the coast, and
in 1879 of the remainder, seem to have been prompted by a fear
of rival colonial powers and a desire to get some grip on the
burgeoning and increasingly lucrative marine industry. Thursday
Island, to which the post was transferred in 1877 on account of
its safer anchorage, also became the headquarters of the
industry, a commercial centre and a port of call. The government's
principal concern was to ensure that the Islanders would not
attack Europeans. There was at least one punitive raid, on the
Prince of Wales people (Moore 1979:12-18), but in 1870 H.M.
Chester travelled around the Western Islands with the intention
of winning over the inhabitants through peaceful trade (Carroll
1969). A few years later he travelled round appointing chiefs; but
since the government lacked a regular patrol boat it had no
option but to leave administration to the LMS (Report of
Government Resident 1887).

Government became more effective after 1886, with the
appointment as Government Resident of the Honourable John
Douglas, following brief terms as Queensland Premier and
acting Commissioner of British New Guinea. Holding this office
for the next eighteen years, he established his own, easygoing
brand of paternalism, which filled the gap left by the increasingly
absentee white missionaries. In 1899 he instituted elected
councils to advise the teacher–supervisors. This seems to have
been designed to counter the influence of the church courts
(Haddon 1908:179), but was nevertheless a remarkable innovation, without precedent anywhere in the colonial South Pacific.
When the first Queensland Aborigines Protection Act was
passed in 1897, Douglas insisted that the Islanders should be
exempt from its provisions on account of 'their marked mental
superiority over the mainland native'. He asserted that they were
'capable of exercising all the rights of British citizens, and ought
to be regarded as such' (1899-1900:35). Nevertheless when he
died in 1904 they passed to the control of the Chief Protector,
becoming subject to the same controls as Aborigines (Hanlon
1939:498).

Queensland's native affairs policy was still in its formative
stage, but it was already assuming the comprehensive and
thoroughgoing character that would make it a model for the rest
of Australia in later decades (Rowley 1971:186). Loos isolates
two of its basic assumptions as

(a)   prolonged tutelage while socially isolated from European society and

(b)   the usefulness of Aborigines as a source of unskilled labour. (1982:183)

The two were not wholly in harmony, expressing as they did a diversity of interests and values. One impulse for segregation came from the White Australia movement, then at its xenophobic height. Aborigines could not be deported as the *kanakas* (South Sea Islanders) had been, but they could be segregated in such a way as to prevent them from threatening the conditions of white workers. The case was all the more compelling because the survivors of conquest were often diseased and living in wretched circumstances that were an offence to a society grown genteel (Evans 1975). Segregation was equally the solution for the small band of humanitarians who wanted Aborigines saved from exploitation and abuse, if not from extinction. Kindly treated and wisely guided in an institutional setting, Aborigines might one day become domestic and agricultural workers, as useful as white employees and perhaps rather more docile. This policy came into conflict, on the one hand with employers – particularly in the pastoral industry – for whom Aborigines were an important source of cheap labour, and on the other, with legislators who were reluctant to allocate public funds for the maintenance of large, unproductive settlements. The outcome was a compromise of sorts.

The official Protectors were soon armed with draconian powers to control the movement and residence of Aborigines. They never succeeded in institutionalizing the whole population although they did establish three large settlements, as well as assisting several missions in the north of the state. However, few of these had the resources or capital to become self-supporting, and with government funds always in short supply, the Protectors had no option but to respond to demands from employers and send the inmates out to work. In doing so they acquired a strong interest in ensuring that wages were substantial and paid in full, since they would have to provide for anyone left destitute. Soon they were controlling employment and rates of pay. During the First World War Chief Protector J. W. Bleakley took advantage of the labour shortage to negotiate a wage agreement for Aboriginal pastoral workers. They would be paid at only two thirds of the rate for white workers, but they would be paid, which is more than could be said for many

Aborigines elsewhere in northern Australia at that time (Rowley
1972:255-87). To ensure that their charges were paid, the
Protectors received the money on their behalf, releasing it to
them only for approved purposes. This policy was justified on
the ground that the money would otherwise be squandered, but
the Protectors did not so much teach the Aborigines thrift as
practise it on their behalf. These powers were just one part of a
control apparatus that penetrated every sector of Aboriginal
life.

The documentary sources do not indicate why the Islanders
were brought under this regime after 1904. Perhaps Douglas's
successor did not share his regard for them; perhaps the Chief
Protector wanted to extend his sphere of influence. Some
Islanders believe that the change was the result of a drunken
brawl on Thursday Island about this time, probably the one
described by 'Banjo' Paterson (1983:19-20). Reports indicate
that the Protector wanted to stop the supply of liquor to them.
There may also have been economic considerations. Up to the
outbreak of war in 1914 the marine industry's foreign labour
supply was under threat from the White Australia lobby
(Philipps 1980). With white divers beyond the means of the
pearlers, Islanders must have seemed the most likely alternative.
There was, then, good reason for controlling their labour and
stopping them from going south to fill the gap left by the
departing *kanakas*. In the 1870s Islanders had travelled without
hindrance, at least as far as Sydney. Henceforth they were to be
kept in Torres Strait, and as far as possible in their communities.
Even their visits to Thursday Island were to be limited to
daylight hours.

Unlike most Aboriginal settlements in Queensland, the island
communities could be self-supporting except in times of
famine. The problem was to achieve the right balance between
commercial and subsistence production, under conditions of
fluctuating shell prices and working conditions. Each community
had its own idea of what was appropriate, some like Murray
limiting their commitment to the cash economy, others
becoming over committed. As Haddon observed on Mabuyag in
1898:

> The advent of the white man has upset the former economic
> conditions on Mabuiag. The men now spend all their time
> 'swimming diving' as it is called, that is, they go in parties
> in sailing boats, and dive by swimming for pearl-shell in

shallow water. Some natives own their own boats, and make up crews on a system of sharing; others hire themselves out to white men. They generally start out on Monday and return on Friday or Saturday. All the time they are away they feed on tinned meat, biscuits, flour, and other white man's food. They get accustomed to this food, and as they are away from home so much, they cannot 'make' their gardens. Thus it comes about that agriculture, as well as fishing, is greatly neglected, and a considerable portion – and in some instances the bulk – of their food has to be bought from the stores. Should the supply of pearl-shell fall off, or the price be lowered, the natives would suffer greatly; and if the storekeepers left the island, the people would practically starve. As it is many are considerably in debt to the traders, and often the traders have to advance supplies of flour and food to ward off starvation. With all their apparent prosperity, the people are really in a false economic condition, and their future may yet be temporarily deplorable. (1901:121-2)

The task of regulating such dangerous imbalances fell to the government. Thus in Mabuyag a few years later we find the teacher–supervisor ordering the people to make gardens, lest a crisis in the industry should leave them dependent on handouts (CPA 1911:20). On other islands the men had to be coerced into going to sea.

This was not the only problem the government faced. In his report for 1907, the Protector on Thursday Island suggested that Torres Strait workers were 'worth' £2 per month, but he had to add that 'of course they have a very inflated idea of their own worth' (Report of the Pearl Shell and Beche-de-Mer Commission:60). In a similar vein, Chief Protector Bleakley described the Islanders as 'shrewd', even 'sea lawyers', remarking on the 'pronounced semitic features' (1961:257)! In plain terms, they had been overtaken by the worldwide tendency towards increased consumption, and were responding by demanding higher pay.

The function of the Protectors was to resist these pressures. Using their official powers they kept a tight hold on the Islanders' money, not just to discourage extravagant gifts to the church — Islanders being 'generous to a fault' in this respect (Bleakley 1961:257) — but to limit their consumption of items that were necessities to Europeans. The policy was rationalized with a gross paternalism: 'The Islanders have not yet reached the stage where they are competent to think and provide for themselves; they are really over-grown children, and can best be managed for their own welfare, as a parent would discipline his family' (CPA 1915:12). The reality is indicated by an incident occurring in 1913. The LMS superintendent, the Reverend O. T. Harris, approached the Protector on behalf of an Islander, with a request that money should be released for the purchase of some roofing iron. The Protector replied that 'he did not like the idea . . . as it would make others wish to do the same; and if this thing is started no one knows where it will end.' With this reply, the missionary kept in his pocket another request for iron to build an entire house (Harris: 18.8.1913).

Special stores for Islanders further protected them against the dangers of consumerism by carrying only the barest necessities. Purchases at these stores were entered against whatever money the customer had in his government pass book, so that he did not even see the money he had earned. And as if this were not enough, the Protector transferred a percentage of each worker's earnings into an island fund, which would carry his community over a period of famine or unemployment. In 1913 the percentage for single men was set at 20%, a rate well above what a European worker paid in tax, as the LMS superintendent pointed out in a letter of protest to the Home Secretary (*ibid.*). The mission may have won this last battle with the government, for the percentage was reduced in the following year. In later years the Chief Protector wrote that this fund had provided for old age pensions, uniforms for village police, medical and sanitary services, and general improvements throughout the years between the wars (Bleakley 1961:68). The government also used its control over Islanders' money to acquire on their behalf boats which they would work, independently of the masters. The scheme had in fact begun with an LMS missionary.

> Revd. F. W. Walker, preaching at one of their church services, had reproached the Islanders for their apparent indolence. He pointed out the great wealth of marine produce at their very doors, the proceeds of which, if collected, would provide for the seasonal 'hungry time'. He was afterwards approached by a deputation of the people who explained that they had no money with which to buy fishing boats large enough to work profitably. (Bleakley 1961:265)

As early as 1897 he had helped the Mabuyag Islanders to buy a boat (Chalmers 1897:4), but the LMS had a policy against commercial involvement, so that it was necessary for him to resign and seek funds elsewhere (Austin 1972). By 1904, the year in which he established Papuan Industries on Badu, the Queensland government was establishing its ascendancy, and it responded to his initiative by establishing a parallel agency for the islands that he was not yet able to serve. The two established a working relationship, and when Walker retired in 1930 they merged to become Aboriginal Industries.

Walker's plan was comprehensive, enabling Islanders to acquire their own boats, selling their produce for them and providing them with store goods at 'fair prices'. The company boats, as they came to be known, proved to be by far the most important part of the scheme, increasing Islanders' involvement in the cash economy by providing work for those who were too young or too old to get on the masters' boats, or who because of family commitments preferred not to stay too long away from home. To accommodate this shifting labour force, each man's catch was separately recorded and paid for.

The scheme was not an unqualified success. The communities at first responded with enthusiasm, paying off the purchase price with surprising speed. But supposing that the boats were now theirs to use as they chose, they were irked to find that the teacher–supervisors could stop them going hunting or visiting. There were also economic problems, for the boats were small and without engines or diving equipment. Operating on narrow margins they were vulnerable to bad weather, falling prices or disagreements among the crew, so that catches often failed to cover running costs. With earnings subject to a complex set of deductions, there was ample room for misunderstanding and disappointment. Some went off hunting in defiance of the teacher–supervisors while others, disgusted, left the boats to fall into decay. In 1910 the Protector complained that 'the venture of supplying the natives with boats is a complete failure. Nothing it seems will move these people – not even fines and imprisonment – to look after their boats and go to work' (CPA 1911:20).

The Protectors, however, were now committed to the scheme and they persevered, even expanding the fleet to take advantage of the boom that followed the First World War. Working trochus, which now had a sizeable market, the company boats were at less of a disadvantage since no diving gear was used. In 1924 twenty-eight boats earned more than £20,000 and, with wages on the master boats raised to between £3 and £4 per month, the communities were more prosperous than ever before, if not affluent (Aboriginals Department 1925). The number in employment also increased from 358 in 1921, when the population was about 3,000 (AD 1922), to 587 in 1923 (AD 1924), approximately half the able-bodied men. Although the great depression cut deeply into earnings, the number in employment continued to rise throughout the 1930s at a rate a little ahead of the natural increase.

As it chanced, the depression, which of course hit the garment industry along with everything else, followed on a glut in the supply of shell, and prices did not fully recover until the end of the decade. The master pearlers, unable to switch to trepang because of the war in China, cut back their operations. The company boats worked on, but their average per capita earnings for 1930 were only £8 (AD 1931:9), forcing the women to redouble their efforts in gardening and fishing. In 1931 the Protector reported unrest and a 'temporary revulsion' against working for the government, so that it was necessary to use coercion (AD 1932:6). In 1933 he complained that 'it is difficult to induce the native to leave home and go to work so long as he can draw money from his savings bank account to spend in the stores' (AD 1934:12). At the same time he noted that the establishment of government stores in some of the communities was a considerable incentive to work, and that the people's level of material wellbeing had improved considerably. Evidently there had been a reversal of the 1913 policy of curbing Islanders' consumption. The priority was now to keep them working, and the Department's boats solvent.

By 1935 the market was recovering and on 8 January 1936, the *Brisbane Telegraph* reported a speech by the Minister to the effect that 'Already the natives of Torres Strait were self supporting and in addition were contributing something towards the support of aboriginals on the mainland.' Even while he spoke the majority of island workers on government boats were beginning a strike that was to last about four months, ending only after the dismissal of uncooperative councillors, the imprisonment of ringleaders, and the temporary posting of armed white police in the most disaffected communities. The Protector's report at the end of the year, that once the workers' grievances had been rectified they 'enthusiastically commenced work' (AD 1937:11-12), was not the whole truth. Nevertheless, he had made a number of important concessions.

Just what the Islanders' grievances were is hard to discover from contemporary sources. The report which the police magistrate of Townsville submitted to the State Parliament has not come to light, while the official reports were somewhat less than frank. Bleakley, the Chief Protector at that time, recorded in his memoirs that the strikers 'wanted to control their own vessels and handle their own money' (1961:270). The Bishop of Carpentaria, who wrote to the Governor expressing some sympathy for them, suggested that the system of payment on the boats was at the heart of the matter (Davis 9.1.36). The Communist *Workers Weekly,* which was the first to report the event on 21 January and 21 February, also expressed this opinion, but went on to suggest that the Islanders' money was being misappropriated. A statement in Parliament revealed resentment against the teacher–supervisors, some of whom were overbearing and intruded unduly into people's domestic affairs. The nine o'clock curfew, enforced throughout the Strait for many years, caused general annoyance.

What Islanders told me later confirmed these reports, but also clarified them. Their statements may, of course, have been coloured by subsequent developments, but they seemed to me to reveal a sense of perspective: for example, they explained that 'citizen rights' did not become an issue until after the Second World War. As one might expect, there was a variety of grievances, and each informant stressed whatever had irked him most. One recalled his bitterness as a sixteen-year-old at being beaten for talking to a white woman. Others recalled the resentment created by various actions of the recently appointed Protector of Islanders. Coming with prior experience in New Guinea, his manner was evidently more overbearing than the Islanders were accustomed to, so much so that one Murray Island councillor hit him. But sooner or later the talk would return to the interference in their economic affairs. It was not just the privations of the depression that made them resentful. Conditions were improving by 1936, and the master boats were not included in the strike. The strike was directed specifically against the government, and the precipitating issue was the discrepancy between effort and reward on the company boats. This was less the result of market fluctuations than of the complicated system of deductions. The hopes raised by a successful year and reports of improving prices could be dashed when officials collected debts incurred in previous years. This is what happened in 1935. Wages on the master boats were not high, but they were predictable; on the company boats 'we never knew where we were'. Failing either to understand, or to believe the explanations given them, some Islanders concluded that their money was being stolen. This was the allegation that the Communist press transmitted when the strike broke out.

The Government had virtually invited this suspicion when it took control over the Islanders' money. The worker, whose debits and credits were entered in a pass book he never saw, was at the mercy of a dishonest or careless official, and discrepancies occasionally came to light. There had been a scandal over the management of a boat on Yorke Island, and everyone knew about it (AD 1916:10). But more to the point, total money held by government on behalf of individuals and communities amounted to a considerable sum. The Minister's statement, quoted earlier, that the Islanders were contributing to the support of Aborigines, could be taken to mean that their money was being officially misappropriated, though this interpretation was later denied. It is unlikely, in any case, that the Islanders heard of it. What they did know, however, was that at any given time, a sizeable portion of their money was being withheld from them.

The translation of resentment into action is harder to explain. Chief Protector Bleakley supposed that the Thursday Island shopkeepers were behind the strike, being resentful of the government's monopoly of retail trade (1961:271). Several Islanders told me that one of the master pearlers had first suggested it. Surprisingly, no one nominated the Communist Party for chief culprit, although to judge from the speed with which its press reported the strike, it must have been in contact with Islanders. A report of some years before suggested that they had learned about strikes from white workers while working the southern end of the Barrier Reef (Bruce n.d.). Townsville was certainly a centre of political radicalism and union militancy throughout the period (Fitzgerald 1984:14-41), but even in the Strait, Japanese divers had staged a strike in 1923, creating considerable alarm (*Age* 19.2.23). Coincidentally or not, 1936 was also the year of an international seamen's strike. Of more immediate relevance was the gathering, at some time in 1935, of a number of company boats around one reef. Talk among men of widely separated communities revealed and perhaps intensified the sense of frustration and distrust, and plans were laid for a general strike to begin in the new year. Letters were then sent to boats working elsewhere, and support was almost complete. [10]

I found general agreement that the Eastern Islanders were the most intransigent, but they were not, as they sometimes later claimed, the leaders. Indeed it seems unlikely that there were any leaders at the regional level. Once the strike started, each community was on its own, cut off from communication with the rest because the boats were no longer moving. It remained then for the government to effect a termination with each in turn. Most proved amenable, once the combination of intimidation and blandishment was applied; but no boats worked from Murray until the outbreak of war.

The 1936 strike was the first organized Islander challenge to European authority, and it is remembered as such (cf. Sharp 1982). Everyone can describe how, when an official came into a village hall to recruit for the new season, 'all the boys jumped out of the window, whistling'. The challenge was limited to striking, however, except for one or two communities where children were withdrawn from school. The Islanders had nevertheless overcome their isolation to win public attention for their grievances, and they had embarrassed a government that prided itself on its native administration. Thus their action produced results, not the least of which was the removal of the unpopular Protector of Islanders. A councillor of the period told me with grim satisfaction that he had seen the man walking around Mackay without a job, a few months later. His successor was Cornelius O'Leary, whose success in restoring harmony to Torres Strait was no doubt a factor in his promotion to department head on Bleakley's retirement in 1941.

In a series of innovations that were without parallel in colonial Australia or Papua New Guinea, O'Leary established mechanisms for regular consultation with elected Islander representatives, and gave the island councils a considerable degree of local autonomy, including control over the island police and courts. At the end of 1936 he reported that 'A greater measure of

[10] The Yorke Islanders did not participate in the strike, possibly because they were running a family business by special arrangement with the Protector, rather than a company boat. The only other boat not to strike was the one commanded by Tanu Nona of Badu (see chapter VI).

responsibility has been given to the councillors and they will now control a considerable portion of the domestic life of their communities which previously were the responsibility of the government teacher' (AD 1937). In 1937 he convened a conference of these councillors at which some unpopular by-laws were cancelled, notably the nine o'clock curfew, and a new code agreed upon. The Torres Strait Islanders Act of 1939 incorporated these changes and, in the process, met the Islanders' desire to be distinguished from Aborigines. Aboriginal Industries now became the Island Industries Board. However, the Government retained its controls over the Islanders' boats and earnings, and its economic regime remained unchanged. Reading between the lines, it seems as though the O'Leary reconstruction was an attempt to achieve by indirect means what the teacher – supervisors had failed to achieve by coercion. Subsistence and commercial production were now to derive their self-sustaining dynamics from within the community, and to be articulated by local institutions.

The new island community

Under colonial rule the island community lost the sovereignty it had formerly enjoyed. No longer oriented towards other communities like itself, it had now to look towards a centre from which its affairs were regulated. The very land on which its people lived belonged to the Crown. Yet its occupation was undisturbed and intruders were kept out. If only because of administrative logistics, it was incorporated and vested with representative authority.

Still partially dependent on subsistence activities, and thrown very much on its own human resources in work, play and religious observance, the community provided both old ways and new for the reproduction of Sider's 'claims and deferences' (see p. 10). The high level of interrelatedness characteristic of a long established, stable population, made possible the retention of kinship as the principal idiom of organization in daily life. At the same time, the ways in which the community was incorporated within the colonial order ensured that specialized function was rarely the primary, and never the only principle in defining the relations between Islanders. Subordinating the circulation of money and commodities to pre-existing social relations, they re-distributed wealth in such a way as to offset any tendency

towards permanent economic differentiation. Economic deprivation was redistributed and so collectively experienced. The
government's monopoly of retail trade left no room for local
entrepreneurs, while its tight control over the supply of cash
saved the subsistence sector from becoming monetized. The
company boat system precluded the emergence of independent
boat owners, while the normal practice was for skippers to earn
only fractionally more than their crew. (Some declined even this
small privilege.) The dominant forms of differentiation were
thus the traditional ones, between young and old, male and
female, both confirmed and in some ways reinforced by an
economy that took men away from the island, and a church that
preferred senior men. Beyond this there was only the prestige to
be derived from a gift to the church or a lavish wedding, which
was fleeting and had no currency outside the community.

The capacity of the island community to influence its
members' conduct was much increased when the council took
over the functions of the teacher–supervisor. Under the new
regime island custom reached its full flowering. The teacher–
supervisors, with their night curfews and work ethic, had kept a
brake on festivity. Now feasting and dancing flourished,
officially approved as the proper way to celebrate secular and
religious holidays, as well as weddings, tombstone openings,
departures and home-comings. After a period of flirtation with
various South Sea styles of singing and dancing, the Islanders
had begun to develop their own, synthetic style which now
became dominant throughout the Strait (Beckett 1982).

Sitting as a court, the island council upheld a code of local by-
laws, partly derived from tradition, but mainly from the LMS,
including offences such as fornication, adultery, message
carrying and domestic squabbling, that were not recognized by
any Australian court. It occasionally heard sorcery accusations,
but it did not enter them in the court books, which were subject
to official inspection. It could sentence those found guilty of an
offence to fines or weeks of imprisonment in the island lock-up.
It also gave great attention to keeping the villages clean and tidy
in the manner established by missionaries and teacher–
supervisors. Even the rocks marking the edge of the streets were
whitewashed.

The Church was organized along similar lines. When the LMS
pastors withdrew in 1914, they left their flocks in the care of the
local deacons, whom the Anglicans quickly recognized and

renamed church wardens. The two European priests who were all the diocese could provide could do no more than visit the island parishes for a few days each year. And when there were priests enough to take up permanent residence, they were Islanders who had undergone training at a special college on Moa Island, and who were accustomed both to the congregational form of government inherited from the LMS, and an Islander way of doing things. Although the proper forms of the Anglican rite were observed, the hymns were in the Torres Strait languages and in a style that had been passed down from the old Pacific Island pastors. Laymen preached in the vernacular, and at meetings after services berated the people for their frivolity and backsliding. The cleaning and decoration of the church, the organization of duty rosters and celebrations were all privileges jealously preserved and fought over by the parishioners.

The Islander clergy, along with the councillors and boat skippers, had the difficult task of mediating between community and European authority, which is to say between universal and particular orders, between the market and the gift economy, and between subordination and self-determination. In situations of conflict, the authorities were of course dominant, at least in the long run; but the community had the advantages of isolation and control over local information.

A colonial society

While still situated in their communities, the Torres Strait Islanders had become part of a society of such extraordinary racial diversity that Thursday Island was known as the 'Sink of the Pacific'. Out of the confusion of the early years, in which native and foreign, white and coloured, mixed freely and sometimes interbred, there emerged a stratified society, caste-like in its rigidity. Around the turn of the century an anonymous Islander summed up the situation with such succinctness that his words have been preserved in the oral tradition:

> England number one. Japanee number two.
> Malayo, Manila bloody fool.
> South Sea all same.[11]

Among the indigenous population there was a similar ordering, the supposed superiority of Islanders over Papuans

[11] I am endebted to George Mye for this saying.

and Aborigines being reflected in the hard cash of wage differentials. Chief Protector Bleakley described them in more rounded terms as 'different in every way from the nomadic people of the mainland, being of much more sturdy build. In fact, many are of magnificent physique. They are very shrewd, but not so alert mentally' (1961:255).

In general terms the hierarchy approximated that of contemporary scientific racism, with north Europeans at the apex, black skinned peoples at the bottom, and the rest distributed according to their position along the colour spectrum. But although most Europeans in Torres Strait would have subscribed to this ideology, the order cannot simply be understood as a realization of it. Closely examined, it appears more complex, and historically must be understood as the product of the marine industry on the one hand and government policy on the other.

The situation can be sorted out in terms of two simple discriminations. Europeans, most Anglo-Australians, occupied the commanding heights of industry, commerce, government, religion and the military. Non-Europeans were subordinate and bound in service to them, by one means or another. (The Japanese divers would undoubtedly have penetrated the upper stratum, by taking control of the marine industry, had they not been prevented by special legislation (Bach 1961:110).) The non-European population was again divided between foreign and indigenous, each group being subject to separate regulations and economic practices.

By the turn of the century the Queensland government was moving beyond the control of recruitment in its efforts to reduce the indigenous population's contacts with outsiders. It transferred *beche-de-mer* and pearling stations from the inhabited islands, and expelled foreign residents, some of whom had lived with local women for years. In 1901 the Protector complained that it was impossible to stop Islanders getting alcohol, since 'a crew, part Malay, part-Islander, Japs etc. go into the pub together' (CPA 1902). Soon Islanders were not only excluded from hotels, but from Thursday Island during the hours of darkness. The introduction of the company boats meant that many Islanders worked only with other Islanders.

These regulations also isolated Islanders from white people. Meeting only the few officials and missionaries who had direct authority over them, many supposed that white people never performed manual work. Since the Islanders were already performing a useful economic role and making no demands on the taxpayer, the government had no occasion to contemplate their eventual integration with the majority Australian population. According to Chief Protector Bleakley, they were 'a race apart, who have nothing to gain by deserting their own people'. Their future was to be that of 'a self-dependent community life in the islands that are their birthright, as an integral part of our great Commonwealth' (1961:299).

In keeping with this policy, and with its general disapproval of 'half-caste' populations (Markus 1982:97-8), the government made sexual relations between Islanders and others an offence, and allowed inter-marriage only with the Protector's express permission. However, there was already a sizeable number of Islanders with European, Asian or Pacific Island ancestry, who posed a problem as far as the legislation was concerned. A number of these were resettled, some at the St Paul's Anglican mission on Moa Island, others at the Roman Catholic mission at Hammond Island. Those who remained on the reserves were declared to be Islanders within the term of the Act, on the ground that they were 'residing habitually' with the Islanders.

Through measures such as these, the colonial order made the Islanders into a formally defined category and bounded group. This group readily broke up into its component communities. Compared with the pre-colonial order they were more like one another, but less interdependent. Warfare had ceased, but so had inter-island trade. Instead, communities were locked in rivalrous exchanges of festive hospitality, church building and fund raising. At feasts the rivalry of the dancers could become so intense as to turn to brawling. Fear of sorcery lingered, and parents still resisted marriages with individuals from other islands; and yet the network of kinship and hereditary friendship provided a basis for unity when the occasion arose. Thus it was that at least once, in 1936, Islanders throughout the Strait were able to act against conditions to which they were all subject.

There was no such basis for solidarity with other segments of the labour force. Not only were their contacts limited by government regulation as well as cultural barriers, but their conditions of work were different. While the Japanese and Malays dealt directly with their employers, the Islanders had to deal through a government that controlled earnings as well as employment, and even some of the boats on which they worked.

One might say that its alienation of their money, in the literal sense of the term, obscured the alienation of their labour in the Marxist sense. Thus the economic problem presented itself to them in political guise and as the consequence of their particular relationship with the Queensland government.

As yet the Islanders' attempts to deal with their problems could be contained within the colonial order, for they had not formulated any coherent alternative. The old life was now too far behind them, and the life of white people still too remote. The seeds of an alternative had nevertheless been sown. Shortly before the strike the Bishop of Carpentaria had publicly proposed that the Commonwealth should take charge of Torres Strait and, to Bleakley's annoyance, Islanders had taken up the idea (Bleakley 17.1.36). It does not seem to have borne immediate fruit, although it may have been connected with the Murray Island council's request in 1939 for the diocese to take charge of their affairs. But when the Islanders finally formulated their alternative, out of the wartime experience, they associated citizen rights with the Commonwealth and colonial status with Queensland.

III Disastrous contact: 'army time' and after

Chief Protector Bleakley's plan for a bureaucratic utopia in which the Islanders could remain forever 'a race apart', was rudely shattered by the war. As the Japanese pressed southwards, the Australian army took over from the civilian administration, brought in hundreds of white troops, and put most of the men of Torres Strait into uniform. As has so often happened, in the Pacific and elsewhere, the military experience gave the Islanders a new sense of competence and entitlement, so that they came to believe that the government propaganda designed for the majority Australian population also referred to them. As Imanuel Wallerstein has observed in another connection: 'The process of maintaining relative social peace in the core areas required the elaboration of various ideological schemes of "freedom" which had the inconvenience that the concept spread to realms for which it was not intended' (1979:125).

The contact was, as an official was later to observe, 'disastrous', not least for the Queensland government, which had lost much of its legitimacy to the Commonwealth, as represented by the military authorities. Even before the war ended a Murray Island councillor[1] had presented the Governor of Queensland with the following petition:

> Torres Strait Councillors Application.
> To his excellency – Sir
> Torres Strait Islanders be self controlled by the people with the aid of the Commonwealth Government.
> When Japan declared war against Australia all our European leaders of Torres Strait were escaped for their lives and

---

[1] I have been unable to establish the identity of this councillor with certainty. Marou, the most likely candidate, was out of office at the time. George Mye has suggested that it was James Idagi, also known as James Williams, who was active in the army strike, and died soon after.

leave us helpless there was no word of evacuation, we were
left as a precious bait for the enemy. And the Governor is
now asked that Torres Strait be self controlled by the aid of
the Commonwealth Government for that purpose. Torres
Strait had volunteered in this present war therefore its people
must be on the same position as the European. That is to
say to have full Citizen Rights. To have full Trade of Union.
To have full European wages for all employment and Labour
condition and to have a higher standard of University
Education (Governor's Correspondence QSA 12257, 13.5.44)

The Governor's outrage at this approach was mollified by the
assurances of other councillors that they did not share its sentiments (*ibid.*). But in fact many of the servicemen did share the
aspirations it expressed, and they returned home at the end of
the war in the belief that the Commonwealth would soon honour
the promises they believed it to have made to them.

They were in for a long wait. Until the Referendum of 1967
Canberra lacked the constitutional power to intervene in what
was a state concern. Its one action was to allow Islanders, along
with Aborigines, to vote in Federal elections, and this did not
happen until 1962. Meanwhile the Queensland government,
through the newly named Department of Native Affairs,
returned to its duties, aware of the changes that had occurred,
but convinced that the Islanders' best prospects still lay under its
continuing tutelage. But economic *force majeure* did not wait
upon constitutional reform. Soon the colonial economy was
threatened by the demands of the mainland for Torres Strait
labour and by the increasing inability of the local economy to
support a burgeoning population. By 1961 it was apparent that
the malaise of the pearling industry was terminal. In that year a
Saibai leader, after a lifetime of working on boats, told me: 'We
very worried people these days. We come a little bit good, but we
look nothing change. Our houses are no good. We got no education. The boys can't find jobs. We like a bird shut up in a box:
we want to come out and fly, but we shut up.' Within a few years
the box would be opened and many of the birds would fly away
south, to join with workers from the poorer countries of Europe
as part of Australia's mobile labour force.

'Army time'

With Japan's entry into the war, Torres Strait became a theatre
of military operations, though not, apart from one air raid, of

actual hostilities. The Australian navy commandeered all vessels and the military authorities in Thursday Island took over administration of the region, interning Japanese divers and evacuating the European and Asian population to the mainland. Only soldiers and Islanders remained.

While the Defence Act exempted persons not of European origin from call-up for war service, but did not exclude them from volunteering, Australian Military Regulations and Orders No. 177 stated that only persons who were 'substantially of European origin or descent' were to be enlisted voluntarily (Hall 1980:28). After the bombing of Darwin, however, the army by-passed these rules to establish the Northern Territory Special Reconnaissance Unit and the Torres Strait Defence Force. The latter, manned below the rank of sergeant by Islanders together with a few Malays and Aborigines, included the Torres Strait Light Infantry Battalion, coastal artillery, a water transport group utilizing small craft, and several other units (*ibid.*:30). By the end of the war some nine hundred men had served in this force, which was almost all those who were physically fit between the ages of sixteen and thirty-five. Although few had been under fire and none had seen active service, they had all worn the King's uniform and borne arms. A number had received training as drivers, clerks and radio operators, and several had been promoted to non-commissioned ranks.

All those who served in the Defence Force were volunteers. Indeed some Islanders insist that its formation was the result of an approach by Marou, chairman of the Murray Island council. This eagerness was not, as Bleakley supposed (1961:72), out of hatred for the Japanese; men of this generation spoke well of their old skippers, who they suggested had dissuaded the Japanese air force from bombing their villages. Rather were they moved by the desire to prove their worth to white Australians, so that they would be entitled to a 'better deal' after the war. Many believed that they had been promised nothing less than full 'citizen rights', but while their expectations may have been extravagant there can be no doubt that recruiting officers spoke in such terms. Marou, a regular and honoured visitor at military headquarters, spent long hours discussing such matters with senior officers. The arrival in 1941 of social service benefits seemed to be a precursor of the new life.

It is worth remembering that at this time the Australian Government was seeking a 'welfare oriented consensus' that would erase the bitter memories of the depression (Roe

1976:217), and there was general recognition that the community would be entitled to a 'new deal' as a reward for wartime endurance (Dickey 1980:167). But hitherto Aborigines and Islanders had been ineligible for social service benefits. The change was urged upon the Commonwealth by various authorities, including the anthropologist A.P. Elkin (1944:53–4) and Chief Protector Bleakley (1944:24.7.41), in terms of social justice and practicality. No doubt the Government also took into account the dangers of a disaffected indigenous population along its weakly defended northern coastline – particularly as this population had been in close contact with Japanese divers.

The status of the Islander recruits was ambiguous. The army had intended that they should be separately quartered and perform duties apart from white troops, being paid less than half the normal rate to which they were legally entitled (Hall 1980:31). In the event, they frequently worked alongside white soldiers, and often did the same work. Islander non-commissioned officers demanded the normal respect from white private soldiers. Men of D Company who had been detailed for special duty at Merauke in Dutch New Guinea told the authorities that they had enlisted on the understanding that they were intended for 'labour purposes', and that since they 'had taken the same risks as the white personnel during the patrol work they should receive equal pay' (Godtschalk 5.1.44). They added that several officers had offered to support their claim. Similar discontents seem to have caused a brief 'sit-down strike' by A, B and C Companies in December 1943. According to the investigating officer (Swain 30.12.43), their complaints were as follows:

1.   The men claim they want equal pay and rights with the white soldier.
2.   They do not want to have any 'Island Laws' in the Army, particularly with regard to punishment for receiving liquor from white soldiers . . .
3.   The fact that white troops who were reported by Native NCOs for drinking in the hold of the boat were not dealt with, and every time any Native soldier does anything of that nature he is severely punished.

The response of the army authorities was relatively mild, milder perhaps than it would have been in the case of white troops. They merely imposed 'extra duties and packdrill' and demoted several NCOs, laying the blame on 'ringleaders' or a 'ringleader' whom they were unable to discover, although they suspected the Murray Islanders (Swain 10.1.44).

The investigating officer noted that the strikers' tactics were 'evidently' those of a trade union, and he suspected that they had been influenced by disaffected white soldiers (Swain 10.1.44). The type of soldier who opted not to serve overseas, known as the 'choco',[2] was often more radical or, at least, insubordinate than the regular volunteer. My own interviews with white veterans confirm that some did indeed sympathize with the Islanders and try to radicalize them (cf. Peel 1946:118). One told me that he had circulated whatever left-wing literature he could lay hand on, though to the semi-literate Islander his sympathy was perhaps more important than the content. The strike bore some fruit, for in 1944 a conference of officials in Melbourne, including representatives of the Queensland government, raised the Islanders' pay, but only to two-thirds of the normal rate, on the ground that to give them the full amount would cause trouble when they returned to civilian life (Hall 1980:31).

The war was only an interregnum; when it was over Islanders once again came under the control of Queensland. But those who had served in the TSLI had become what Renato Rosaldo has called a 'cohort' (1980:110–20). Their experience of what they called 'army time' had left them with a distinctive consciousness of their worth and the means to construct an alternative to their present situation. Down-playing their second class status in the army, they echoed the tropes of Australian militarism to speak of 'sacrifice' and 'comradeship'. Having fought for 'King and Country', they were now entitled to a share of the 'better deal' that had been promised to all who had 'served'. As one veteran ruefully explained some years later, 'we all came out of the army with swelled heads!'

The restoration

At the end of the war the military authorities returned the Islanders to the keeping of the Protector and the newly named Sub-Department of Native Affairs.[3] The Torres Strait Islanders Act

---

[2] Choco is short for 'chocolate soldier'. Derisive in its implications, it was presumably coined by volunteers (Wilkes 1978:78).

[3] The Sub-Department of Native Affairs came under the control of the Minister for Health and Home Affairs, along with two eventide homes, an institution for inebriates, an institution for the blind and the State Tourist Bureau. Native Affairs became a full Department in 1963. It was renamed the Department of Aboriginal and Islander Affairs in 1968.

of 1939 was once again in force and stayed in force without substantial change until 1971. However, the government realized that the clock could not be turned back to 1939.

> The serious disruption occasioned by the advent of war to the long accustomed mode of life practised by the Torres Strait Islanders had had a profound effect on both the economic and psychological aspects of their make up. From a cultural point of view the war contact was disastrous, in that it was swift and all-enveloping. In its aftermath came various degrees of bewilderment, for the rehabilitation of these people embodied not a return to pre-war conditions, but a return to conditions forever changed by the wave of unprecedented prosperity that has swept over the entire area. (DNA 1947)

The same report set out the perspective in which future policy must be formed.

> Complete conversion to the life of the white races must come, and all concerned should realize the implications of such a transition and be ready to deal with any eventuality that may arise. The change has come rapidly, and to prevent disillusionment a carefully thought out plan of education must be instituted.

It cannot be said that any such plan emerged, for subsequent reports confined themselves to practicalities. From 1956 on the annual reports declared a commitment to the national policy of assimilation. Thus in 1958 the Director stated that Queensland aimed 'at the ultimate assimilation of all aboriginals and half bloods into the state's community life. Nothing in that policy, however, can be construed as an impetuous forcing of people to change their environment while they are unwilling to accept the responsibility of full citizenship' (DNA 1958:2). The Department took this qualifying clause seriously, particularly where the Islanders were concerned. The niche that the Islanders had occupied in the colonial economy would simply be enlarged to accommodate their rising numbers and aspirations. This would be effected by putting them into the positions left vacant by the Japanese divers and boatwrights at the outbreak of the war (DNA 1947). The master pearlers were unhappy with this arrangement, but the Department was able to silence them by mobilizing the public hostility to the Japanese which had been aroused by the war.[4] Outside the region, Islanders would be

---

[4]   The pearlers were permitted to import divers from Okinawa in 1959, but they proved no better than Torres Strait workers.

allowed into the labour force only at points where they would not be in competition with white workers.

In the event it was the 'wave of unprecedented prosperity' that saved the day. This lasted just long enough to draw the Islanders, along with their wartime savings and post-war gratuities, back into the marine industry, and when it broke Islanders were still on the average better off than they had been before the war, though lagging far behind white Australians. The combination of rising population and static employment opportunities only gradually became apparent, and meanwhile some individuals could earn what was, by local standards, big money. Thus the disillusionment that the Protector feared came only by degrees, and was distributed unevenly.

Controlled emigration to the mainland served as a safety valve, both for growing pockets of unemployment and for political discontent, but the numbers had to be kept small so that the boats could be manned at home, and a mainland backlash could be avoided. Those who remained in the Strait lived a life that was supervised, if less strictly than a generation earlier. The Department still regulated employment and managed their money, although it imposed fewer restrictions on how they spent it (DNA 1950:29). Alcohol was forbidden. Islanders had no vote and no access to government other than through the Protector, so that opposition was bottled up in the communities, or dissipated in abortive attempts to form alliances with sympathetic Europeans on the mainland. Coincidentally or not, liberalization followed the collapse of the marine industry in the 1960s.

Pearl shell and plastics

War in the Far East had put an end to trepanging as early as 1936, and there was no resumption after 1945. The post-war industry dealt only with gold-lip and trochus shell, commodities which varied in their relative importance until 1962, when plastics displaced the latter in button manufacture and made serious inroads into the demand for the former. Pearling continued on a reduced scale throughout the 1960s, sustained by the need of local pearl culture stations for small quantities of live shell. A few enterprises stayed in business, but the numbers of boats and men employed were fractions of those of a decade earlier.

After six years of war, shell had been in demand and easy to get. Islanders and Europeans rushed to buy boats of all sorts and sizes from which to pick up trochus. But two years later the demand had shifted to gold lip, for which luggers with diving equipment were required. The total earnings of the industry climbed steadily to a peak of £520,000 in 1950–1, falling off in the following year, recovering briefly in 1956–7 with a figure of £632,000 before going into a long if uneven decline (Queensland Year Book *passim*). If we make allowances for inflation, it becomes apparent that the industry had reached the limits of its post-war expansion by 1951. This is reflected in the number of boats at work, which never regained the 1950–1 peak of 125, and the number of men employed, which peaked at 1,360 in the same year. (Incidentally, these figures were far below those of 1904, the high point of the century, when 378 boats employed 2,509 men.)

The labour for the industry now came entirely from the islands, together with a few Aboriginal communities on Cape York. As a result, Islanders were able to move into the more skilled and better paid positions of skipper and diver. In addition, the Department negotiated new basic wage agreements across the board which were in real terms substantially above the pre-war rates, though still below average earnings on the mainland. Thus on the trochus boats the basic rate in 1947 was £15 per month, plus keep and the possibility of bonuses. During the good years divers could earn as much as £500, and in 1957 one skipper made £4,000. However, there were always boats which, because of bad luck or mismanagement, failed to rise above the minimum. Moreover, although rates of pay were adjusted from time to time, they failed to keep pace with increases in the cost of living. Thus by 1958 the basic monthly rate for trochus workers had reached only £19.[5]

The government fleet followed much the same trajectory as the private. During the post-war boom it reached forty boats, but by 1957 it had fallen to twenty-two, by 1961 to fifteen and by 1967 to six (DNA *passim*). The casualties of the first two years were boats which were poorly suited to pearling, but subsequent casualties were mainly caused by bad luck and inefficiency. As

---

[5] Comparing these cash earnings with movements in the North Queensland retail food price indices (QYB *passim*), it becomes clear that while Islanders were earning more in real terms than they had in 1939, they were well below the 1947 level.

competition intensified the masters equipped their luggers with engines and those working gold-lip with diving compressors. To keep up, the government fleet had to follow suit, which meant choosing only those enterprises that seemed capable of covering the increased running costs (DNA 1948:26). The rest either went out of operation or continued as marginal concerns with negligible earnings. In the event, not all those in which the government had invested were able to stay out of debt, and it gradually reduced its commitment, concentrating the surviving boats in the hands of those who could run them most profitably. In 1961, eight of its fifteen boats worked from Badu, whose success I shall discuss in a later chapter.

The effect of these trends was an increasing inequality among communities. For example Saibai, which by 1960 was without boats, could send its men to work for Badu or Yorke Island skippers, but it would not see them all year and would not have the benefit of the turtle and dugong that the boats brought back to base each month. Instead the people of Saibai bought canoes from their Papuan neighbours, gave more time to hunting, and secured yams and bananas in exchange for store goods bought with their social service benefits. The Murray Islanders, situated further from Papua, either cultivated their gardens or emigrated south.

Although the Islanders' economic situation had been much improved after the war, the market imposed a limit to expansion and, consequently, to the amount of labour that could be absorbed on the boats. After the peak year of 1951 the number of men employed never again reached 1,360. In 1958 it fell below a thousand, in 1961 below six hundred, declining further throughout the decade (QYB *passim*). Meanwhile the population was increasing rapidly.

The published population figures for Torres Strait are unreliable. The Queensland government's figures of 5,000 in 1948 and 7,250 in 1960 are in excess of my own estimates. On the other hand, the methods of racial and ethnic identification employed by the Commonwealth census from 1961 lead me to believe that its figure of 5,217 was an underestimate.[6] This in turn would cast doubt on Caldwell's estimate of 3,698 for 1947 (Caldwell 1974). But if we arbitrarily adopt a middle point be-

[6] See the explanatory notes to a recent census of Aboriginal and Torres Strait Islander population. (Australian Bureau of Statistics 1982, also pp. 177–80.)

tween the two sets of figures, and take into account data from later censuses, it is still clear that the population was increasing rapidly. It is also evident that, while the marine industry provided employment for just about every able-bodied male between the ages of fifteen and forty in 1951, it could absorb only about one third of them ten years later.

The marine industry was no longer the only field of employment for Islanders. The State government had expanded its operations in the Strait, creating positions for teachers, medical aides and assistants in its retail stores. It also hired Islanders to work in its bulk and retail stores on Thursday Island, its boat repair yards, its administrative office and hospital. To house those who now lived on Thursday Island it built a new settlement a short distance from the town, and the carpenters and plumbers who worked on it went on to put up new houses and public buildings in the islands. There was more building to be done at the new settlement at Bamaga on Cape York. Originally established to resettle flood victims from Saibai, it eventually attracted people from other places, who came to work in its agricultural and sawmilling projects.

There are no indications of the number of Islanders in government employment, but by my own calculation the figure would have reached between three hundred and four hundred by 1960. Although they mostly did the same kind of work as Europeans, they invariably lacked qualifications so they could not get similar employment outside the government sector. Correspondingly, their pay was well below the rates for white teachers, clerks, carpenters and the rest, as though geared to the going rates in the marine industry. The only Islanders whose earnings approached those of European employees were the handful who carried managerial responsibilities in the government trading agency, the Island Industries Board.[7]

Given the generally low level of cash earnings, Commonwealth social service benefits constituted a significant subsidy for most households. Before the war, support for the aged and indigent had come from the island fund, which was financed by taxing the Islanders' earnings. Now the Commonwealth provided child endowment, invalid and old age pensions, and maternity allowances, though not unemployment benefit. State government assistance was as yet not appreciably above pre-war

[7]   The Island Industries Board was the successor to the pre-strike Aboriginal Industries Board, which replaced Papuan Industries in 1930.

levels, except for the installation of radio communication between Thursday Island and the outer islands and the provision of housing and medical facilities on Thursday Island and Bamaga.[8]

Certainly, average cash incomes were appreciably lower than on the mainland, particularly when the much higher prices of commodities, due to freight costs, is taken into account. This relative poverty was accurately reflected in the quality of housing, much of which was of bush materials or unlined corrugated iron. Nevertheless the changes in the regional economy and in government practice had been such as to create a greater degree of economic differentiation than had existed previously. A handful of outstanding boat skippers occupied the apex of the pyramid; below them were their less able colleagues and the upper grade of government employees. The families in these brackets who lived in the islands gained considerably by escaping rent and having access to fresh vegetables, fish and meat. Boat skippers, particularly, consumed or disposed of large quantities of turtle and dugong. Those on Thursday Island were not so well off in that they usually paid some rent and could get little by subsistence production, the ground being unsuitable for cultivation and the seas around being over-fished. Towards the bottom of the scale were those who lived in the communities, without jobs and dependent for cash on the endowment coming to their children or the pension of some relative. But worst off were those who lived on Thursday Island by casual work, or as dependants of kinsfolk in employment. The Department periodically rounded them up and repatriated them, but there were usually a hundred or so at any one time, unwilling to face some trouble at home or clinging to the meagre sophistication of life in town.

Only a lucky few could hope to earn the same as even an unskilled white worker. Apart from this, 'proper wages', as the Islanders called them, could only be got by emigrating to the mainland. In 1947 the Department had responded to requests from the Eastern Islanders by allowing eighty men to go down to the cane fields, where there was a shortage of cane cutters (DNA 1948:2). The experiment was successful and repeated several years running. Each time some of the men found other jobs at the end of the season and stayed on. Presently their numbers

[8] This estimate is based on visible evidence of expenditure. The Department's published financial statements have never been such as to permit any kind of breakdown. My guess is that Banga and the Tamwoy Town settlement on Thursday Island were taking the lion's share of the Torres Strait budget.

were augmented by young men who, absconding from trochus boats at Townsville and Mackay, came seeking their hospitality. Except for a few trouble-makers, the Department made no attempt to repatriate them. Once cane cutting was mechanized, the majority of the immigrants found work as railway fettlers, an occupation unattractive to white Australians on account of its low wages and working conditions, but paying standard rates regardless of race or colour. With overtime, a man could earn five or six times what he got at home, and the money was his to spend as he pleased, for the government made no attempt to regulate the employment or earnings of Islanders once they left Torres Strait.

News of life down south soon spread back to the islands, producing further restiveness. There was an obvious risk that the trickle, if not controlled, could become a torrent, and that the marine industry would then be deprived of the cheap labour on which it depended (DNA 1952:2). The government had the power to regulate movement, in the sense that no Islander could step on the Thursday Island plane without a permit, but in practice it used these powers selectively by delegating them to the councils. Communities like Badu, which still needed labour for the boats, forbade emigration; those like Murray Island, which no longer ran boats, encouraged it.

By 1960 there were, by my count, no more than 500 Islanders working on the mainland, the great majority of them single males from the Eastern Islands. In the decade that followed, employment opportunities in the Strait declined, despite the opening of some relatively well paid jobs in the new pearl culture industry. Meanwhile on the mainland the demand, not just for labour, but for Torres Strait labour, escalated. The Eastern Islanders, who had been derided back home for laziness, established a reputation for being first-class tropical workers and were in demand on construction projects across northern Australia from east to west. A memorandum in my possession, written for a major Australian company active in northern Australia at that time, gave a good account of Islander workers. Among its comments, it stated that they were superior to European migrants in learning to handle equipment; their hygiene habits were also superior to those of European migrants and some Australians; and their behaviour around the camp was good. Supervisors wished they had more 'Thursday Islanders'. Pearl culture companies were now flying Torres Strait workers on short term contracts between Thursday Island and their new farms in Western Australia. By this time the pressure was too strong for councils to block migration. Nor, given the depressed state of the local economy, was there much point.

Colonial politics and some alternatives

The ex-servicemen had returned to their communities with a sense of entitlement to a new deal, and in the years that followed they talked endlessly of 'freedom' and 'citizen rights', ideas that I shall analyse in the next chapter. But there was no lack of specific demands. In place of the Department's schools, run by one white teacher and untrained Islander assistants, they wanted 'proper schools' like those on Thursday Island, and the opportunity for secondary education. They wanted the same pay rates as white workers, and to handle their earnings without government interference. They wanted to be able to move about without restrictions, to go into hotels and consume alcohol, and to vote. In short, they wanted an end to 'the Act' (i.e. the Torres Strait Islanders Act of 1939) and to the Department of Native Affairs, which they came to regard with increasing resentment.

The ex-servicemen also came home with a sense of political strength, having used the weapon of the strike, to effect, twice in the last ten years. Reading between the lines of the government's report quoted above, one suspects that the Department resumed its powers with some apprehension. Yet there was never another strike, nor any other mass demonstration of discontent. Despite the mounting dissatisfaction through the 1950s, the biennial conferences of councillors became increasingly docile.

The trend is well illustrated in the case of voting rights, to which I referred briefly at the beginning of this chapter. Prior to the amending legislation of 1961, Queensland had the power to determine who would vote in Federal as well as State elections, since the Commonwealth Electoral Act gave the vote to those whom the State accepted as voters. (In fact ex-servicemen were an exception to this rule, but no one had intervened to get them their rights.) In 1949 the report of the Department of Native Affairs had conveyed to the Queensland Parliament the resolutions of a recent conference of island councillors, particularly

> the desire of the people to obtain a greater recognition as citizens of the state. The councillors were unanimous in

> their request that civil rights as applicable to white citizens
> should be granted them as tax payers of the nation. Already
> social service benefits, to an even greater extent than
> applies to Aboriginals, are enjoyed by the Islanders, but
> these people have not yet attained their desire for the
> franchise. (DNA 1949:23)

These aspirations are consistent with what we know of Islanders
in the years immediately following the war, and are not
inconsistent with the position of the Department quoted above.
The Queensland government nevertheless denied the request,
perhaps on the advice of the retired Bleakley, who wrote in
his book:

> It would be a sorry day for their happiness as a race if the
> franchise were extended to them and they were subjected
> to the disturbing influence of political partisanship, which
> actually could have little meaning and interest for them.
> (1961:299)

The 1958 conference of councillors not only accepted this
denial, but unanimously declared that Islanders were 'not ready'
for the vote (minutes of Torres Strait Councillors' Conference,
5.1958). Yet within three years some of the same representatives
were telling a Commonwealth Parliament Select Committee on
Voting Rights for Aborigines, that they did after all want it. The
1958 resolution was certainly contrary to the wishes of many
Islanders with whom I discussed the matter; conversely, not all
those who requested enfranchisement in 1961 were privately
happy at the prospect. The most likely interpretation of these
sudden reversals is that once the Queensland government had
set its face against enfranchisement, the Department of Native
Affairs and in turn the councillors fell into line. By 1961,
however, it was apparent that the Commonwealth was about to
override this opposition, and the councillors' statements were
an indication that Queensland was bowing to the inevitable.
(Even so, it was not until 1964 that Islanders voted in State elections, and only after the possibility of a special, non-voting
parliamentary representation had been considered.)

Although the level of public concern over Islanders and
Aborigines was still relatively low, Queensland evidently preferred to contain Islander representation within its administrative framework, leaving the responsible minister to speak on
their behalf in Parliament or to the world at large. In closed

meetings such as the biennial councillors' conference it was easier to control what was said. Islanders at first did press for citizen rights, and Marou of Murray Island went on doing so into the 1950s, but the general trend was towards caution, at least in public. It is not hard to see why this should be. Firstly, senior officials of the Department presided over the meetings and drew up the agendas. Secondly, they knew the Islanders personally, and so were in a position to play on their loyalties or call in debts of gratitude.[9] Moreover, an increasing proportion of the councillors worked for the government as teachers, store managers and boat skippers, and so had reason to fear for their livelihoods, should they openly defy the authorities. Finally, in the Cold War climate of the period, the risk of being called a Communist was often enough to silence dissent.

In any case, from 1949 the Department worked increasingly through three Representatives, from the Eastern, Western and Central Island Groups. The Western and Central Island Representatives, who were both boat skippers in the government fleet and followed the official line, held their position for life, by some arrangement that I have never been able to elucidate. The Eastern Islanders, by contrast, went on electing their Representative, who for several years was the intransigent Marou.

By the mid-1950s, however, even the Eastern Islanders were working within the system, and the most radical demands were for better education. Discussions were taken up with such mundane if important matters as the building of houses, the installation of water systems, the delivery of supplies to the stores, and so on. Once or twice the possibility of opening a beer canteen on Thursday Island was considered, but left undecided. Between conferences, the representatives and councillors were kept busy as intermediaries between their people and the DNA office, handling endless petty problems. If one could help a constituent to get a pension, or a government job, or a new house, or even sort out a problem with a pass book, one could claim to have done 'something for the people'. A radical councillor might promise more, but was more likely to come home empty handed.

[9] The Queensland Department has been dominated by long serving officials. Between 1914 and 1986, it has had only three Directors: J.P.W. Bleakley, C. O'Leary and P.J. Killoran. All three served for extensive periods in Torres Strait, and O'Leary ran the Department from Thursday Island from 1948 to 1953, so that they were known personally to many Islanders.

With these tangible rewards in mind, voters increasingly gave their votes to candidates who had an acquaintance with the bureaucracy, or at least an effective grasp of English – men who, as they put it, 'know how to talk to white people'. More often than not, these men were already government employees.

The dreams of 'army time' had almost vanished from public discourse by the mid-1950s, but privately they remained very much alive. Some, like my informant, concluded that they had been suffering from swelled heads and were not after all ready for the responsibilities of citizenship. But many still believed that change would come sooner or later, and that the Department of Native Affairs would go (see pp.101–5).

Those who wished to carry on the struggle for freedom had to find ways outside the official framework of representation. Some talked of striking again, as in 1936 and 1943, but the necessary conditions no longer existed. When Islanders met on Thursday Island they were divided by inter-community rivalries, which when fired by alcohol led to brawling. The social and economic differentiation that had occurred within the communities undermined the old solidarity. Moreover, there was a greater degree of differentiation among the various enterprises that made up the government fleet. Those which were the most important to the Department were also the most successful and the least discontented. A strike by the Eastern Island boats would scarcely be felt.

Powerless to act on their own account, the radicals were sustained by the belief that there were still white people, like their wartime comrades, who would help. Many believed that the Federal government would give them a better deal than the State: it had been the government of 'army time', and some believed that it had administered Torres Strait in the freer times before Islanders came under the Queensland 'Act'. But while Islanders continued to receive its social service benefits, Canberra seemed remote and inaccessible. No Islander had yet been there. Meanwhile there were other possibilities.

The earliest approach came from the Australian Communist Party. Whether or not contacts had been established during the 1936 strike, they were certainly operative at the end of the war when an Islander who had been seconded to the United States Navy visited a Communist journalist, Gerald Peel, on a visit to Sydney. In the following year Peel published *Isles of Torres Strait*, a short history of the region ending with a draft programme which articulated the kind of aspirations that had been expressed in the petition reproduced at the beginning of this chapter. It proposed immediate improvements in educational and health facilities, award rates of pay and assistance for Islander boats. Subsequently, Torres Strait should be made an autonomous region under the Commonwealth, with marine and other natural wealth reserved for the exclusive use of the Islanders (Peel 1946:134). It is not clear how widely this book circulated, but a prominent Island leader told me that it was 'the true heart of Torres Strait'. In 1948 another Communist journalist visited Thursday Island and published an exposé of conditions in a party newspaper (Devanny 28.2.48; 3.3.48; 6.3.48; 10.3.48). But while she made contact with a number of Islanders, including Marou, the chairman of Murray Island, there were no political consequences. They found the interest gratifying, but did not respond to, or perhaps were unaware of, Communist doctrine. Had they been inclined to keep up the contact, it would have been impolitic once the Cold War set in for they knew that mail was liable to censorship as it passed through the DNA office. Thereafter political outlets were limited to the occasionally sympathetic ear of the State member. Institutionally the parties were uninterested in people who could not vote.

Instead the radicals turned towards an organization that corresponded more directly to their experience, the Australian Legion of Exservicemen and Women. This organization, much smaller and less influential than the Returned Soldiers League (RSL), had been formed to cater for veterans who had not served overseas, as well as for some political dissidents who had been denied membership of the larger body. Around 1949 one of its members, who happened to be working on Thursday Island, established a branch for veterans of the Torres Strait Defence Force. The prospect proved attractive in that it seemed to re-create the comradeship of 'army time' and promise support well beyond what the Legion could in reality give. Membership soon became synonymous with opposition to the DNA, and several councils banned it on this account. However, there were sizeable branches on Thursday Island and on Murray, which busied themselves with fund raising and writing letters to the Legion headquarters in Brisbane. Attempts by Department officials to set up an alternative organization for veterans came to nothing.

Torres Strait radicals did not confine their attentions to the Legion, but sought out visiting journalists, clergy, politicians

Plate 4. Meriam ex-servicemen perform an army dance

and anyone else who might put them in touch with the higher authority they were sure would recognize the justice of their cause, if it only knew. Learning that I came from Canberra, some supposed that the Federal government had sent me to gather information, preparatory to intervening on their behalf. By 1960 the sense of frustration and expectation was oppressive, intensified by the economic downturn but also by a number of unconnected developments. The *Aussie Legion Journal* of April 1960 had carried a feature which called the Torres Strait veterans a 'lost legion', unjustly denied 'full citizen rights and repatriation benefits'. Word spread that these benefits, which were small sums given to white troops on demobilization, would amount to thousands of pounds for each man. Someone claimed that the money had already reached Thursday Island, but was being held up in the Department office. People had also got wind of the Commonwealth's initiative on voting rights, and of the formation of a branch of the Aborigines and Torres Strait Islanders Advancement League in Cairns. A Christian Cooperative established in 1958 by a Sydney–based Anglican priest, the Reverend Alf Clint, seemed to promise an alternative both to the pearling industry and to the government's Island Industries Board (Tennant 1959). On Murray Island that Christmas the leaders of the local Legion ordered their members to dance in celebration of their impending freedom. At New Year I heard a speaker declare that henceforward black and white would mix together as equals, my presence in the crowd was an indication of the future. There would be unrestricted intermarriage and Islanders would no longer get 'half pay' and 'half pensions'.

The more sophisticated Islanders dismissed these ideas as the delusions of the gullible and uneducated, and indeed those who clung to them were often both. But ironically, most of what they hoped for was realized over the next decade. By 1970, although wages were still low, Islanders could vote, enter hotels, move as they pleased and spend their money without restriction. Even the repatriation benefits had materialized, albeit much smaller than imagined. By this time, however, many of the radicals had already left Torres Strait.

There was an undeniable element of protest in the emigration. Of course, many other considerations influenced the decisions of those who made this difficult and often painful step. Some left for reasons that were purely personal; others acted on the spur of the moment, in anger or out of a love of adventure. Nevertheless, many Islanders saw the emigration as a collective statement of dissatisfaction with conditions in the Strait. On the mainland they would get 'full wages' and their children would be able to get a 'proper education' in place of the 'gammon schools' at home. Religion and politics were free. Back home the Department of Native Affairs was allowing the councils to 'spoil the islands'.

Anglicans and Pentecostalists

The adversary relationship that developed between the Legion and the Department of Native Affairs had its religious counterpart in the conflict between the established Church of England and the Assemblies of God, a Pentecostal sect introduced by

Islanders from the mainland. Both can be seen as expressions of the mounting contradiction between the colonial and mainland social formations, as well as reactions to the increasing social differentiation among Islanders.

Anglicanism in Torres Strait had taken on a distinctively colonial character over the years. It was closely identified with the DNA and, since both of them claimed legitimacy under the Crown, Islanders tended to regard them as a unitary establishment. Such an impression was reinforced by their appearance together on ceremonial occasions such as the enthronement of a new bishop or the visit of a State Governor. Occasionally one heard of disagreements, but the division of spheres established when the Anglicans took over from the LMS in 1915 was such as to ensure that these were minor and settled in private. Bishop Davis had criticized the government at the time of the 1936 strike, but his successors remained silent. Not until 1959 did the Church venture a public policy statement, and though its cautious wording might suggest some dissatisfaction with the economic and educational conditions of the Islanders, there was no challenge to the Department's authority (Diocese of Carpentaria 1960 a,b). Even had it wished, the Church lacked the means of offering any kind of alternative; indeed it was dependent on Government assistance in the conduct of its three missions on Cape York, and would soon surrender them to the DNA.

Torres Strait Anglicanism was also colonial in the sense of adopting a distinctively Island style in the conduct of its services and the running of its parishes. This was in part a consequence of the early period when the shortage of clergy had left the island parishes with an unusual degree of autonomy. The subsequent predominance of Islanders among the clergy favoured its perpetuation. But it was also a matter of policy. A priest who served the diocese during the first ten years described how they reversed the former LMS approach:

> There was sometimes too much of the idea of requiring the new converts to abjure that which was not actually out of harmony with Christian precepts . . . Our policy was to 'christianize' old customs where possible, and to retain native forms of expression (rather than so called 'white man custom') instead of arbitrarily cutting out everything. (MacFarlane, 1959)

Under the new dispensation, not only were feasts and dancing an appropriate way to celebrate religious festivals such as Christmas and Easter, but 'island hymns' – in fact of Samoan composition, though in the vernacular – and even drums were acceptable inside the church. Similarly, unique forms such as the tombstone opening emerged with full patronage and participation.

When Islanders began settling on Thursday Island after the war, the cathedral was the only place for them to worship in. The bishop did not discourage them, but their appearance prompted the withdrawal of part of the white congregation, whose preserve it had long been, while those who remained soon became a small minority. The bishop's response was to let services take on some of the distinctive character of Torres Strait Anglicanism: Island priests alternated white Island hymns with *Hymns Ancient and Modern*, and when the organ broke down it was replaced by a drum which accompanied both.

Viewed in the context of the culturally diverse, worldwide Anglican community, this was simply a sensitive adaptation to local conditions. But in the colonial context it posed the question whether this was a 'proper' church or a mission to people still not fully civilized. The Diocese of Carpentaria was organised like others in Australia, but it was also affiliated to the Australian Board of Missions. Islanders were baptized, confirmed, received communion and were buried like Anglicans everywhere, and yet they surrounded these events with island custom. Some had been ordained priests, and one was an archdeacon, but everyone knew that the standards of St Paul's Theological College were low by mainland standards. One diocesan official described these clergy to me as 'good chantry priests', with the clear implication that they served a very limited purpose. Finally, when all was said and done, Islander priests were still under the Act. This was impressed on one priest who came upon two white priests drinking wine and was himself offered lemonade.

As long as Islanders lived isolated in their communities they could ignore such problems, but once they began to travel on the mainland they could not escape the fact that Australian Anglicanism was both unfamiliar and unwelcoming. As we shall see in the next chapter, this weakened the legitimacy of the Church of England and enhanced the attractions of the Pentecostal Assemblies of God who, while welcoming Islanders, made no attempt to cater for their cultural idiosyncrasies.

This sect came out of the robust tradition of north American evangelical fundamentalism (Anderson 1979). Established in 1914, it reached Queensland in 1929, becoming the largest of the Pentecostal sects (Sommers 1966:167–9), though miniscule by comparison with the major denominations. Its meetings are enthusiastic, emotional, even exuberant in the revivalist mode. There is a minimum of ritual and only the simplest of forms. Though a pastor usually conducts the meeting, he leaves ample opportunity for members of the congregation to make spontaneous testimonies, confessions and prayers. These alternate with the singing of hymns and well known revival choruses. Faith-healing is a prominent feature, with the sick always remembered in prayer if they cannot be brought out before the congregation. The *glossolalia*, which are believed to be the same 'gift of tongues' that the Holy Spirit brought to the disciples on the first day of Pentecost, can occur at any time though more appropriately in the closed 'tarry' meetings.

Traditionally a religion of the dispossessed and the displaced, which goes on to the streets to rescue the drunkard and sinner, the Assemblies of God in Queensland had already established a following among the Aboriginal and *kanaka* populations. Islanders coming to the mainland found a church ready not just to receive them, but also to seek them out on the streets and the remote railway sidings where they worked. The white 'brothers and sisters' were not only friendly and informal, they invited them into their homes. One Islander told me with some feeling how on his arrival in Mackay, white Pentecostalists had met him, taken him home and fed him 'free of charge'. This was 'proper love'! The informality also extended to the meetings, which gave Islanders the opportunity to participate as they did in the Anglican churches at home but could not on the mainland. The songs and choruses were easy to learn and their guitars welcome. The set phrases, out of which most prayers and testifying were composed, placed no great demand on their limited English.

Two emphases of the Assemblies answered the particular needs of Islanders on the mainland. One was their classically Protestant rejection of worldly pleasures combined with the doctrine that economic success was a sign of grace. Islanders, who had come to the mainland to improve their economic circumstances, found that if they could earn more they could also spend it faster, particularly on alcohol. Pentecostalism, so they claimed, gave them the power to resist such temptations and to save their money. It also had the power of healing. This proved important to Islanders, who distrusted European medicine and missed the ministrations of their priests and folk healers back home.

On the mainland becoming a Pentecostalist was a matter of individual choice; in Torres Strait it had far reaching social and political implications. The Islanders had long been aware of religious diversity, but since the Roman Catholics and Presbyterians, who were represented on Thursday Island along with the Church of England, observed a tacit agreement not to poach on one another's flocks, it was not an issue. It quickly became an issue when the chairman of Murray Island, Marou, allowed Pentecostalists to erect a meeting house on his land and invited the Assembly to send a pastor, though without himself joining. The circumstances surrounding this action will be considered in chapter VI, but we may note now that he was a leading exponent of citizen rights. This fact may not be irrelevant to the speed and severity of the response. The bishop immediately excommunicated him, and the synod resolved that other denominations should be banned from the reserves. Confirmation from the councillors' conference provided the necessary sanctions, and the Assembly was stopped from spreading to other islands. But while the Murray council soon passed back into Anglican hands, the sect survived, attracting some who had not been on the mainland but liked the form of services and the emphasis on faith healing.

There are local aspects of this dispute that will be considered in chapter VI. The point to be made here is that, while the Assembly was confined to Murray Island, and to the township on Thursday Island where the councils had no authority, the question of religious choice was posed for all Torres Strait. Radicals recognised a parallel between their own struggle and that of the Pentecostalists, even when they were not attracted by the sect. The latter, often ex-servicemen, developed the point, some even asserting that theirs was a 'Commonwealth church', with the implication that their eventual triumph would coincide with the disappearance of the State administration and the coming of freedom. But their non-conformity brought to the surface other aspects of the underlying contradiction. The argument that there should be the same freedom of religion in the islands as existed on the mainland called into question not just the Church of England's monopoly, but the authority of the councils and the local government system. At another level, Pentecostalists

challenged island custom, indirectly through its close connection with Anglicanism, and directly through their condemnation
of worldly pleasures such as dancing. They went further and
required their members to wear pants and shoes in church; to go
barefoot and in *lavalava*, as Anglicans did, was 'not civilized'.
These prohibitions not only offended Anglicans but on occasion
troubled Pentecostalists, particularly those of the older generation. When in 1960 the head of the Legion on Murray ordered
his members to dance in celebration of their imminent freedom,
the Pentecostal members forgot their vows and joined their
comrades on the dancing ground.

Natives or citizens?

'Army time' drew the men of Torres Strait out of their
communities to perform a new and more worthy role in the company of white comrades. Peacetime sent them home again and
back to their old occupations. Colonialism restored offered
more scope for advancement than before, drawing Islanders into
its command structure and channelling them into a wider range
of occupations. But the rates of pay for these were geared to the
marine industry, and thus well below what any unskilled white
could command.

Moving into Thursday Island, Islanders could gain some sense
of urban living and pursue some of these new occupations. But
in doing so they exposed themselves to the inequities of
colonialism to a far greater degree than at home. Thursday
Island was becoming increasingly like a company town, except
that the 'company' was the Queensland government, which soon
employed more people than the whole of the private sector. The
power of the DNA was not confined to Islanders but included,
directly or indirectly, those who had to do with them as
employers or even as suppliers of goods and services. Moreover,
the legal distinction between Islanders and others provided the
basis for a social discrimination that pervaded every area of life.
Contacts between black and white tended to be clandestine and,
because of the restrictions on sexual contacts and the supply of
liquor, tinged with illegality. The regime appeared all the more
arbitrary in that South Sea and Asian 'half castes' from the two
missions, though often in the same occupations as Islanders and
earning the same wages, were not subject to legal disabilities.

Uncertain of their own status, these marginal people alternated between recognizing their Torres Strait kin and being 'flash'.

Conditions on Thursday Island may have intensified Islander discontent. What converted that discontent into a challenge was the recollection of 'army time' and the experience of life on the mainland, where Islanders enjoyed equal wages and freedom from supervision. They may have suffered some discrimination, and the white friends they made might not have been the most respectable of citizens, but they chose, as with their military experience, to remember the goods things.

Given the limited scope for political outlet in Torres Strait, the challenge most often found expression in the communities. But these were no longer as easily mobilized as they had been before the war. Though still closed to outsiders they had become diversified in terms of their past and present linkages with the outside world. The ex-servicemen were the most clearly defined and militant cohort, claiming special wisdom and privilege. However, they found themselves opposed by the boat skippers, and also by the teachers and store managers who owed their advancement to the government. This second group also formed something of a cohort, since many of them had attended a special school for bright pupils just before the war, run by the former teacher–supervisor, P.R. Frith. Ironically, though claiming 'more education', they were prevented by their jobs from visiting the mainland, and they were consequently threatened by those of lesser attainments who came back full of urban sophistication and subversive ideas. Race was also beginning to divide the communities as Islanders with a South Sea or Asian ancestor emulated their mission 'countrymen'[10] in claiming superiority over 'Torres Strait natives'. As though to support their claim, 'half castes' (anyone of mixed descent) were disproportionately represented in the ranks of boat skippers, government servants and community leaders.

The communities were simultaneously becoming differentiated from one another, in terms of their place in the colonial system and their links with the world outside it. As I shall show in the cases of Murray Island and Badu, the internal differentiations

---

[10] 'Country' – short for countryman – was the term of address among men from the same place in earlier years, and it has been perpetuated among their descendants. People with a grandfather from Samoa, Rotuma, Tanna etc., recognize others with the same links as quasi-kin.

I have been discussing manifested themselves in varying strength and in differing configurations.

The community's capacity to domesticate these intrusions also varied, but was in every case strained. In an island which had no more than one or two boats calling each month, it was possible for the big issues to fall out of focus, becoming confused with family rivalries and local squabbles. Acting against this tendency, however, was the Islanders' love of talk. The world and their place in it were topics of inexhaustible interest. Just as an earlier generation had made themselves a new culture, so now their descendants were working out a way of debating the issues which concerned them.

IV   Reflections in a colonial mirror

July One, the date in 1871 on which the LMS brought the 'Light', which is to say the Gospel, is the one festival in the year that is distinctive to Torres Strait Islanders. It might be called their national day, for it has been celebrated as far away as Sydney. The story of the first landing on Darnley Island is often told, and on special occasions, notably the centenary celebrations in 1971, it is re-enacted.[1] The sight of a dinghy carrying missionaries from their ship causes a crowd to gather on the beach. As it approaches it is challenged by men in traditional fighting gear who, after some parley, lower their bows and display the leaf that signifies peace. The party then comes ashore and proceeds to the church where, after a short service, there is a feast and dancing.

Although the Islanders believe that this dramatization represents the actual events, it owes more to the romantic picture the Reverend McFarlane wrote for his supporters in faraway Britain (1888:33–6). As noted earlier (p.33), a European trepanger and his workers had been in occupation of the island for some years, and the people knew the effects of firearms too well to offer any kind of resistance. July One is, then, not so much a reconstruction of events as an articulation of meanings, one of many to be considered in this attempt to describe Islander consciousness after three generations of colonialism.

Ceremonial representations, such as the first landing, readily lend themselves to interpretation, but everyday conversation also provides a point of entry into Islander thought. Islanders have a great love of talk, both the stereotyped joking and storytelling that characterizes large gatherings, and the spon-

[1]   The celebration of July One was instituted by the Church of England soon after their takeover of the islands, as a tribute to the LMS and perhaps as a means of ensuring continuity (MacFarlane 16.7.59).

taneous yarning that passes away the evening hours at sea or at home. As I moved from circle to circle and community to community, I began to perceive recurring themes underlying the anecdotes and the gossip, all directly or indirectly concerned with their present and future place in a world dominated by white people.

Identifying the individuals referred to in these conversations provided an initial difficulty for me, but the terms in which they were discussed proved broadly familiar. My companions seemed to have relegated traditional forms of thinking to the edges of their minds, utilizing them only rarely and discretely for matters of purely local concern. The dominant modes of thought derived from mission Christianity and official teachings concerning the state, together with a work ethic that had its origins in the industrial revolution. What was lacking was a sense of the market or of *Realpolitik*: the world as the Islanders understood it was governed by a moral economy, and their place in it would finally be determined by their worthiness as Christians, loyal subjects and good workers.

These modes of thought had their origins in colonial ideology. Though not always speaking with one voice, missionaries, pearlers and government officials had brought with them and propagated doctrines which, whatever their transcendental meanings, carried the message that colonialism was good, right and part of the natural order of things. In the early stages, indoctrination had proceeded through dramatic demonstrations such as the discharge of firearms, punitive raids, the distribution of gifts, silent trade and the quaint pantomimes the missionaries performed to communicate their intentions to people whose language they did not yet understand. Soon, however, the missionaries were conducting formal indoctrination, not only in church but more intensively at the Papuan Institute (see p. 35); and one of the Gospels had been translated into Meriam Mir and into the two main Western dialects.[2]

The LMS also provided secular education, but its Pacific Island teachers were inadequately trained for this work and had dif-

[2] The translations were the work of the Loyalty Island teachers (Haddon 1907:187–9; 226–7). By the 1950s only the Mabuyag Gospel of St Mark was available, having been reprinted, and none of them was in regular use. In church Islanders struggled with the seventeenth century English of the authorized version and the Book of Common Prayer. Father Wilhelm Rechnitz spent many years translating the Communion service into both Eastern and Western languages, but the clergy used them rarely.

ficulty in enforcing regular attendance (Langbridge 1977:74–5).
It was this failure that led the Government Resident Douglas to
intervene, and by the turn of the century to maintain a chain of
government schools, and compulsory attendance for all children
from the ages of six to twelve. These came under the control of
the Chief Protector after Douglas's death, and remained the
responsibility of his successors until 1984, paralleling but
separate from the Queensland public education system. Instruction was of variable quality, particularly during the early years,[3]
producing few graduates with anything like an adequate grasp of
written or spoken English. But if nothing else, it inculcated a
respect for the monarchy, an awareness of the British Empire
and, after the Second World War, some sense of Australian
nationhood. School houses displayed pictures of British royalty
and maps of the world, large areas of which were coloured red to
indicate that they were British possessions. Anzac Day, Empire
Day and, later, Australia Day, as well as the monarch's birthday,
were all observed, and some teacher–supervisors made a daily
ritual out of raising and lowering the flag.

Royalty and the flag, indeed, figured largely in the emerging
colonial order. The Anglicans made much of being the established
Church and routinely offered up prayers for the reigning King or
Queen. The government, likewise, proclaimed its connection
with the monarchy. Before the Second World War it arranged
for Islanders to appear before members of the royal family, and
after the war it presented Island leaders to them. In the meantime, viceregal parties periodically toured the Strait, and in 1958
the Queensland Minister for Native Affairs distributed pictures
of Queen Elizabeth II to each island community, 'as a symbol of
their freedom'. Members of the Torres Strait Defence Force
underwent a further round of indoctrination from their officers,
and for them these symbols assumed a heightened importance.

As for the work ethic, it came in the preachings of missionaries,
the scoldings of officials and the urgings of employers, as well as
in the daily hazings of skippers. It took on a new legitimacy when
the Church of England reversed the old LMS sabbatarianism and
allowed crews to work on Sundays. From another quarter, both
the teachings of clergy and officials and the example of Euro-

---

[3] Mr Alan Williamson is currently writing a doctoral dissertation on education
in Torres Strait up to 1941. I am indebted to him for permission to read his
preliminary drafts, which discuss the teachers and curricula in some detail.

Plate 5. *'One King, one Flag, one Fleet, one Empire'*
(courtesy Cairns Historical Society Collection)

peans in general, reinforced the importance of commodities in 'civilized' living.

From the late nineteenth century, then, the Islanders were subjected to a steady barrage of indoctrination, the gist of which was that they were indebted to white people for the benefits of British rule, the Christian Gospel and the opportunity to earn the wherewithal for a 'civilized' way of life. At the same time, it was made clear to them that they were not the equals of Europeans and could not expect to enjoy the same freedoms or material wellbeing. Whether they would ever do so was left unclear, but whatever was said in public, many Europeans believed that the Islanders were inherently inferior. Wartime propaganda offered a more sanguine view. But as late as 1960 both clergy and officials worked on the assumption that the colonial order was there for the duration, fortified by a pseudo-evolutionism that declared 'It will take them hundreds of years to catch up!'

We cannot, of course, assume that colonialism wholly captured the Islanders' hearts and minds. Given the sanctions at the regime's disposal, an absence of dissent cannot be construed as consent. There are, nevertheless, reasons for believing that the

Islanders soon accepted a good part of what they were taught. I have already suggested that they were culturally predisposed to accept new things, while their religious pluralism made it easy for them to take on a new cult. Although the two religions were not close, there were points of similarity, such as a myth that paralleled the story of Christ's death and resurrection (cf. Beckett 1975). The LMS may also have been right in supposing that its Pacific Island teachers, being recent converts, were 'better able to get at the heathen of their class' than Europeans (McFarlane 1888:138; cf. Langbridge 1977:88–114).

The missionaries' own accounts have to be taken with a grain of salt, written as they were to impress superiors and financial backers (cf. Langbridge 1977:128–9); but Strachan's description of the church meeting on Saibai in 1885, quoted earlier (pp. 40–1), suggests that it was not all wishful thinking. And when the Anglican Bishop of Carpentaria made his first tour of the new island parishes in 1915, he declared the Islanders 'not only Christian in name, but also to a large extent in practice' (White 1.8.1915). Their faith may at first have been ingenuous. In 1960 a Badu churchwarden could chuckle over the unsophisticated zeal of the 'old people'; but he also recalled the tears they shed as they heard the story of Christ's passion. If the simplicity of South Sea Congregationalism had given way to the pomp of High Anglicanism or Pentecostal enthusiasm, there were still those who saw visions and believed in miracles, attributed misfortune to divine anger and sought the aid of priest or pastor when sick. Similarly, Bleakley's description of the Islanders as 'intensely loyal' (1961:293) was confirmed for me by the emotion Islanders displayed while listening to the radio broadcast of the funeral of a Governor of Queensland whom they had never seen. Indeed the only part of Australian culture about which they expressed some doubt was its medicine.

Finally, anthropology has no way of determining internal mental states. What is certain is that the Islanders came to *use* the doctrines and ideas they had been taught. This use may initially have been opportunistic, a means of winning European favour and discomfiting rivals, which would have been encouraged by the authorities' reliance on local mediators to relay their teachings. But this same mediation enabled the ideology to become part of everyday life, and so increasingly taken for granted. As Islanders came to live, and, even more, to think with their work ethic, their loyalty and their Christianity, colonial culture became hegemonic, 'a lived dominance' (Williams 1977:108–14).

Living and thinking with the ideas the Europeans gave them, the Islanders were coming to see themselves as reflections in a colonial mirror. I have adopted this metaphor from Michael Taussig's powerful analysis of the culture of terror in the rubber-extracting regions of the northwest Amazon, early this century (1984). Taussig uses it to illuminate the 'mimesis between the savagery attributed to the Indians by the colonists and the savagery perpetrated by the colonists in the name of . . . civilization' (*ibid.*:495). Similar constructions characterized the early encounters between marauding trepangers and 'savage' Islanders in Torres Strait, with the Pacific Island crews playing a curious mediating role. As the colonial order emerged, the cultural backwardness attributed to the Islanders reflected the under-developed economy which needed them to remain that way.

My concern here, however, is with the other side of the equation, which Taussig is unable to consider in his article for lack of data. It entails a shift from the active to the passive voice, since the Europeans were dominant culturally as well as politically. Thus the Islanders saw whites as themselves in reverse: independent where they were dependent, responsible where they were irres-ponsible, worthy where they were unworthy. Yet the mode of Islander incorporation into the colonial society saved them from getting caught in a descending spiral of submissiveness and self-abnegation. As we have seen, it left them in occupation of their islands and partially dependent on local resources to which they had traditional rights. Interacting with people of their own kind, in the practice of a custom that was theirs, gave them an alternative mirror in which to see themselves. 'Army time' gave Islanders a glimpse of another kind of European who was like themselves – or perhaps like the idea of themselves that had been conjured up by the wartime interregnum. His reflection lingered in the glass after Queensland had restored the colonial European to his rightful position, creating a confusion of images that made it impossible for them to undertake a consistent critique of colonial culture. But it could not prevent them from debating the issues among themselves, albeit in a piecemeal and con-tradictory fashion, discovering in the process ambiguities and dissonances in the ruling ideology.

Ideology, if it is to bind together the various elements of a society in relations of dominance and subordination, must establish the primacy of some bond, in terms of which all people are the same. It is the doctrinal equivalent of, and may find expression in, rituals that express what Victor Turner has called *communitas*: a 'modality of social relations' which suspends hierarchy and division to reveal 'an essential and generic human bond, without which there could be no society' (Turner 1969:96–7). Thus the Anglican rite of Holy Communion reveals each as a sinner, saved only through God's grace and Christ's redemption. What is less certain is whether such doctrines lead to the acceptance of inequality in everyday life or to its questioning. Genovese writes of Christianity:

> When it proclaimed a single nature, endowed by God, for every man, it also proclaimed all men brothers. But in so doing, despite every attempt to separate the Kingdom of God from the kingdoms of man, it illuminated the chasm that separated the equality of men before God from the grim inequality of man before man. (1974:166)

To understand how established 'truth' can be reinterpreted and turned against those who established it, without committing the heresy of changing it, we must distinguish between the code and the message it is used to convey (cf. Hunt 1977:258–9). Codes, be they language or some other symbolic form, are susceptible to regulation; indeed their strict enforcement is a notorious feature of authoritarian regimes, just as their flouting is a sure means of defiance. The messages that they carry are harder to police, so that political repression may simply result in people learning to express dissent through the codes of deference. Indeed, the more authority values code as a thing in itself, the easier it will be to turn to subversive ends. By means such as this the hegemonic impact of a ruling culture can be dulled, if not withstood.

Colonialism established mission Christianity, loyalty, and the work ethic so firmly that no one dared flout them, or perhaps even thought of doing so. But they inevitably suffered changes of meaning in the process of being transposed to the community setting, the more so since their local custodians were Islander priests, teachers and skippers. The wartime interregnum virtually necessitated reinterpretation because of the dissonance that had crept into the voice of authority. Even then the Islanders conducted their critique within the framework of the colonial ideology, emboldened perhaps by the very inviolability of its codes.

Darkness and light

The principal message of July One is that Islanders are Christians. And inasmuch as this is the most important thing that can be said about them, it means that they are essentially the same as white Christians. Yet the ceremony also contradicts this equality, for those who bring the Gospel are white, while those who receive it are black: having received this 'gift beyond price', they are forever indebted. The very concept of mission – something that is sent – implies the existence of people who lie beyond the boundaries of the Church, and must be brought into the fold. We must therefore probe beneath the surface to discover the unstated meanings of this transaction.

The Light metaphor, current throughout the South Seas, refers first and foremost to the Gospel. However, the story of its coming records that the old people could not understand what the missionaries said, or make much of their mute pointing to heaven. It goes on to describe how the missionaries gave them rice and biscuit, and there is great amusement over their suspicion of foods that have since become staples. The implication is that European products won Islanders for Christianity in this first instance. In the same vein, an old churchwarden showed me a stoneware bottle of the kind used by way of payment in the early days, with the comment: 'This is what civilized Torres Strait!' In reality it was the pearlers and trepangers who introduced such things, so that its appropriation into the Light story is remarkable. Explaining why their forefathers had accepted Christianity, my friends often said it had 'more power', a term that included temporal as well as spiritual power. The Gospel made Islanders 'civilized', but the term meant more than religion as it is normally conceived. In the early days, preachers likened heaven to the Burns Philp store on Thursday Island (MacFarlane 16.7.59). According to one of my informants, 'civilization is to know everything and make your living by it.'

The Light image implies the existence of a Darkness, which in Torres Strait was used to represent the heathen state in which the missionaries found the Islanders. Around 1960 'Darkness Time' still occupied an important place in the consciousness of their Christian descendants. Those who had experienced it were long dead, and those to whom they had spoken were a dwindling number, but there was a lively if sometimes inaccurate oral tradition, quaintly primed by the novels of Ion Idriess (1938; 1950), and by occasional dance-dramas depicting 'olden time' people (Beckett 1982).

There was no question of going back to the old ways. It would have been socially ruinous for anyone to suggest such a thing; but the Islanders were unwilling to forget their past, or to let the missionaries appropriate it. Instead they took refuge in the picturesque and the dramatic, celebrating the warfare and the ritual in a way that revealed a nostalgia for lost male power. It was said that the 'old people' were bigger than their present day descendants and – unlike the latter – merciless killers, a quality that enhanced their sexual powers. As for the old cults, they were described as 'heathen' but not bad, and the fetishes as 'idol gods' but not false. Islanders began as religious pluralists, only gradually giving to Christianity the exclusive devotion it demanded. In the past they had unceremoniously thrown away a skull that lacked power; now they 'threw away' the old religion, allowing the missionaries to destroy or take away many of the fetishes. But the spiritual essences that animated the fetishes were not thereby destroyed, they had simply 'gone away'.[4] Thus it was said that when the missionaries burned the Malu headdress on Murray, onlookers heard a sudden shriek and 'something' flew up into the air and disappeared. Similarly, when a schoolteacher took the old god Waiat from his hiding place on Waier island there was a storm. Islanders did not, it must be emphasised, go on practising the cults; but they were not willing to disown them altogether.

Recognizing that the Islanders considered their cults to be authentic, we can perceive another message in the July One ceremony. Islanders voluntarily gave up their old powers to accept Christianity, just as they lowered their bows to let the missionaries land when they might have killed them. Since they were not starting from a position of total spiritual deprivation, their debt to the missionaries was that much less. Even so, they were prepared to pay the missionaries for the religion they had brought, just as they paid their affines and trade partners or, in the past, those who brought new rituals and songs. And yet this was not a relationship of balanced reciprocity. White mission-

---

[4] The many Torres Strait masks in museums around the world are evidence of the massive cultural loss that occurred during the early and mid-nineteenth century. But, according to tradition, several of the most important fetishes disappeared of their own accord, or were hidden by their custodians.

aries retained control of the Church. Indeed there were some who believed that they were withholding the core secrets of Christianity. Why should this be so?

The July One story describes an instantaneous transformation: the Light shone and Darkness was dispelled. But its annual commemoration might suggest that the process was still going on. Darkness remained a potent image in the rhetoric of parish leaders, representing the antithesis of Christianity, much as the Devil is often made to do. Its most evil manifestation was sorcery. This resided in the past that the Islanders had foresworn, but lingered with a few wicked individuals who had inherited the knowledge from earlier generations. It also existed on the margins of the present in the still 'uncivilized' peoples of Papua and Cape York. These 'bushmen' were ridiculous in their unsophistication, but also dangerous, using sorcery against Torres Strait, and even teaching Islanders how to use it. Here was the Achilles heel of Island Christianity, for while white people seemed not to be vulnerable to it, Islanders still were.

Although I did not hear anyone articulate such an idea, it seemed as though Islanders, by being locked into their ancestral communities and kept partially dependent on traditional sources of livelihood, could not quite disengage themselves from the past. It was consistent with this that some still used magic in gardening and hunting. However, there was never any magic for pearling, though divers prayed before they went down, and wore phials of oil that had been blessed by a priest. The community, then, was for some at least a battlefield on which the forces of Darkness and Light still contended.

This was how the LMS had seen the situation, and the ever-present danger of backsliding had provided a justification for the imposition of restraints and punishments well beyond what prevailed amongst white people. This was nowhere more in evidence than in the regulation of sexuality, which had been relatively free in the old days, and elaborated into a thoroughgoing eroticism. The Protestant missions of the South Seas seem to have been particularly preoccupied with this matter. But in Torres Strait it became a means of controlling young men's labour so that, as the pastors gave way to government teacher–supervisors, the restraints continued, albeit with some mitigation of the cruel and unnatural punishment employed by the LMS. The elders of the Church had long supported these controls, and when the councils took charge of the communities and sat as local courts, they enforced by-laws relating to 'immorality', mainly fornication, but also, occasionally, adultery. When a European, or an Islander who had been to the mainland, pointed out that there was no such law among white people, the elders replied that 'black people' needed restraint, otherwise they would 'go any way'.

The issue was posed in a novel way with the introduction of ballroom dancing after the Second World War. This not only brought unmarried persons of opposite sex into previously unacceptable proximity, but actually required them to make physical contact. When reminded that this was 'civilized' practice, the elders replied that black people were different. Just as island dance was not fit for white people, so the waltz was not fit for black people. Some communities eventually accepted it, though never for married women. But there was widespread relief when rock-and-roll replaced touch dancing in the mid-1960s.

The question underlying these debates was whether Islanders suffered from an inherent defect which left them incapable of self-control and so forever morally inferior to Europeans. It seems that some of the Polynesian pastors had told them that they were the children of Ham, and so eternally doomed to be the 'hewers of wood and drawers of water'. The Church of England gave no support to such ideas but manifested the kind of paternalism that represented Islanders as perpetual children. The idiom was certainly current. In 1910, the Protector had declared them children, in need of a wise but firm parent (see p.49). Bishop White recorded with evident gratification the words of an aged Saibaian leader, on the occasion of the Church's takeover from the LMS: 'We are like children who have lost their father and mother. We do not know what to do or where to look. You will be our father and show us the way to go and how to live' (White 1917:54). The requirement that white priests, like white teachers, should be called *baba* (father) and their wives *ama* (mother) must be understood in similar terms.

The practice of calling Island priests by their given names rather than Father indicates their ambiguous situation in this scheme, as in the colonial order as a whole. Islanders themselves were sensitive to these ambiguities, and unsparing in their exposure of educational shortcomings, social pretensions and moral frailties. Several priests had had to abandon their vocations following denunciation by their parishioners. Yet

Francis Bowie and Poey Passi were revered for their blameless lives and piety, being credited with the powers of healing and clairvoyance. One, it was said, had received a ghostly Communion, just before his death in Thursday Island hospital; and the account of it, supposedly from a witness, would not have been out of place in the lives of the saints. Both were said to be able to ward off sorcery and call down retribution on the sinful, but perhaps the most instructive example comes from the youth of one of them:

> Teased for his chastity by a group of young people, who had been talking about love magic, he replied: 'Alright, I'll match my *puripuri* (magic) against yours – *inside the church.*' After the service was over he found one of the girls waiting for him. She suggested a 'secret wedding' (i.e. sexual intercourse), but he sent her back to her parents.

In this and other matters, these priests could do 'Christian way' what others did by magic. What is remarkable is that no white priest was credited with such powers, and it is tempting to argue that they derived from the very intensity of the contradictions massed around the position of the Islander priest living in the traditional community. But the point I want to emphasize here is that they had negated Darkness by carrying the power of God into domains of which Europeans were ignorant or uncomprehending. In the same way, Islanders sought the service of Islander priests rather than their white colleagues, in time of illness, which might or might not have been caused by sorcery.

Such attainments were at least implicitly subversive of the colonial order, since they showed – as one man put it – that 'Island people have more faith (i.e. miraculous power) than white people'. The implication of this was that Islanders no longer needed white people to mediate between them and God. One might see here a resurgence of the separatism that had asserted itself on Saibai in 1913 through the German Wislin cult (Haddon 1935:46–8). The good things of the world were made by the ghosts, not by white people, who simply intercepted what was intended for Islanders and forced them to work for it. However, Jesus Christ was now on Saibai, as well as in heaven, and the ghosts would soon return to free them of their dependence on Europeans. By 1960 few people had heard of these ideas, and fewer would have believed them if they had; but the same separatism could be heard in the claims cited above, and in such statements as 'black people believe money is the root of all evil. They don't care about money. In the islands they have everything they need' or, more simply, 'We no belong money. White man belong money.' In the post-war period, those who had gone to live on the mainland returned with reports of religious observance neglected, divorce, drunkenness and gambling. The implication of this discovery was that white clergy had misled, even made fools of, Islanders.

Communities still dependent on subsistence production and whose key relations remained outside the market, seemed to nurture such utopianism. However the reality, even for them, of economic and political dependence forced them towards another kind of formulation. This same suspicion of bad faith also undermined the Church's long established position in the gift economy. The point is illustrated by the following anecdote, which probably refers to events occurring around 1900.

> A Boigu man told me how they got a white man's boat off the reef. When that white man come to pay, Mr Walker (F.W. Walker, LMS missionary and founder of Papuan Industries – see above p.49–50) said, 'They don't know about money, their reward is in heaven.' So he took the money for Papuan Industries. That Boigu man said, 'If we got that money today, we might be alright. We never know that time, money cover the world.'

In a more direct way, people became increasingly reluctant to pay their Church dues, complaining that 'bishop too much ask money.'

The new formula that emerged cut across the colour line to oppose 'good people' and 'bad people'. Christianity still provided the criteria, but it was now used to challenge the colonial order it had once supported. This was the solution that Pentecostalism offered, making acceptance of 'the Lord Jesus Christ as one's personal saviour' the supreme value. Islander Pentecostalists claimed that the Assemblies of God had more power, both in terms of the miracles their pastors – black and white – could perform, and their capacity to regulate the lives of their members without resort to external sanctions. The older generation recalled that the LMS had placed prohibitions on worldly pleasures such as dancing and smoking; the difference was that these applied to white as well as black. Moreover, backsliding resulted not in fines and the scoldings of village elders, but in the rejoicing with which confession and repentance were received. Such testimonials, the very lifeblood of revivalist Christianity, placed black and white on the same footing, as 'brothers' and 'sisters', not parents and children. Further, the regular reaffirmation and renewal of personal salvation negated the imbalance implied in the July One commemoration, since it applied equally to everyone.

From its July One beginnings, then, Islander Christianity had faced three possible directions. Of these three the separatist was the least articulated, amounting almost to a yearning for a freedom that was irretrievably lost. Between the other two, represented by the Anglicans and the Pentecostalists, there was a continuing debate. For the former, the Assembly of God was a 'gammon church', only recently formed and without standing among 'normal' white people, whereas the Church of England was santified by the apostolic succession and was headed by Her Majesty the Queen. The latter replied by identifying the Church of England with Queensland and its colonial regime. The Assembly was – by a logical leap that I could never follow – a Commonwealth church. Its ways were those of white people, rejecting 'uncivilized' customs such as dancing and wearing *lavalavas*, which Anglicanism still tolerated. Pentecostalism also enabled Islanders to attain a European way of life by its prohibitions on worldly pleasures.

What is perhaps most remarkable about all this, is that the emigration to the mainland and, so to speak, the mainland's invasion of Torres Strait, did not result in a secularization. Instead Islanders re-thought their Anglicanism or sought out other versions of Christianity that seemed to accord more closely with their new situation. At the same time, they were thinking along similar lines with the ideas they had acquired from school and in the army.

Subjects and citizens

There is no secular equivalent of July One. Both in ceremony and tradition the Church gets virtually all the credit for 'civilizing' Torres Strait. However, I recorded one account of pacification from Mareko Maino, grandson of the *mamoose* of Warrior Island (Tudu).

Captain Banner (a pearler, resident on Warrior Island at the time) talk to Kebisu (the head man of the island). 'I been call this man o' war to quiet you people. All time you kill. Better you come good. Better you try civilize these people. If I say yes, man o' war come wipe out all people belong Warrior Island.' So skipper tell Captain Banner, 'I'm going to leave Union Jack, first place in Torres Strait.' So that man o' war leave two-three bag of flour. That night he come ashore, they put a flag pole. 'Tell that old man come here. We'll show him we got different arrow.' They show them that rifle. They give a rope to Kebisu. 'When I tell you pull, you pull.' So old Kebisu pull that rope and Union Jack come out. 'That flag means you no more fight. If you do, this boat going to come back.' So Kebisu say, 'No more fight.'

This appears to be a conflation of several distinct events. Captain Banner established a trepang and pearling station on Tudu in 1868, banishing some of the inhabitants until they undertook to be of good behaviour (Chester 1870). However, it was the police magistrate, Captain Pennefather, who in 1879 'fired five shells from the guns, close to the island from a distance of 2000 yards which had the effect of showing them what could be done if necessary' (Pennefather 19.12.1879). Pennefather was visiting Tudu in order to inform the inhabitants that their island was now part of Queensland, and they 'amenable to the laws of the white man'. As a further object lesson he put the chief and several other men in irons overnight, under suspicion of having poisoned a European (*ibid.*; see also Sharp 1980). Whatever the facts, the linking of the Union Jack, the Royal Navy, firearms and flour, with pearling and pacification is highly significant. The underlying theme of submission is the same as in the Coming of the Light story, but duress is admitted – although the few hours that Kebisu spent in irons have been omitted.

The first political event to find a place in the folk memory is Queensland bringing Islanders 'under the Act' in 1904, after the death of the Government Resident Douglas. In 1960 there were still some who remembered this, but the story had gone into general currency that up to this time they had been ruled by the Commonwealth government. I suspect that this was a recent coinage, deriving from their 'army time' experiences. At all events, it led them to ask the question, Why had the Commonwealth abandoned them to the State? How had they fallen from grace? Many found the answer in a drunken brawl that occurred around that time, resulting in the sacking of a Filipino jewellery shop (cf. Paterson 1983:19–20). Having abused their freedom, they must find a way of redeeming themselves before it could be restored.

Japan's invasion of New Guinea provided just such an opportunity. It also brought to life words such as loyalty, sacrifice, and motherland, which had long been the currency of school lessons, but were now being addressed to Islanders in recruiting speeches. An English language song composed at the time, and sung repeatedly in later years, echoes these sentiments.

> I think for the country.
> I think for the country and motherland.
> All volunteer army.

The formation of the TSLI at a time when the colonial order was virtually suspended, brought them together with white people into a state of communitas. And the response of at least some white soldiers led them to believe that their bid for equality had been recognized. This is the message of another Meriam and English language song composed around the same time.

> Australian boys *wi tabara ged dekaereta*
>   (they left their country)
> *Pei bakeauda*
> (came here)
> TSLI they going to fight for their own freedom and liberty.

It was consistent with such sentiments that army veterans should have made freedom, along with citizen rights, their watchword. During the 1936 strike such talk had been considered premature; after 1946 it no longer seemed so. Out of the debate that engaged Islanders over the next twenty years, two opposing positions emerged. On the one hand were those who supported the colonial order, insisting that the Queensland government, like the Church, was acting in good faith and would introduce material and social improvements piecemeal, as Islanders showed themselves worthy and capable of handling them. A Saibai councillor hearing that Western Samoa was about to get its independence, wondered whether there was a plan for all Pacific territories, including Torres Strait, to get independence in due course. Their adversaries questioned Queensland's good faith. Islanders were already civilized, they insisted, and by serving 'King and Country' in the 'hour of need' had redeemed the debts that their ancestors had incurred when white people brought them the Pax Australiana. They had now earned, and should immediately be given, their freedom. This term I initially understood to mean the removal of the disabilities and restrictions they suffered under the Queensland Act. But it entailed economic as well as social and political change, and for some amounted to nothing short of a total transformation of the life they knew. According to one explanation, 'The main thing in freedom is white people's living: only little bit work and plenty wages. No get a hand dirty.' With this would go not only full wages but full pensions, which in fact they received already, and handsome repatriation benefits to ex-servicemen. Island councils, courts and by-laws would give way to Commonwealth law enforced by white magistrates and police. Small wonder, then, that some Islanders became angry when the Minister told them that the Queen's picture was their freedom!

Some even imagined, or dreamed perhaps, that their islands would be transformed into modern cities, with tall buildings and busy traffic. Their enemies ridiculed such notions. One even likened them to a cargo cult he had read about in a magazine. But in fact they were working on sound, if selective, understandings of how the world worked. Industrial capitalism was certainly capable of transforming a remote, undeveloped region into a bustling metropolis, and during the 1950s it was giving a practical demonstration of this capacity at the Weipa bauxite mines on nearby Cape York. They failed to grasp the economic conditions that would cause the commitment of resources on such a scale, but they were not wrong in supposing that political influence and social policy were also considerable factors. And their belief that wealth would be distributed according to some principle of social justice was not far from the rhetoric of the welfare state. Islanders had already had some experience of this in the form of pensions and child endowment, which had come to them about the time when the Pacific War was beginning. These inspired an old man to address a party of army recruiters, visiting Badu, in the following terms: 'When I was a child I got no friend. This time I got plenty friend.' His use of the term friend was not accidental. What he was doing was to apply the principles of the indigenous gift economy to relations with the Australian government. This, however, was not just a survival of the past, but something that had been sustained by the moralism of mission Christianity, and now by the rhetoric of the recruiting officer and of the welfare state. Together these combined to create a sense of a *moral economy*, which is to say a belief that the workings of the economy were subject to the recognition of certain rights and obligations. However, whereas the moral economy of E.P. Thompson's English poor of the eighteenth century (1971) or James C. Scott's Southeast Asian peasants (1976), was grounded in tradition, that in Torres Strait was based upon a developing relationship between Islanders and white Australians, and conceived of in positive terms of growing entitlement.

For the sceptics, such talk was just 'silly', the confused fantasies of minds too uneducated to understand what white people told them. Indeed the Islanders' defective education was the principal ground for rejecting talk of freedom. They lacked sufficient education to vote in elections, determine their own future, or even work on the mainland. This touched on a sensitive nerve, for all Islanders felt themselves uneducated compared with white people, particularly when it came to speaking standard English. Children finished their schooling at fourteen, and while a handful of bright scholars had received an extra year of education in the late 1930s, others had missed their normal complement during the war period. Thus, men who were eloquent and acute in the vernacular, or in Broken English, became tongue-tied and incoherent when trying to communicate in the standard English required in official situations. Voters in council elections searched for candidates with better-than-average competence, since so many of their representatives returned from conferences without any understanding, or with a wrong understanding, of what had gone on. This created a sense of helplessness which found release in jokes;[5] but it also undermined the Islanders' confidence in their ability to cope with freedom. Critics of the colonial order, however, turned this argument around:

> They say we can't get freedom till we better educated. But that same talk since before the war. When my father was councillor they ask more education. How long we been ask that thing and never got it yet? Torres Strait people never

[5] These jokes follow a fairly stereotypic pattern, according to which some self-important man, usually old, attempts to make an impression by airing his English, only to commit some absurd blunder of pronunciation or usage.

> will get education while they under the Act. While we
> under the Act we'll always be down.

Getting a better education for one's children was, indeed, a
common justification for emigrating to the mainland.

Like the Pentecostalists, these radicals had come to distinguish
between friendly white people, who recognized the justice of
their cause, and unfriendly whites who wanted to keep them
down. Given its commanding position in the Strait, the DNA
was inevitably cast as the villain of the piece. All ills were laid at
its door. Since it negotiated wage rates with the master pearlers,
it was to blame if these were not higher. Since it managed
Islanders' enterprises, it was to blame if they failed. Some even
alleged that the Department was withholding the ex-servicemen's
repatriation funds. Given this bad faith, the hospitality traditionally offered to visiting politicians and officials, in which
Islanders had taken such a pride, was perceived as gullibility.

> We always think that when visitors come to the island we
> respect them. But when we go to Thursday Island they
> always look one side. And most of them, you'll find they
> won't take any coloured people into their home.

In the same vein, a man refused to practise dances to welcome a
visiting dignitary, asking, 'Why should we make ourselves
monkeys for him? What's in it for us? Nothing good.'

The Commonwealth was not included in these strictures.
Remote from everyday affairs, it had come to represent friendly
Europeans much as the Assembly of God had done for the
Pentecostalists, which may explain why the Assembly was called
a Commonwealth church. Known to have 'more power' than the
State government, it had appeared as an alternative patron at
least since 1936 when the bishop had proposed that Islanders be
transferred to its care. And just as the Pentecostalists could
revolt against the Church of England without compromising
their status as Christians, so the radicals could revolt against
Queensland without bringing their loyalty into question.

'The laziness of the native'

More than other parts of the colonial ideology, the work ethic
had been thoroughly domesticated. This was at least partly due
to the fact that those working on the boats were the younger
males. Since the married men had dependants to support, it was

mainly to the unmarried workers that the parish and the older generation looked for help; thus, when men were discharged from the boats, they were expected to make donations and distribute gifts. Bleakley describes young men in Mabuyag passing through the village with bolts of calico, tearing off strips for this relative and that as they went (1961:258). I myself have seen a young diver take the new watch from his wrist and place it on the wrist of a favourite uncle. Church leaders and the parental generation had material reasons for urging the value of work.

But the boys had their own reasons for going to sea, for it had become a test of masculinity. Indeed there was more than a passing resemblance between boat work and the old time initiation. Parents put their sons under the care of an older kinsman who would 'teach them how to work', a process that commonly included some hazing. Removed from their families, the boys came under the control of older men and formed close bonds with age mates. The very harshness of the life was a matter for pride: swimming for trochus off Mackay on a winter's morning, walking barefoot on the sharp coral, rowing long distances back to the lugger after a day's work. There was the risk of attack from shark, stingray and stonefish. But 'it made your body strong'. This might also be a boy's first chance to see Thursday Island, or perhaps one of the north Queensland port towns. And when he returned at the end of the season it was to form gift ties with kin and perhaps win the approval of some prospective parents-in-law who wanted a good worker for their daughter. In the words of a Darnley man, 'Trochus work was something you wanted to do; boys took a pride in it.'

But the social pressures on the boat workers virtually forced them to put a monetary value on their labour. As early as 1907 they evidently thought it was worth more than they got (see p.48). The response of the authorities was to compare their work unfavourably with that of other races; and like colonialists the world over, they pronounced the natives lazy. The older generation were not above repeating this reproach by way of rousing up their sons, though they were unwilling to admit that they had been similarly culpable in their young time. But they had themselves been recipients of 'black man's wages' in years gone by, and since they were the principal recipients of the boy's earnings, they were reminded each year just how meagre these were.

The system of payment according to productivity allowed the

authorities to argue that those who wanted more money should simply work harder. But the best workers were often the most disappointed, and unrealistic expectations sometimes gave way to suspicions such as those that gave rise to the 1936 strike.

The years following the Second World War gave grounds for optimism. If Islanders were not yet to do 'white man's work', they had a chance to show that they could be as good at diving as the Japanese had been. Young men took up the challenge, becoming something of an elite among their peers. The work was less arduous than swimming for trochus, but it carried a new element of danger. Finally the Islanders declared themselves unwilling to match themselves against the daredevil Japanese divers, whose many gravestones in the Thursday Island cemetery bore witness to the claim that 'they no fright death'. But Islanders had to experience fatalities almost every year before they reached this conclusion.

The official wisdom was that diving was good work 'as long as you are careful'. Correspondingly, the cause of death was attributed to the victim himself, he was 'too greedy to pick up shell' and overstayed his time underwater. I sometimes sensed a touch of fatalism, even a morbid fascination with danger that may be characteristic of people in such occupations. Talking of the places divers called 'flash bottom', one man told me:

> There are places like a garden, with different coloured corals – they can send you crazy – like flowers: one red, another yellow. And pearl shells open like a woman's thing, when she's lying naked on a bed. The shell lies thick everywhere, like in a *copper maori* (i.e. an earth oven). But it's very dangerous, like a temptation. You must go steady to get that shell, and not stay down too long.

Only rarely, however, did the divers reveal a tragic sense of their life. Joseph Bowia, a Baduan, wrote this lament for a kinsman who had died in a diving accident. (He himself was later to die under similar circumstances.)

> Mother, was it for this that you cut my umbilical cord,
> That I should spend my life out here on the sea?
> I am a castaway, the seabirds my only companions.
> Alas, this is a bad life out here on the sea.
> We have been sad like this a long time,
> Floating on the water like gulls.
> Our homes, where our fathers and mothers and sisters stay,

Are far away on the horizon,
While we set our feet on an alien place.[6]

This was the only song of this kind; though most songs were
about boats and the sea, they revealed no such melancholy. Most
young men simply said, 'You feel proud to be a diver. You are
somebody – you feel a man.'

Among the skippers there was a similar tendency to explain
failure in terms of personal inadequacies. A man was a weak
leader, he was 'woman sick' and so unable to leave his island. The
failures themselves were more likely to plead the straitened state
of the industry, or suggest that the master pearlers or government officials were discriminating against them. Of course the
top skippers could afford to take a complacent view, for they
were almost the only Islanders to get into the same income bracket
as Europeans. But, their men, whose incomes fell far short of this
level, accused them of cheating and exploitation in collusion
with the authorities.

If there was one matter on which virtually all Islanders agreed
it was that they were poor. True, they were better off than their
Papuan neighbours or most Aborigines; but what mattered was
that they were worse off than white people, who, so it seemed
from their perspective, never risked their lives or exerted themselves. Some accepted this as the proper state of things, pending
the Islanders' advance to a sufficient level of education and
economic responsibility. Others, remarking that the DNA fixed
the wages and controlled education, concluded that their
economic conditions were the consequence of political decision
rather than the real value of their labour in the market place.
This suspicion was strengthened when they got to the mainland
and found that, when free from government supervision, they
could command the same rates as European workers for
equivalent work. And far from being lazy, they found that they
were in demand as 'good tropical workers'. For the moment, at
least, it did not matter that they were at the bottom of the labour
hierarchy. Citizenship legitimated wage labour.

A question of balance

Islanders saw the division between black and white as the fundamental fact of their existence, and their dependence –

---

[6]   A rendition of this song can be heard on Beckett 1982. The translation is by
Ephraim Bani.

economic, political and cultural – on Europeans was a problem that exercised their minds continually. This condition was not altogether unprecedented, economically and culturally, if not politically, they had been dependent on their Papuan neighbours before colonization. Indeed, without the canoes which their trading partners sent them they could not have lived on their islands. They were able to deny this reality by setting it within a framework of gift exchange that was delayed and conducted between hereditary 'friends' who might never meet. The same principle of balanced reciprocity existed between in-laws within island society.

Colonial ideology was also based on the principle of transaction, but one that was characterized by asymmetry and inequality: the Islanders were indebted to white Australians for the benefits of civilization, but nothing that they could give or do was of sufficient worth to redeem this debt – or at least, not for a very long time. The recipients, however, reinterpreted these doctrines in terms of balanced reciprocity. The exchange was to be delayed, but their conformity to civilized standards, their work, and their demonstrations of loyalty and Christian faith were the earnest of what they would presently achieve. Military service seemed to be just such a redemptive act, and army propaganda seemed to confirm this interpretation. Thereafter the model offered two possibilities: either black and white would continue to exchange with increasing velocity or, by a radical stroke, the achievement of balance would dissolve the division as well as the inequality of the races, putting an end to exchange, at least in the old form.

Islanders were discovering the contradictions between the colonial and national ideologies at a time when the colonial and metropolitan orders were themselves coming into collision, not just at the regional level but in the communities. As we shall see in the next two chapters, both the debate and the collision took a distinctive form according to the particular setting in which they occurred.

V   The Murray Islanders

It is possible to discuss the transformation of Torres Strait in regional terms because the same influences were at work throughout and were, to a considerable degree, coordinated by the Queensland government. But while the Islanders all brought the same kinds of cultural resources to the colonial encounter, they experienced it not as an undifferentiated mass but as members of small face-to-face communities that were more or less isolated from, and independent of, one another. In this setting the forces that now dominated their lives were mediated by a dense fabric of claims and deferences and a distinctive tradition, so that each island may be said to have experienced them in its own way. One might also say that, inasmuch as each community retained some capacity to redistribute the effects of colonialism and transform its meanings, it was able to negotiate the terms of its surrender. Thus to locate the discussion of previous chapters in the setting of a particular community is to 'thicken' the description in a way that is essential for an understanding of the Islanders' history.

Murray Island as I first saw it in 1958 seemed like a realization of Redfield's Little Community. It was distinctive, small, homogeneous and, to a degree, self sufficient (Redfield 1956:4). It was 260 km east of Thursday Island and, though in daily radio contact, was visited by only one or two boats a month. In the village that stretched along 1 km of foreshore, each house was within sight and usually within earshot of its neighbours and, since the inhabitants spent most of their waking hours out of doors, there was little that passed unnoticed. The Meriam seemed forever to be gathering for some church service, meeting or entertainment, organized by one of the many associations. Informally, too, they saw a lot of one another. Along the road that ran the length of the village there was a continuous traffic, by day of people going to the gardens or the store or the medical aid post, and until late at night of families visiting relatives. Walking back from church at noon on Sunday one was sure to be invited by two or three parties, gathered for dinner within sight of the road. Small wonder that any little event was broadcast by what Meriam called the 'village wireless' within a few hours of its happening.

Murray's response to the outside world seemed almost contradictory. On the one hand it was open to new things; on the other it was cautious of commitment and retentive of old ways. It was the one island in the Strait where one could see an old cult re-enacted, albeit as entertainment. And yet the clamour for citizen rights was nowhere louder than on Murray, and the same people who declined to leave their gardens for the luggers were spearheading the entry of Islanders into the mainland labour force. This impression was broadly in keeping with Haddon's sixty years earlier, and perhaps in a general way consistent with what we know about the Meriam before contact. According to the mythology, just about everything came from somewhere else, even the original inhabitants and the dugong shaped hill that dominates the island of Mer, not to mention the twin deities, Malu and Bomai (Haddon 1908:1–63). When Europeans began coming the Meriam seemed equally receptive. In 1802 Matthew Flinders found them friendly and eager for trade (1814 II:110). In 1834 they rescued a young British castaway, surrendering him regretfully two years later (King 1837). In 1868 they allowed a Jamaican, Douglas Pitt, to establish a *beche-de-mer* station (Pitt 13.5.1882), and in 1872, they received two LMS teachers, Tom and Mataiker (Murray 9.12.1872:32–3). The Meriam strategy was to domesticate what they accepted. Just as Malu and Bomai had been contained within fetishes and confined within shrines, so iron was integrated into the subsistence economy and foreigners were adopted and assigned kinship statuses. Of course, once colonization began in earnest, domestication was a matter of mitigating intrusive forces rather than neutralizing them, and in the long run the Meriam must be judged to have been fighting a losing battle. But out of this battle they developed a sense of a domain that was theirs from time immemorial, which they could and should defend against all comers.

The Meriam domain expressed itself in several modes. Territorially, it meant that they continued to occupy and use the land according to the traditional rules of inheritance. Politically, it meant that they made decisions about the matters immediately affecting their lives, including religion and local government. Culturally, it meant that they maintained a body of practices which they called Meriam custom. As in other communities, this included much that had been adopted from Europeans and Pacific Islanders. But there was a conscious effort to maintain continuity with the past, powerfully symbolized by the sacred drum Wasikor, which they had repeatedly refused to yield up to missionaries or collectors and now used in church.

Their domain was based in their continuing commitment to the subsistence economy. Using the garden places, the beaches and reefs kept alive the myths and stories associated with them. Gardening and fishing as their ancestors had done kept alive the meanings of these traditions. That the land they cultivated had been inherited from their ancestors reaffirmed their control over their means of production. The subsistence economy not only left each family in command of its working life, but also enabled the people to participate fully in local affairs, underwriting the turbulent democracy for which Murray was known throughout the Strait. The Meriam themselves said that among them, 'everybody *mamoose*', which is to say everyone was a chief. What this meant was that becoming a leader was the birthright of every man, with the rider that making followers out of men who believed themselves also to be born leaders was no easy task.

On this foundation, the Meriam maintained a sturdy tradition of resistance to white domination. In 1888 they shot arrows into the missionaries' cattle, which were spoiling their gardens (Haddon 1888); in 1913 they walked off the company boats when they found they could not use them as they wished; in 1935 a councillor felled the Protector of Islanders in a dispute over compulsory medical inspection; in the post-war years they insisted on keeping resident European teachers out of their affairs. Nor were the Meriam only capable of defence: they were active in the 1936 strike, and stayed out until the war began. They were again active in the army strike of 1944, and in the years after the war repeatedly pressed the government for improvements and reforms. Murray was the home of an active Legion branch and, somewhat unwillingly, of a breakaway Pentecostal church.

The post-war developments are to be understood as manifestations of the mounting contradiction between the colonial and metropolitan systems, and they subjected the Meriam domain to considerable strains. When ex-servicemen claimed special privileges, and when Pentecostalists rejected dancing and claimed moral superiority, they challenged the Meriam way of life. And when voters opted for delegates who 'know how to talk to white people' they undermined the principle that everyone was *mamoose*. As one such delegate exclaimed in a moment of exasperation: 'Everybody *mamoose*; no one to follow. Everybody savvy; no one to learn.'

Meriam ethnography

To be accurate one should speak of the Murray Islands using the plural, for there are three: Mer, Dauar and Waier.[1] But they are situated within 1 km of one another, and their inhabitants have always constituted a single society and population. Waier is the smallest, the crescent shaped shell of an old volcano, its outer walls rising vertically out of the sea. Supporting no vegetation beyond a few coconuts, it has never been inhabited on a regular basis, though it once concealed an important shrine. Mer and Dauar are more hospitable. They are surrounded by coral reefs and fringed by sandy beaches which extend back some distance before the ground begins to rise, on Mer to as much as 250 metres. Mer is approximately 2.79 km in length and 1.65 km at its widest point. The corresponding figures for Dauar are 1.58 km and 0.762 km. Before colonization, the population seems to have been quite dense. In 1802 Flinders estimated it at 700 (Haddon 1935:95), while the LMS records of 1873 suggest 800 (Murray 9–12.1872:34). Even the lower figure amounts to a fairly high level of density and explains why infanticide and abortion were practised. Parents limited the number of their children, not just according to their own circumstances, but in response to a societal norm that cast ridicule on couples with more than four (Haddon 1908:109). In fact, Haddon's figures suggest an average of 2.6, although this would seem to refer to surviving children (*ibid.*:108).

These islands are, nevertheless, the richest in Torres Strait. The waters abound with fish, which can be trapped in the large stone fish weirs that lie off Mer and Dauar (Johannes 1984). At certain seasons the beaches are flanked by shoals of 'sardines',

[1] For an excellent map of Mer see Lawrie 1970:284; also Haddon 1908:170–1.

and during the laying season numbers of turtle clamber ashore to hide their eggs in the sand, at which time they can be caught by the simple expedient of rolling them on their backs. The rich volcanic soil also supports a luxuriant vegetation, including many edible species such as coconuts, various fruit and nut bearing trees, and some roots and wild aroids. It is also excellent gardening land.

In contrast to the Central and Western Islanders, the Meriam made gardening the basis of their economy, perhaps as a response to the favourable conditions, to population pressure, or to the difficulty in obtaining canoes. Bananas and several varieties of yams were the staple foods, cultivated by a slash-and-burn technique that must have been considerably facilitated when it became possible to replace shell axes with iron blades.

Here, as elsewhere in Torres Strait, the problem was to get through the Norwest Monsoon (January–March). Gardeners had to exert themselves to the utmost during the planting season (September–November) to have enough yams in their storehouse to carry them through the 'hungry time'. Should the yams fail they would have to fall back on the less nutritious and acceptable green banana and wild aroids. Such an eventuality meant not only privation and perhaps sickness, but the reproach of improvidence (*Memeg kurup*).

Gardening took clear priority over fishing. Indeed, land and sea were represented as incompatible elements. One should not go fishing until the planting was finished: instead of the dirt under one's fingernails drawing one back to the gardens, the salt water would draw one back to the sea. Contact with salt water must be followed by washing in fresh, and a day's rest before returning to the bush or the plants would spoil. Cultivation was also in a general way identified with the Malu–Bomai cult and its leading officiants, who controlled some of the best land, were supposed never to go fishing.

In production, the domestic mode prevailed (cf. Sahlins 1972:76–8); the core of the household being a conjugal pair, or occasionally a polygynous marriage, together with the unmarried offspring. The wedding ceremony represented the wife as subordinate to her husband, and she was enjoined to work without ceasing, weeding, carrying firewood, fishing, cooking, weaving mats and caring for the children. Her girlhood would have prepared her for such a role. Boys, however, had few responsibilities before marriage, and even after marriage they were expected to spend much of their time in dancing and amorous adventures. However, the work of their maturity would be gardening, in particular the solitary cultivation of the great *usari* yams, the performance of rituals and occasional headhunting expeditions.[2]

A gift economy, which required the redistribution of food when life crises were celebrated or rituals performed, intensified agricultural production beyond the needs of the domestic unit. Marriage, in particular, required the man's and the woman's kin to make exchanges of food, small and large, as long as it lasted. A man's reputation was at stake in these exchanges, which could take on a competitive edge and frequently resulted in quarrelling. Land might be owned individually. Alternatively, brothers might hold their inheritance jointly, and occasionally their sons continued the arrangement, either because relations among them were particularly close or because land shortage made division difficult. Owners were expected to leave the bulk of their land to sons, but they might disinherit one who had given offence, and commonly placed it all in the hands of the eldest. (This inequality was unlikely to be transmitted to the next generation, since a man without land could not get a wife.) A daughter might receive a small marriage portion, which she could pass on to her heirs; and if she had no brothers she could inherit all the land, before more distant kin in the male line. The latter would inherit if there were no children, but this eventuality was commonly avoided by adoption. The outcome of the system was that, while an area of garden land might be mainly owned by agnates (people related in the male line), it was likely to have a number of owners who had inherited through a female connection at some point in the past. A garden place was thus a genealogical record, and the word for path (*gab*) was also the idiom for a kinship connection.

Residential land, situated on the foreshore, was inherited in the male line. This provided the basis for social placement. The association of people with named stretches of beach provided the means of dividing the society into units for the regulation of marriage and the practice of various cults. The minimal units, which Rivers called 'villages', numbered twenty-seven (Haddon 1908:169–84). One could not marry into one's own village, or

---

[2] Haddon could gather little information on actual raids (cf. his detailed descriptions of warfare in the Western Islands, 1904:298–319) and he suspected that the Meriam were not in fact particularly warlike (1908:189–90).

that of one's mother or father's mother. Villages might have their own shrines; but the more important cults grouped a number of villages together, some occupying a continuous stretch of foreshore, others situated at various points around the three islands. Since there was a profusion of cults and most villages belonged to several, the division of ritual labour was kaleidoscopic rather than segmentary.

Whatever the intermittent importance of the hereditary cult and territorial units, daily life was organized so as to leave room for personal preference. Although marriage formally transferred the woman to her husband's village, they did not have to live there, but might live with other kin elsewhere, even borrowing their garden land. Weddings and the exchange of gifts that followed engaged the kin of bride and groom, called 'sides' (*doge*), rather than villages as such.

Although Murray was remarkable for the richness and diversity of its religious life, the cult of Malu–Bomai seems to have become dominant, in the sense of pervading all branches of life and engaging all but a few immigrant villages in a ranked division of labour. The chief officiants, who controlled the fetishes, are supposed to have wielded awesome magical powers, and terrorized the rest of the populace through a secret society. They had more wives and larger holdings of land. Haddon understood them to be 'a sort of hereditary government whose authority no one could question' and this is the way they were remembered by later generations (Haddon 1908:78). 'Everything quiet: no one sing out. Everyone keep to their own place. That was the law of Malu. If they break that law: *Malo-ra ib*!' The Meriam phrase meant that an offender's jaw bone would end up decorating the mask of Malu.

Whether power really was monopolized to this extent, or whether the leaders of other cults and sorcerers exercised a countervailing power, we shall never know, for the old religion was the first casualty of European contact.

Colonial reconstruction

Murray's encounters with Europeans began early and were intermittently intense. During the first half of the nineteenth century they were peaceful and brief, leaving little discernible residue other than a need for iron. The arrival of trepangers in the 1860s initiated relations with the cash economy, but also trouble, including several Meriam deaths and the destruction by fire of one of the two sacred drums of the Malu–Bomai cult (Haddon 1908:190–1). Missionaries were continually in residence from 1872, including several Europeans during the twelve years of the Papuan Institute. And when they withdrew in 1890, they were replaced by a succession of government teachers.

As a result of these intrusions, Murray acquired a centre. The north-west side of the island, which provided the best anchorage, became the location for church, mission buildings, school house and store. Eventually the Meriam came to live near these facilities, but they were the last people in the Strait to form a nucleated settlement, preferring until the 1930s to live near their gardens and fish traps around the periphery of the two islands. Thus situated they were less subject to the scrutiny of the missionaries and able to cling to their old ways a little longer. The LMS declared war on the 'idol gods', burning the Malu fetish and sending others away to museums. When Haddon recorded the chants of the Malu–Bomai ceremonies in 1898 he was told that they had not been performed for more than twenty years, but the revival aroused considerable emotion (1901:47). Some say that the Bomai mask was saved, and one or two of the smaller cults may have gone underground. Although the missionaries claimed complete conversion, there were the *apek le*, people living on the other side of the island, who kept their distance. A white school teacher claimed that two old men had taken him through some kind of initiation as late as 1926 (Davies n.d.). He also discovered the Waiat fetish which had until then remained hidden on Waier (Haddon 1935:398–9), although its decayed condition suggested that it had been neglected for years. If the old religion persisted by this stage, it was as a private practice. Under the more tolerant Anglicans some of the Malu–Bomai rites could come out into the open again, not as religion but as ambiguous folklore. That this much survived the LMS suppression is perhaps due to the fact that the Meriam still spent much of their time in their gardens, secluded by dense vegetation from the eyes not only of Europeans but also of their fellows.

The subsistence economy was in some ways strengthened through contact. Iron axes, knives, crowbars and fish hooks increased the efficiency of labour and possibly the volume of production. The introduction of new crops, such as sweet potato, corn and cassava, as well as new varieties of yam and banana, diversified the economy and provided some insurance against the failure of one of the staples. The availability of flour and rice in times of famine could keep up the gardeners' strength through the time of new planting, when previously they had been debilitated. Finally, the decline of population through exotic disease, to a low point of 406 in 1913, eased the pressure on land. Securely based, the Meriam could afford to keep the labour market at arm's length.

In words that might have found a place in E.P. Thompson's essay on time and work discipline (1968), Haddon summed up the Meriam attitude as follows:

> The natives certainly do not like to be made to work. One can always get them to work pretty hard in spurts, but continuous labour is very irksome to them; but after all this is pretty much the same with everybody. Nature deals so bountifully with the people that circumstances have not forced them into the discipline of work. (1901:19)

For all its sympathy this observation loses sight of the Meriam strategy. From the middle of the nineteenth century they had shown themselves ready to make a limited commitment to the cash economy. In the early 1900s they deployed some sixty men to work off the price of three company boats, only withdrawing them when they found that the cutters were not their to use as they wished. Around 1911 as many as 120 were working on boats – more than half the male population – only to stay home when earnings dropped.

Again, Haddon's statement that 'the people are not avaricious, their wants are few and easily supplied' (*ibid.*), glosses over the complexities. The Meriam were certainly less dependent than most others on commodities. Men who grew up before the Second World War told me they did not taste flour or rice until they went onto the boats. But they had an inescapable need for iron tools and cloth, and the beginnings of an addiction to tea, sugar and store tobacco. Since the coming of the South Sea men, bride price was paid in trade goods, and there were the demands of the Church to be met.

But while married men were prepared to gather shell on the home reef, or to go out on the company boat for a week or two, they were reluctant to absent themselves for long periods. Instead they sent their sons, who being single or newly married were still under their authority, and whose contribution to the subsistence economy was in any case negligible. The government pressed them, but they resisted, and in doing so made the subsistence economy not only the basis for resistance, but a symbol of it.

Gardening was not simply a way of making a living. It remained a source of prestige, won by a successful 'show garden' located by the bush path where everyone would see it, and by a display of crops at the annual harvest festival. It was also a source of aesthetic satisfaction, for even secluded gardens were planted with multi-coloured crotons and hibiscus. Men and women returning from the gardens would often put flowers in their hair.

Spending so much time ashore, the married men were able to exert some control over parish affairs and local government, while being complete masters of their own work. The rules of land tenure had been maintained by the teacher–supervisors and councillors, and the domestic mode of production now organized not only gardening, fishing and crafts, but the allocation of manpower to the marine industry and the expenditure of cash income. The domestic unit itself had changed only to the extent of excluding polygyny. The authority of husband over wife, and parents over children, was sanctioned by church and council: wife beating might now be an offence, but so was it for a wife or child to leave home.

Although the young unmarried men were the principal money earners, they were expected to yield the bulk of what they got to their parents, and the Protector, who controlled their money, automatically transferred a portion of each month's wages to their mothers' pass books. This left them dependent on their parents when they needed to assemble bridewealth. There was, as we have noted, a resulting tendency to delay marriage on one pretext or another.[3] Correspondingly, some girls' parents held out for more bridewealth.[4]

The parents' conduct need not be attributed solely to avarice, for they were under new pressures, resulting from demographic

---

[3] According to Haddon, boys originally married between the ages of eighteen and nineteen, girls between sixteen and eighteen (1908:115). However, the figures he collected from the turn of the century suggest that the age of first marriage was, or had become, more variable, and the averages were twenty-one and eighteen respectively (1935:113). My examination of the marriage register for the years 1927–41 revealed average ages of twenty-four for males and twenty-one for females.

[4] I was told that before the First World War £5–10 was a good bride price; between the wars it rose to between £15 and £20.

changes. The outlawing of abortion and infanticide, combined with some improvements in hygiene and health care, increased the number of surviving children. Adoption enabled parents to space their children and redistribute part of the overall burden among childless couples, but my genealogies reveal that families of ten children were by no means uncommon.

To begin with, a couple might live with the husband's parents, particularly if he was still in employment. But they would establish their own household after the birth of the first or second child, entering a phase of low per capita production and maximum vulnerability to sickness or accident. Their survival would to a significant degree be dependent on the customary distributions of food surpluses among kith and kin, and the members no doubt looked forward to feasts. A household with several unmarried grown-up children was correspondingly at the peak of its productivity, contributing more than its share to the extra-domestic economy.

What with neighbourhood food distributions, convivial work bees, church fund raising and a festive complex burgeoning under church and government patronage, island custom offered numerous ways of converting surplus wealth into social values. In doing so it dissolved the distinction between the cash and subsistence economies in such a way as to advantage the older men, who were dominant within the community but dependent on their sons for money. One might say that the yam displays held on July One served to subordinate wage-earning sons to gardening fathers. Paradoxically, government practice also favoured the prestige economy. By controlling the Islanders' monetary surplus and investing it on their behalf, it denied individuals the possibility of accumulation. Again, by limiting the circulation of cash within the communities it removed the possibility of petty trade in garden produce, fish or handicrafts, so that there was no alternative but to redistribute them against the possibility of future need.

Though the prestige economy aroused a keen rivalry, it produced no fixed hierarchy. A family was best able to participate at the moment when it was about to break up into new households. There was also an element of chance in that anyone, however humble, might be lucky enough to find a turtle or even a pearl, and become for a day the community benefactor. Political ambitions were better pursued through the church or local government.

Whether or not remnants of paganism lingered in hidden places, the Church had won control of the public domain long before the century was out, and was soon closely integrated with daily life. Particularly under the Anglicans, the Christian calendar coincided harmoniously with the subsistence cycle: Christmas with the turtle season, Lent with the 'hungry time', Easter with the first of the new crops and July One with the main yam harvest. The church also provided a hierarchy of local rank for men. Under the LMS one passed through the seekers' class to membership and, perhaps, to deacon. The Anglicans had their own more elaborate array of offices, ranging from sidesman, through lay reader to churchwarden, though women could hold office only in the auxiliary mothers' union and girls' friendly society. Entry to the ministry was a possibility for men with a strong vocation and a capacity for study, but lay office was open to anyone of good character and it was widely coveted.

Nor were the offices empty honorifics. Though the Church of England in Torres Strait inclined to a hierarchical mode of government, its lack of priests during the early years left it no alternative but to rely on the congregational forms left by the LMS. By the time it had been able to train sufficient priests, the island parishes had been under local control for twenty years. In Murray, as elsewhere, each incumbent had to come to terms with parish officials who were jealous of their 'customary' powers, and some found themselves unable to exert any significant influence beyond the limits of the church yard. A priest who tried to assert his authority found himself the subject of complaints to the bishop.

There were similar developments in the field of local government. Before annexation a Queensland magistrate had visited Murray and appointed two *mamooses* on the advice of the missionary Samuel McFarlane, who was also requested to guide them in their maintenance of law and order. In the 1890s this responsibility passed to the government teacher. Remarkably, one of the *mamooses* was Passi, heir to a senior office in the Malu–Bomai cult, though by now a church leader. (The other appointee, known as Harry *mamoose*, was not heir to any important ritual office, and the reasons for his elevation are obscure. He seems, however, to have been a forceful figure.) Whether the colonial regime was co-opting the indigenous leadership, or the old leadership was perpetuating itself through the new structures must remain in doubt.

However, political office became openly competitive when, in 1898, the government established an elected council. Evidently the voting proceeded smoothly, but within a short time one of the four councillors had been convicted of various offences and there was a clamour for his replacement. The resident teacher–supervisor suspected that the charges had been laid with this in mind, and feared that 'there would be continual trumped up charges of a trivial kind, in order to get the coveted places' (Haddon 1908:179–80). He was not wholly wrong, for in the years that followed incumbents were replaced with fair regularity, average tenure being two three-year terms, with no one holding office for more than two terms consecutively. But while the issues seem to have been ephemeral– Meriam political history is a virtual blank before 1936 – we need not suppose that nothing more was involved than self seeking and popular caprice.

Initially the councillors had only an advisory role, but being relatively young, they soon took over the functions of the ageing *mamooses*. When the company boats were introduced they were given responsibility for their running, and when the government approved a code of mission-inspired by-laws, they became assessors (*ibid.*:178). As 'first line supervisors' they found themselves required to implement unpopular policies, and a number were dismissed for yielding to popular pressure. Sitting in court they became subject to a different kind of contradiction, being required to uphold the law among people towards some of whom they had particular obligations as kinsmen. If they were severe on their kin they eroded their electoral support, but if they were partial their rivals might complain to the Protector. This, together with a general notion that office should circulate, was probably enough to secure a steady turnover. It seems that there was some preference for younger, more go-ahead men, but the duties of office were not overly demanding and the talents required were widely available. When the teacher–supervisors withdrew from local government in 1938 and the councillors' conferences began, a wider range of talents was called into play, but the effects of the change were not felt until after the war.

Colonization resulted in the instituting of new structures and the re-ordering of old structures. Its major innovation was to incorporate the community, so that the Meriam dealt with the outside world as a parish and a local government unit rather than sectionally, as members of territorial and cult groups. In the early years, the government had utilized the territorial principle to divide the community into three 'tribes' for the election of councillors and the management of boats. But these no longer had any connection with cult organization, and by the 1930s had ceased to correspond with residence; so that in the end it was the Meriam themselves who requested their dissolution. Henceforth, advancement was to be a matter of what one was rather than who one was: offices in church and government were to be filled according to the rules, either by election from below or appointment from above.

Kinship emerged as the counter to these atomizing tendencies. While the territorial and cult groups had atrophied, the principle of filiation by which they had been recruited remained active in the inheritance of land and the regulation of marriage. The principle now gave rise to a grouping, usually small but of variable span, that I shall call the family. Increasingly referred to by the English word, it corresponded to *no sik*, the indigenous term for the descendants of a conjugal pair, as well as to the more restrictive *kimiar no sik*, meaning descendants in the male line. With the adoption of patronymics after the war, the latter became the point of reference although for many purposes, such as weddings and tombstone openings, the family included all descendants. Since brothers and sometimes first cousins might hold their land undivided, they were occasionally involved in ownership disputes with other families; and they might combine forces to put on a competitive display of food for some celebration. But these confrontations were relatively rare, and most families remained dormant for long periods, while their members severally organized cooperation as the occasion arose, from the whole range of bilateral kin, called *boai*. In one form or another, kinship organized the subsistence sector, and became available as the alternative principle for organizing participation in the cash economy, local politics and the church. Since the recognition of kinship identified the parties with the original inhabitants of the three islands, it was the appropriate idiom for domesticating intrusive institutions. Providing form and legitimation for the claims and deferences of daily life, kinship also made possible the occasional outbursts of resistance for which the Meriam were famous.

A community in crisis

At first glance, Murray might not have seemed very different after the Second World War. There was still a strong commitment to gardening and a steady round of public and private festivities. Everyone seemed to be on friendly terms, to judge by the easy banter and small talk that went on at public gatherings. This indeed was the fiction that community leaders tried to maintain, not just for outsiders, but for the people. That the reality sometimes fell short of this ideal was a cause for unease.[5] Thus, when I remarked to the council chairman on certain absences from the customary Christmas feast, he replied bitterly that some people thought they were 'more clever than Satan'.

Murray had always had its personal and family rivalries, but now there were enduring divisions. Throughout the 1950s and 1960s, the council suppressed Pentecostalism in the name of the Anglican majority. At the same time, the Legion of Ex-servicemen proclaimed themselves a privileged group, with special entitlements that council and government were unjustly denying them. I have described these conflicts in earlier chapters as manifestations of the contradiction between the colonial and metropolitan systems, but in the Murray setting they were aggravated by conflicts that were specific to the community. Murray had its own problems, including a mounting pressure of population on land, increasing cash dependency in a context of economic stagnation, and increasing socio-economic differentiation, partly resulting from these developments.

The discontents to which these gave rise provided a fertile ground for politicking, and in 1959 a private dispute quickly became a public issue that brought Anglicans and Pentecostalists, soldiers and civilians into open confrontation. Rumours of an impending tidal wave seemed to loosen people's grip on the present; and the coincidence of the collapse of trochus fishing with news of the visit of the Commonwealth commission on voting rights and talk of repatriation benefits, persuaded many that freedom was imminent. After some months people began to realize that there was to be no sudden transformation, and life seemed to return to normal. And yet, almost without realizing it, the Meriam had come through their crisis, and throughout the

---

[5] For an account of similar tensions in another Torres Strait community, see Beckett 1971.

1960s they took their destinies into their own individual hands, many by emigrating.

The economic crisis

Murray's ex-servicemen returned from the war with high hopes. The post-war boom, coupled with the steady income from social service benefits, lured them into a new set of dependencies on the cash economy that could not easily be reversed. Powdered milk became the proper food for infants; flour and rice became the preferred diet of children; the dim light of hurricane lamps gave way to the grand illumination of the kerosene pressure lamp.

By 1958, however, the average per capita income was only around $104 (£52) and it had not been much higher over the preceding ten years. The Meriam were better off than they had been before the war, but they were now more aware of their poverty relative to white Australians. There was also more economic differentiation within their own ranks. The majority living in their palm leaf and thatch huts looked enviously on the fortunate few who had houses of sawn timber and fibrolite. Even a galvanized iron roof, valued for the rain catchment it provided, was beyond the means of the majority. A mere fifteen households out of 73 owned dinghies, and only the store manager had an outboard motor. That many had such things by the 1970s confirms my own impression that they already had them in their sights at this time.

The store manager was the only one who could be considered well-to-do, even by Islander standards, a condition that could be directly attributed to his earnings. Among the rest there were small but considerable differences. I estimated the annual incomes of forty households, with an average of seven members, as follows: 45% received less than $300, 70% less than $600. Only three households received more than $900, that of the store manager exceeding $2,000. These differences were largely due to contingent factors, such as the number of children bringing in endowment, and the number of old people and invalids bringing in pensions. Overall, the welfare input exceeded that of wages, even before the collapse of the trochus market, amounting in 1958 to 58% ($60 out of the total per capita income of $104). The relatively small contribution from wages was due to the low rates offered, coupled with the fact that only 55% of able bodied males between sixteen and sixty were in employment. Of those employed 39% worked on the boats and the rest in government service, ranging from sanitary workers and policemen through teachers and medical orderlies. These last two occupations brought higher wages than could be earned on the boats, and since they left time for fishing and gardening were much in demand.

The Meriam dealt with the marine industry after the war much as they had done before. During the post-war boom they bought only two luggers, investing less per capita than almost any other island, and as before it was the young men who went to sea. As before also, these boats made little money. Disgusted with their meagre earnings, the more ambitious workers opted for the master boats; but on several occasions the council, unable to get crew, conscripted them. Their response now, however, was to run away to the mainland at the first opportunity.

The island boats epitomized Murray's economic frustration. The crews blamed the skippers and refused to vote them in for a second term; the council also blamed the skippers, sometimes dismissing them in mid-year. Skippers and crew blamed the council for using the boats for public purposes without pay, and everybody blamed the government. In other words, the result was divisive and destructive, and there was no possibility of any skipper establishing himself. In the end the boats lay idle. Had the Meriam been able to think up some other type of enterprise they would doubtless have leapt at it, but they were at a loss. They knew there was a market for fresh fish and vegetables on Thursday Island, but transportation was too slow, too irregular and too costly to make it a paying proposition. When I asked them what scheme might solve their problems, they could only think in terms of getting a boat, but without any clear idea of what they could do with it. By 1958 some had already concluded that if the State or Commonwealth governments did not recognize an obligation to them, they would have to emigrate. The collapse of the trochus market at the end of 1959 clinched the matter. By 1960 the number of emigrants to the mainland had increased by 38% on the 1958 figure, and the flow continued thereafter.

That the Meriam were the first Islanders to work on the mainland in any number was the result of a council approach to the government. The forty men who went south in 1947 had contracted to cut cane, returning at the end of the season with a lump sum towards a house, a tombstone or some other major item. In subsequent years some of them stayed on in other kinds of work. By the mid 1950s some men were bringing down their wives and children rather than returning home, but as late as 1960 the great majority were male, approximately 60% of them unmarried.[6]

This migration was a response to a great diversity of factors, including no doubt intangibles such as taste for adventure. Among the attractions my informants cited were higher wages, better education and medical attention, freedom from government and council restraint, and freedom of religion. The young, single men were also beginning to think of themselves as repressed and exploited by their elders. But these reasons for migration should not obscure a push factor. Although families were ashamed to admit it, a number had or would soon have insufficient land.

The population, having bottomed out around 1913, began to rise at an ever increasing rate. In 1960 there were, by my own count, 682 Meriam, of whom 146 lived elsewhere. At 536 the resident population was still well below what it had been at contact, but of this number almost 50% were under twenty. Overall, there should have been enough land for everyone, because there were sizeable tracts which had not been cultivated for at least twenty years, to judge by the dense vegetation. But some families were already reduced to borrowing, with the prospect of virtual landlessness in the next generation. These, as one such man put it, would have to 'fly away like birds'.

This solution threatened the domestic unit, for if the young men earned more money on the railways than they had earned on the boats, their parents saw little of it. With endowment, children were not the burden they had once been, and a pensioner was an adequate substitute for a wage earner. But almost three-quarters of the households had no pensioner members, while the income from child endowment began to fall away at the point where a family head would normally have been making his greatest contribution to the community. Some sense of the extent of the problem can be gained from the fact that the average number of able-bodied males (16–60) per household was only 1.2, as compared with 1.9 females.

---

[6] In 1958 71 Meriam males and 11 females were said to be residing on the mainland. In 1960 the figures had risen to 95 and 13 respectively.

The subsistence economy was scarcely affected by these changes, inasmuch as the young men had never made much of a contribution to it. People occasionally sold such items as fish, firewood, and coconut oil, to meet a need for cash, but they continued to distribute the bulk of their surpluses through the festive complex or among kith and kin. When it came to money, however, the 'inherent contradiction' that Sahlins finds between the household economy and the greater institutions of the society (1972:101–2) was very much in evidence. Many were unable or unwilling to pay their island tax and church dues, and even the ex-servicemen found it difficult to find their Legion subscriptions. A common response to such problems was to organize sales and entertainments, to which a small admission fee could be charged. The problem was that there were no fewer than seven organizations competing for a tiny cash surplus, so that income was often minimal.

Parents were also finding it increasingly hard to put together the $200–300 bride price, ring and feast required for a 'proper wedding'. Some simply failed to produce the bride price; others delayed until the girl had conceived and the council had ordered the couple to marry, at which point they could hold a 'quiet wedding' and waive the bride price altogether, either way setting the marriage off to an inauspicious start.

The contradiction between domestic and other needs also found more virulent expression through the emerging sectarian division. Pentecostalists took advantage of the resentment caused by the bishop's constant demands for money, by claiming that the 'brothers and sisters in the south' would soon send them money to build a church. Required by their religion to shun worldly entertainments, and encouraged by it to question customs such as bride price, they could say that 'in Pentecost you only look out for your family'.

Anglicans and Pentecostalists

Not everyone who resented the Church of England's demands joined the Assembly of God, nor was this a primary concern for those who did. The schism had its origins in the same contradictions that gave rise to the economic crisis; but it precipitated its own crisis, for the Meriam had to come to terms with the fact that church and community were no longer coterminous. Some Anglicans, unwilling to accept such a possibility, mounted a harsh repression, to be met with stubborn resistance.

Pentecostalism seems to have begun in an individual quest for supernatural power. The church, like the old cults, had never fully absorbed this quest, so that there were always healers and clairvoyants who worked in a clandestine way with their own combination of Christian and traditional lore. I was told that it began in 1938, when two men met some Pentecostalists while their trochus boat was undergoing repairs in Mackay. They came home with a new set of songs and a belief in faith healing. At first they kept these things secret, but when one of them 'raised a girl from the dead' they called meetings and taught their friends the new songs. The priest protested and the council promptly gaoled the singers 'for creating a disturbance'. One of the leaders subsequently claimed to have caused the priest's death by a curse, but no more was heard of the new religion until after the war.

The Assembly gained a permanent foothold in 1950 when an Islander, long absent on the mainland, returned as a self-appointed missionary. This time the very chairman who had suppressed the sect allowed it to practise, even providing land on which to build a meeting house. This chairman was Marou, and it seems that this change of heart was connected with his campaign for citizen rights.

Marou's action brought down the combined weight of the colonial establishment. The bishop excommunicated him, and the DNA dismissed him from the council. Later, councils refused to allow a pastor to conduct services, restricted Pentecostal meetings, and inflicted various kinds of disabilities on members. But although without the means of baptising, marrying or burying, the Assembly survived and even grew, at one point claiming 30% of the adult population.

The relative merits of the two churches were much debated, for many were undecided which had 'more power'. Some Pentecostalists said that they joined the Assembly after having been healed, but Islander priests also prayed over the sick and annointed them with oil. (Oil blessed by certain revered individuals was regarded as particularly efficacious, and used long after their death.) At a more worldly level, some men expressed themselves unwilling to give up the offices they held in the Church of England. The parish had been accommodating in this matter, and some 70% of men over the age of thirty – about the age at which one began to consider one's public standing – held some title. The fact that a lay reader was illiterate and never actually read the lesson in church did not mean that he was

ready to relinquish his office: 'If I join Pentecost I got no name.'
An overzealous young priest who tried to prune some of the
dead wood, precipitated a run of defections. Correspondingly,
few of the Pentecostalists had held church office before converting. Moreover their ranks included a disproportionate number
of women, to whom the Church offered little in the way of
recognition, and who could take a much more prominent role in
meetings than in the formal Anglican services. (In 1967 a woman
headed the Murray Assembly.)

But more was at stake than the feelings of a few office holders.
The offices were the means by which the Meriam could exercise
some control over the Church, and their multiplication served
to distribute this control through the community. Pentecostalism
not only threatened these mechanisms, but called into question
the customary means by which the Church and other intrusive
institutions had been domesticated. Nor could the Assembly
easily be domesticated, since it branded dancing and the festive
complex as worldly pleasures. As if this were not enough, some
of its members called for the council to be replaced by white
magistrates and police, who would enforce only Commonwealth
law. It was not altogether surprising, then, that staunch
Anglicans became enraged when they saw Pentecostalists walking around in shoes and trousers; island custom was being
denied.

But while the Assembly might look forward to the day when
they could practise their religion in its full rigour, their
immediate problem was to lift the council restrictions. Thus
they were forced to participate in community politics, and,
being a minority, to seek allies among the Anglicans. Murray's
political crisis gave them the opportunity.

Council politics

While the Anglican Parish of St James could no longer claim to
be the Meriam at prayer, the council remained the sole secular
authority within the community, and its only legitimate delegate
without. As such it also carried the main burden of defending the
Meriam domain. The sectarian issue had fractured the consensus
on which it had previously been able to rely, and given rise to
several noisy ructions; but otherwise local government ran
smoothly. Murray's political crisis stemmed rather from the
increasing importance and complexity of its external relations.

As the people came to see the government as their only hope for economic salvation, they fell into ever greater dependence on a few skilled and experienced spokesmen. Council office, still less that of Eastern Islands Representative, was no longer something to which every man – if not any woman – could aspire. As one former incumbent observed, 'You've got to be a smart man to be councillor these days; not like before'. For the same reason, it was no longer possible to keep the kudos and power of office from becoming concentrated in a few hands.

Although the local autonomy of the council depended on satisfying government requirements, it was never at serious risk. There was a running squabble over the boats, but since these had not been equipped with engines they did not amount to a serious liability, and the DNA let things drift. There were occasional rows because the council did not report for medical treatment those sick who did not want it, but they usually ended in a stand off. Otherwise, since Murray remained clean, orderly and peaceful, it was left to itself. Keeping it this way absorbed a good deal of the council's energies on a day-to-day basis. Like most other villages in the Strait, Murray's was a model of neatness, maintained by frequent 'village days' that were compulsory for all able-bodied men and single girls. The council's police supervised the work and kept a lookout for untidy yards and foreshores. On their nightly patrols the police also kept an ear open for sounds of drunkenness and domestic discord, and used their long flashlights to discover trysting couples among the bushes. If they chose to report what they saw, the council would then consider summoning the offenders before the island court. After a public hearing, the verdict would be delivered, and if it were 'guilty', fines or a few weeks in the lock-up would be imposed.

The court heard an average of twenty cases a year, covering much the same offences as before the war, but with 'drinking methylated spirit' now the most common (34%).[7] 'Immorality', i.e. adultery and fornication, accounted for 28% and various forms of quarrelling for 17%. As before the overwhelming majority of the offenders were young, though occasionally an

---

[7]   The Yorke Island conference in 1938 had drawn up a code of by-laws based largely on what the LMS had instituted at the end of the nineteenth century. Later conferences of councillors revised it and the tariff of punishments. Drinking alcohol was in breach of the Act, but many councils only invoked it in the case of methylated spirits.

older person suffered the ignominy of exposure. A councillor, several skippers and some minor church officers lost their positions following conviction. Once every few years, someone was convicted of attempted sorcery and imprisoned or banished.

Although some young men muttered that drinking and 'immorality' were not offences among white people, the public consensus was that Islanders needed these controls. There might be anger over an excessive punishment, and doubt over the inevitably circumstantial evidence for sorcery. Land cases usually left the losers unsatisfied. But generally the complaint was against a particular councillor, who might be dismissed at the next election, and emanated from a faction of close kin which would dissolve as new issues arose. The sectarian issue would not go away. The dissenting group had all the features of permanence; it was large and had the potential for expansion. Moreover, it challenged the integrity of the community. It was in this sense that the Representative, acting as electoral returning officer, refused to accept the nomination of a Pentecostalist for council office saying, 'councillors must be for everybody; not just for one thing'. How, he asked, could a Pentecostal councillor organize the celebration of the Queen's Birthday, which entailed feasting and dancing?

Murray's other sectional group, the Legion, was equally subversive of the colonial order, but less easy to oppose. Its forty-odd members asserted a right to 'preference in everything' and they sponsored candidates to represent their interests, rather than those of the community at large. At the same time, their charter of service to 'King and country' was impeccable, and their day-to-day activities took customary forms such as work bees and dances. Nevertheless, their membership of an association which did not have the blessing of the authorities, and their real if somewhat tenuous affiliation with the Brisbane headquarters, amounted to participation in an alternative moral and political order.

While participation in the Legion might seem to promise an end to the colonial order, the existing political reality was the system of local government and representation controlled by Queensland. Murray's relations with the government alternated between challenges to its authority and attempts to extract material benefits from it. For the first ten years after the war, the former had been dominant; but with freedom still a remote prospect, some began to drop their sights and think in terms of more modest but attainable improvements, such as the housing and piped water that other islands were getting. Either way, external representation had become far more important than it had been before the war, and Murray increasingly felt the need for leaders who, as they put it, 'know how to talk to white people'. Their problem was to assess the effectiveness of delegates in a political arena of which they had only a limited understanding, whose activities they were unable to monitor. Often enough they were dependent on the delegate himself for an account of what he did, leaving him in a position to claim credit for improvements in which he had no part. The Meriam were aware of the risk that they might choose candidates whose real talent lay in knowing how to talk to their own people, not to whites.

The tensions arising from external representation compounded those that had long operated in local government, and they produced a volatile electorate. In the nine elections held between 1946 and 1965, eighteen individuals filled the four council positions, only two replacements being caused by the death of the incumbent. On no occasion did the same candidate manage to top the poll in two successive elections. Nine served only one term; five served two terms; one four, one five and one six. This last three between them held the chairman and Representative positions for all but a few months of the twenty years. The oldest of them, Marou, held office for ten years, in addition to the seven years he served before 1946, being chairman for eight years and Representative for five. Sam Passi served eleven years, most of them as chairman; and apart from four years' absence continued in office until 1976. The record, however, belongs to George Mye, who was first elected to the council in 1953, retaining the position until he left Murray for his native Darnley in 1976. He became Representative in 1956.

I cannot hope for a complete explanation of why the Meriam repeatedly elected these three while rejecting others. In a small, stable community, one knows the whole person, not just a public persona; consequently judgements tend to be complex and shifting. Nor are the dramatic issues that periodically electrified Murray a certain guide, for they were often the catalysts for underlying discontents, less easily articulated. All I can do is attempt to interpret what Meriam said to me about their political history in the light of observable developments in their community and the region as a whole.

Marou emerges as the most complex of the three leaders, for

Plate 6. *Sam Passi, former chairman of Murray Island, displaying an*
usari *yam*

while he was a product of the colonial era and committed to
island custom, he retained a vivid sense of the old Mer which
perhaps enabled him to conceive of a life free from colonial
domination – some now say, independent of Australia. Certainly, he was the most fearless of the Department's critics, not
just in the safety of his own community but in the presence of
senior officials and ministers. In the words of a longstanding
opponent, with a lifetime of government service behind him:

> Marou was a brave man, always fighting the government.
> He spoke up for the people. This time it's all government
> men (i.e. employees) who can't speak up because they're
> frightened they'll lose their jobs. Marou was never a govern-
> ment man. When Mr O'Leary (Director of Native Affairs)
> came with some big people during the war and sent for

Marou, that old man told him, 'If you want to see me, you come to me'.

He was born in 1886 on the other side of the island, among people who still kept Christianity at arm's length, and who taught him the old lore. He nevertheless attended the government school, assisting the teacher as a monitor. Like other adolescents he went to work on a lugger, but managed to escape to the mainland and was about to become a sharecropper when the authorities discovered him and sent him back. Never a member of the LMS church, he was baptised when the Anglicans arrived in 1915, and soon after went to Darnley Island to study for the priesthood. When the diocese ran out of funds he returned to Murray and worked as an assistant teacher. In 1928 he was elected councillor and in 1931 became both chairman and a church-warden. Put out of office in 1933 he was returned in 1936 in time to take a leading part in the strike, for which the Protector dismissed him. 1939 saw him chairman again, and petitioning the bishop to take over Murray from the Protector and run it like St Paul's Mission.[8] He claimed, and is widely believed to have made the approach that led to the formation of the TSLI, and he certainly accompanied the recruiting officer around the Eastern Islands. Though too old to serve, he visited Thursday Island on a number of occasions, and eyewitnesses report that the European officers entertained him and accorded him every respect. At home, however, people found him increasingly autocratic, and he was dismissed following a violent quarrel over land. But when the servicemen returned they made him their spokesman. He told me that they had wanted to do away with the council and go 'under Commonwealth law', but he had persuaded them to work through existing structures.

At home Marou made enemies through his severity in punishing infringements of the by-laws, but at the councillors' conferences he became the leading advocate of citizen rights. He was enough of a thorn in the Department's side for one official to nickname him 'old Stalin', partly because of the pipe and moustache he affected at the time, but also perhaps because of his brief contact with Communists in 1948. It was this stand that enabled him to stem the tide of domestic discontent, and he topped the poll in two more elections. But by 1950 the DNA had

---

[8] Marou showed me the letter in which the bishop politely declined his request.

consolidated its hold and was hardening in its attitude towards reform. Marou, with nothing tangible to show for three years in office and with Murray falling behind in the pursuit of prosperity, looked for new strategies. Realizing that the Communists were both ineffective and embarrassing allies, he again turned to the Church, but was again refused – this time quite sharply. Increasingly aware of the limitations of the colonial structure, he now conceived the idea of becoming Torres Strait's delegate in the Queensland Parliament. However, when one of his supporters formally proposed this at a meeting on Murray, it evoked a sharp challenge from the parish priest Poey, son of old *mamoose* Passi, and possessed of considerable prestige in his own right. Although Marou denied it, many believed that his subsequent invitation to the Pentecostalists was an act of reprisal. If so, it was a grave miscalculation.

Emboldened by the indignation of the Anglican synod and the other Torres Strait councillors and, so it was said, with the approval of the Director of Native Affairs himself, Marou's enemies took round a petition for his dismissal. The Torres Strait Islanders Act of 1939 (section 10, part II) provided that the Director of Native Affairs might dissolve a council on receipt of a petition of at least two-thirds of the electors, and the numbers were sufficient for him to act. In the election that followed, the priest's nephew, Sam Passi, took first place, and with it the offices of chairman and Representative. Born in 1912, he had spent his adult life as a school teacher in various parts of the Strait. For this reason he had escaped the radicalizing experience of the 1936 strike and army service. Consistent with his experience, he was unimpressed by talk of freedom, and at one election I heard him inform the people that he would not pretend to 'lead them into a land of milk and honey'. A 'government man' himself, he seemed content with the existing state of affairs, as long as Murray's local autonomy was respected. He spoke excellent English and was curious about the outside world, although at that time he had never been beyond Thursday Island. He was absorbed in the life of the community, as a churchman, a gardener, and as guide, philosopher and friend to countless kith and kin. Had he remained Representative beyond the one term, this orientation might have changed; but in the short run he failed to fill the external role that Marou had virtually created.

Although Marou had lost his place to Sam Passi, he had come a

close second in the election, and it seems that some who had
signed the petition to unseat him later voted him back. More
rallied to him in the election of 1953, restoring him to his former
offices. But this was his final term, for in 1956 he failed to win a
place on the council. As late as 1960 he was hoping for a come-
back; but while people spoke highly of him as a preacher and
authority on traditional lore, few came to see him any more.
They said that at seventy-four he was too old, Murray needed
councillors who were 'better educated'. Although, after the petition, he had ceased to protect the Pentecostalists, some still
blamed him for letting them in; others held bitter memories of
his severity in court, and these faults were no longer offset by his
activities as a Representative. Some considered his talk for
citizen rights an embarrassment to the pragmatic politics of the
1950s, while the ex-servicemen who still pursued this goal had
their own leaders with links to Legion headquarters.

George Mye took Marou's place as Eastern Islands Representative in 1956, after only one term on the council. Born on
neighbouring Darnley Island in 1923,[9] he had come to Murray in
1948 to manage the government store. By marrying a Meriam
girl he acquired affinal ties on Murray which, combined with his
kin connections on his home island and neighbouring Stephens
Island, stood him in good stead when he ran for this position.
But the Murray people said they voted for him because he was 'a
good educated man'. On Darnley the government teacher had
trained him for store work while he was still a schoolboy, and he
had subsequently attended the special school of Mabuyag.
Following a short period of training with the Island Industries
Board after the war, he was sent to take charge of the Murray
branch store, which was the largest in the Strait. Essentially,
however, he was self-taught, studying for the school leaving and
bookkeeping certificates by correspondence, and cultivating
the kind of Europeans who could broaden his outlook. Subscrib-
ing to the *Pacific Islands Monthly* and the *National Geographical
Magazine*, he had a better grasp of political and financial matters
than any other Islander in the Strait, and people knew it.

Mye's political perspectives were very different from those of
either Marou or Sam Passi. He had been too young to join the

---

[9] Like most Darnley Islanders, he was of mixed descent. His surname came from
    his grandfather, who came from the Vanuatuan island of Maewo. He was also
    descended from the Jamaican trepanger, Douglas Pitt, and from a Niuean
    seaman.

1936 strike and had worked on a cargo boat throughout the war, thus escaping the two radicalizing experiences of the period. At the same time, he had a much closer acquaintance with the workings of government. Learning from Marou's mistakes, he formed a strategy more appropriate to the colder political climate, pursuing limited but attainable material improvements. Citizen rights such as the franchise could wait. Yet, identifying himself with Murray's traditional intransigence, he spoke of himself 'fighting the government', pointing out that he did so at the risk of his job.

Noting the antagonism that Marou had built up through his involvement in local affairs, George Mye disengaged himself by passing the position to his runner up, Sam Passi. Hearing only appeals from the island court, he was sometimes able to mitigate sentences that seemed overly severe. For some years he even declined church office and was rarely seen about the village. However, he saw everyone in the store, where his expertise in money matters and his indulgence in the matter of credit were in constant demand.

The improvements that he could win during the early years were relatively small, and neither he nor the government seemed to promise a solution to the burgeoning economic crisis. This, at any rate, was how it seemed to the Legion members, who were looking instead to their former white comrades for repatriation funds and much more. The Legion, originally formed around 1949, underwent a revival in 1957 with the return of one Tom Tapou. Born in 1908, and with experience of the 1936 strike as well as 'army time', he had been living for several years on Thursday Island. There he had been converted to Pentecostalism, along with others of his large family, and had attended Legion meetings. He arrived on Murray as a committee member of the Thursday Island branch, an office which he claimed entitled him to be leader of the local sub-branch. There was already an elected committee, but his official connection with Brisbane headquarters won him initial acceptance, which he was able to maintain through his energy and enthusiasm. As it happened, both he and his wife were invalid pensioners, and they spent a good part of their income on entertaining members at large and small gatherings. Tom Tapou had another constituency, for although the bishop had brought him back to the Church of England by appointing him churchwarden, he made no secret of his sympathy for the Assembly. For the moment, however, his primary commitment was to the Legion, and in the run-up to the 1958 council elections he told me that if the ex-servicemen did not get control this time there would be 'civil war'. He also had a private score to settle, for in a land dispute with one of the councillors the decision had gone against him. In the event, George Mye, acting in his capacity as returning officer, found occasion to disqualify all their leading candidates, either because they were Pentecostalists, or for failing to pay island tax or committing some breach of the by-laws.[10] Thus it was George Mye who topped the poll, followed by Sam Passi, and two other men generally in sympathy with their politics. (This result was facilitated by the returning officer's decision to change from the old one-voter-one-vote rule, to giving electors as many votes as there were seats on the council.) The ex-servicemen, after a brief exclamation of protest, went along with the election, and only a few die-hard Pentecostalists declined to line up and shake hands with the new team. Yet within six months the electorate had dismissed all four.

The affair began with an obscure dispute between two men which came into the public arena when one accused the other of an injury which was also in breach of the by-laws. This was unremarkable in itself, except that the offender was related to two members of the council and the rumour got about that they would not prosecute him on this account. The aggrieved party was a Legion member and he went to the committee, which took up his case with alacrity. Within a few days they had circulated a petition and secured enough signatures to unseat the council. They then drew up a list of complaints against the incumbents, mostly unrelated to the precipitating issue and often designed to discredit them with the DNA rather than to right local wrongs. Some complaints revealed a mistrust of the very expertise that made George Mye an effective delegate, even his possession of a typewriter was subject to innuendo. There was talk of sending him back to his native Darnley.

The DNA duly dissolved the council but it was ten months before an official arrived to conduct a new election. This left the Meriam time to rediscover their individual and collective dependence on George Mye, if not the other councillors, and there was a steady trickle of people coming privately to make their peace with him. Thus he was able to regain a seat on the new council;

---

[10] These disqualifications were set out in part III, section 11(3) of the Act.

and although he only took third place, the councillors of the other Eastern Islands secured his reappointment as Representative.

The other three members of the incoming council were all ex-servicemen and one was a declared Pentecostalist. However, Tom Tapou had won only second place, the chairmanship going to another committee member who had no particular sympathy for the Assembly. After a private conversation with the government official this man performed his duties with circumspection, distancing himself from his more radical associates. Tom Tapou had also been closeted with the DNA official after the election, and it was said that he had been warned not to cause any more trouble. But in fact there was little that he could do within the existing political framework. He lacked the expertise to represent the people in external affairs, and in any case lacked the opportunity to do so. His fellow councillors impeded his efforts to help the Pentecostalists and denied him the opportunity to re-open the land case that irked him. There was nothing for him to do, but to return to his bailiwick, the Legion, to await the coming of freedom.

The Legion, along with the two churches, had been the unofficial government of Murray during the interregnum. Tom Tapou now announced that when 'Commonwealth law' came in, the ex-servicemen would be put in charge of the island. It was a heady time, in which rumours of imminent freedom ran throughout the Strait; but there was nothing the Legion could do to hasten the process, so they busied themselves with dancing and feasts throughout the Christmas of 1960 and into the New Year.

In the event, freedom did not come as a single, all-transforming cataclysm, but piecemeal; and by the time the next council election came around, while Islanders had the Federal franchise, their material circumstances had deteriorated. Even the Pentecostalists were disappointed in their hopes. Thus no one was surprised that George Mye was the only member of the outgoing council to be returned. With Sam Passi once again chairman, and his cousin in fourth place, the community seemed to have returned to a more moderate style of politics. The ex-servicemen still had one councillor, and they usually managed to get at least one of their members elected in subsequent contests. But with the emigration of Tom Tapou and most of his family, and the gradual flow-through of improvements, the Legion confined itself to more limited objectives. While Meriam regularly voted out some of their councillors at election time, there were no more petitions.

The Meriam domain and its enemies

Although the Meriam were well aware that most of their problems derived from their relations with the outside world, they tended to talk politics in terms of the local personalities involved. Their problem was that they had to visualize the world that seemed about to engulf them with understandings that they had formed on its outer margins. Lacking any clear guides as to the likely outcome they were liable to excesses of optimism and pessimism which became focussed on local bodies such as the Legion, the two churches and the council, and the individuals identified with them. Similarly, they found it impossible to think about changing relations with the outside world without considering the possible implications for their relations with one another and their ability to control them. Thus when an ex-serviceman made a speech about the benefits of freedom, someone muttered that these included divorce, an unkind reference to his turbulent domestic affairs.

By the end of the 1930s the Meriam had constructed a domain within which they were able to maintain continuity with the past, conduct relations with one another according to the canons of custom, and run church and council as though these were community bodies rather than instruments of external control. To the outside world they presented a unitary personality that was hospitable yet fiercely jealous of its autonomy.

In the years following the Second World War this domain came under threat, arising on the one hand from the increasing dependence on external representation, and on the other from links with the metropolitan society which brought subversive ideas. In 1951 the Meriam had had to weigh the advantages of having Marou as their external delegate against his severity in court, and his introduction of a new church. In 1959 they had had to make a similar kind of choice. No doubt there were a whole host of considerations that induced people to dismiss the council they had elected only a few months earlier, but the one that stands out among the ephemera is the suspicion that they had been prevented from choosing freely.

While the Representative was conducting the election according to the book, the grounds for disqualification by a returning officer who was also a contestant were open to misinterpretation. However, the people's discontent focussed less on the result than on the form. Over recent years the Meriam had established an uneasy balance between the principle that everybody was *mamoose* and the need for delegates who knew how to talk to white people, by conducting elections as though there was still open competition.

Political participation was nowhere higher than on Murray. People of all ages did not hesitate to declare that the council was 'doing nothing for the island' or, alternatively, 'ruining the island'. Women, although nominally eligible, did not run for office; but almost every man thought of himself as a potential candidate, although a direct question would always produce the modest disclaimer: 'It's only up to the people'. A casual observer at an election might indeed have supposed that the contest was wide open. There were scores of nominations, some seemingly made on the spur of the moment; and there was no shortage of candidates. In the 1960 election, following the petition, no fewer than thirty offered themselves – as though to make a point. Most polled only a handful of votes and several were deserted even by those who had nominated them. But while a long serving leader might be mortified at such a defeat, the ordinary individual took it in his stride; he had exercised his right to put himself forward for the people's consideration. Nor was this simply an empty charade, for once in a while a new candidate did take the popular fancy.

Even those who managed to gain election time after time were not allowed to become complacent, for their votes fluctuated from election to election. This was most marked in the case of the external delegates, whose performance could not be monitored. Significantly, they were the principal targets of both petitions, suggesting that the precipitating issue may have released more general unease.

A puzzling feature of both petitions was that a significant number of those who had voted to unseat a councillor voted him back at the very next election. When I asked how this had happened, I was told that they were all the 'silly ones' who were easily swayed. But their reversal could also be interpreted as sending the delegate back to his duties after suitable chastisement. Even if the Meriam had in reality only a limited choice as to who their councillors would be, they wanted to be able to give their consent. The decision must be 'up to the people', so that they could line up and shake hands with their new leaders without dissembling.

The Legion's move to overthrow the 1958 council was an adroit move which raised it from being a sectional interest group to a guardian of community values. As though to hold its position centre stage, it dominated the Christmas celebrations with a large dancing team that performed throughout the holiday. And to reinforce its standing, it ended the season with a presentation of the Malu–Bomai dances. Even the Pentecostalists were persuaded to join, 'because we've got our freedom'. The position, however, was impossible to retain: the ex-servicemen councillors proved to have the defects of all councillors, and could not produce the benefits they had promised. There was also an increasing unease over the political costs of the upheaval. That the DNA had had to send in a European official to conduct the election suggested that the Meriam could not manage their own affairs. The ex-servicemen's talk of a Commonwealth takeover, with white magistrates replacing the council, was no more reassuring to those who still valued their island's independence. However, it was the Pentecostalists who ended up carrying the blame. The word went about that they had fooled the Legion into supporting the petition simply in order to get freedom for their church, and hard line Anglicans began saying that the government was going to banish Pentecostalists to an uninhabited island.

Although the majority of Pentecostalists were inoffensive citizens who simply wanted to worship at the church of their choice, their existence did constitute a threat to the Meriam domain, perhaps without their realizing it. Not only did they deny the institutions that enabled Murray to face the world as a community, but they threatened the bonds of kinship that tied one domestic unit to another in the daily round of petty sharing and cooperation.

Kinship was still the principle by which the Meriam organized their everyday life, conceptually and to a degree in practice. The couple with whom I lived found it convenient to 'adopt' me; and they took the time to point out to me my 'kin', explaining the genealogical connections. It was usual, in referring to particular relatives, to append a kin-term to the given name; for example, 'John-*awa*' or 'Wais-auntie'.[11] These were the people, they gave me to understand, from whom I might ask favours and should entertain requests.

But while it was usually possible to discover a kin link between parties to a transaction, the kinship system did not enable one to explain why certain individuals collaborated rather than others. Since almost everyone had at least one Meriam parent and most had two, it was possible to find a 'path' to many more kin than one needed, at least for everyday purposes. Nor could they be differentiated in terms of the type of link; even distance was an uncertain guide. Meriam would admit that they had a particular liking (*lag*) for certain kin they called 'mates' (*kaimeg*) but they were less ready to admit dislike of those with whom they did not associate, insisting that these were people whom they could approach if they needed to do so. Correspondingly, it was proper to refuse an unwelcome request as long as one did not deny the kinship connection on the basis of which it had been made.

Elections placed this system under a certain amount of strain. I was sometimes told that people voted for their relatives, as though to deny the personal and ideological divisions that became manifest on these occasions. But since personal kindreds overlapped and candidates needed scores if not hundreds of votes, rather than the handful mobilized for a housebuilding or a family feast, one had often to choose among kin. However, the secrecy of the ballot saved the system from open breach; and while a candidate might suspect or even know that a particular relative had not supported him, it was wiser to pretend ignorance and work for a change at the next election. Reversing the statement that elections were a matter of kinship, some claimed that the modern way was to 'think of the island, not just your own family'. This disengaged politics from kinship in such a way as to deny that any particular ties were being broken.

I was sometimes told that religion too 'goes by family', as though to deny the intrusive doctrinal dispute. The assertion seemed to bear some correspondence to the facts, for there was a marked tendency for Pentecostalists to be close kin of some

---

[11] Traditional Meriam kinship terminology is of Iroquois type, the basic distinction being between siblings of the same and opposite sex. In recent times these have been replaced by *bala* and *sisi*, which are modified versions of the English terms for brother and sister. The English term, auntie has also come into use. However, the Meriam *awa* remains in use for mother's brother, along with the vernacular terms for sister's son, cross cousin and grandparents.

other Pentecostalists. Correspondingly, converts returning from the mainland tended to revert to Anglicanism if their families were of that denomination. Where close kin differed over religion, they had quarrelled earlier over land or some family matter. Nevertheless, while religion might be embedded in customary relations, it gave them a new dimension and at points changed them. Bonds and divisions took on an appearance of permanence through association with eternal doctrines, and were reiterated every time people went to church.

Changes in the mode of recruiting work bees were particularly indicative of what was happening. The custom was for a family to invite kinsfolk to help in some task such as building a house or clearing bush, in return for food and the promise of reciprocal help at a future date. Pentecostalists continued to respond to such requests from Anglican kin, but in organizing their own bees they invited their co-religionists, making a contribution to the local Assembly by way of recompense. In so doing they denied their Anglican kin a means of reciprocating, and threatened the ties that sustained Meriam cultural unity.

A crisis passed

During the years of crisis, the Meriam lived in the shadow of impending changes which, still undeveloped, filled them with extravagant hopes and fears. The 1960s saw the Meriam coming to grips and to terms with the actualities. The phantasm of freedom dissolved into a number of particular reforms that left the colonial order intact, if less pervasive in its influence. The Meriam came to realize that, while they might expect a steady trickle of government assistance to improve their living conditions, there would be no economic miracle. If they wanted to live like white people they would have to go to the mainland. This prospect became less alarming as it became a reality for increasing numbers. Fears that the family would be disrupted were calmed as men sent for their wives and children and sons for their parents, to join them in the south. The prospect of adapting to urban living also became less daunting as sizeable Islander communities formed in centres such as Townsville, re-establishing some of the institutions of island life in the new setting. There was enough movement back and forward for the people at home to be able to make realistic judgements as to the pros and cons of emigration. Some spent a limited period away working, to return when they had enough money to build a house and buy a boat. A greater number left for good, in search of higher income, better schooling for their children, the right to practise their preferred religion or a generally less restrictive way of life.

In 1967, when the Commonwealth Film Unit made its documentary *The Islanders*, Murray was able to muster some eighty dancers in a magnificent display of their cultural heritage. Ten years later this would have been possible, if at all, only during the Christmas season when the emigrants made visits home. It is still possible to speak of the Meriam domain. But, as we shall see in later chapters, while Murray has greater bargaining power in external affairs it has reduced its capacity to regulate the lives of its citizens. In particular, the council no longer forbids the consumption of alcohol or contacts between the sexes which once made up the largest part of the court's business. This is explained as being 'modern way', but it can also be seen as an admission of impotence. In the past these by-laws had enabled the old people to control the young, particularly the young men; now these by-laws are more likely to drive them away from the community.

VI The Baduans

I often heard Baduans say, 'We were the last to be civilized, but now we're the first.' Badu had been 'last' in the sense of receiving missionaries later than most islands; it was 'first' in the sense of having the finest church in Torres Strait. It was also first – and the two were connected – in having the biggest and most successful pearling fleet. When I came there in 1959, this community of less than five hundred was base for no fewer than thirteen boats; and the monthly cycle of movement, to the working grounds, from thence to Thursday Island and home again, set a rhythm to which the whole community moved. Badu was dedicated to 'hard work',[1] the paramount good from which all other benefits flowed. Not the least of these was the favour of the DNA; indeed the steady flow of official visitors bore witness to the fact that the Queensland government regarded Badu as its success story.

At the beginning of the century Badu had been a community much like any other in the Strait. Not until the 1930s did it embark on the course that was to distinguish it from the others and transform its internal structure. At the heart of the transformation lay the replacement of the old task-oriented pattern by a work discipline that had its origins in the Industrial Revolution. As in England, according to E.P. Thompson (1968:80), this involved the whole culture: 'In all these ways – by the division of labour, the supervision of labour; bells and clocks; money incentives; preachings and schooling; the suppression of fairs and sports – new labour habits were formed and new time disciplines imposed' (*ibid.*:90).

By the 1950s there was little sense of continuity with the past. The current generation set more store by the foreign descent to

---

[1] Hard work seems to constitute a single word in Torres Strait Broken, as in the phrase '*ardwork for nothing*'. However, it has a counterpart in Kala Lagaw Ya – *zaget* – as also in Meriam Mir – *dorge*.

which many of them could lay claim. The council had taken control of the land, cancelling the traditional system of tenure. Subsistence production was no longer an alternative to wage labour; and though hunting remained important, its practice was firmly subordinated to the routines of pearling.

Notwithstanding these changes, one could still speak of a Badu domain. If many things were done 'modern fashion',[2] there was still a recognizable island custom. When it was time to go to sea, skippers stayed for neither Sabbath nor feast; but they bought opulent furnishings for the church to commemorate their dead, and their weddings and tombstone openings were the most lavish in the Strait. Although the community was closely integrated with the colonial economy, it retained control over the conduct of its everyday affairs, local government and church were firmly in local hands and the great majority of men worked under local skippers. The colonial authorities were content that it should be so, since Badu was politically quiescent, paid its church dues promptly, and regularly fulfilled its norms in the production of pearl shell.

Badu's success was likewise located within the community; but not so much with the people at large as with the skippers, and most of all with one man, Tanu Nona, who had 'taught Badu how to work'. Strong leadership, as he himself said, was the keynote of his career, applied not only to pearling but to the council and the parish. There was no question of 'everybody *mamoose*' on Badu: in the words of a Meriam, long resident on the island, 'They just put their heads down and say Yes. All they know is how to say Yes!'

If Badu was 'first', then, some Baduans were – to adapt Orwell's satire – more 'first' than others. And while the changes had been legitimately effected through community institutions, there was some feeling, particularly among the have-nots, of alienation from the domain as it was now defined. These parochial tensions were exacerbated by the tensions arising from the contradiction between the colonial and metropolitan systems. The strength of Badu's pearling enterprises saved it from the effects of the economic crisis until the mid-1960s, and made the prospect of citizenship seem less alluring than it did to the Meriam. But 'army time' had left its mark, and if strong leadership stopped the Legion and the Assembly of God from

---

[2] Fashion – more nearly rendered *pasin* – is the Broken counterpart of the Kala Lagaw Ya *pawa* and the Meriam *tonar*.

gaining a foothold, it could not stop Baduans from hearing such talk on their regular visits to Thursday Island. These tensions were also expressed through the kinship system, which remained the chief idiom in which claims and deferences were defined. On the one hand certain families differentiated themselves from, and claimed superiority over other families; on the other hand individuals claimed kinship with members of other families in such a way as to deny inequality.

Badu ethnography

Badu is an irregularly shaped island, measuring some 9.7 km in diameter.[3] Much of its area is taken up by low hills, covered with great granite boulders, but there are open grasslands, which are lightly wooded and well watered. Around the circumference, long sandy beaches alternate with dense mangrove. It was here that the people lived, building temporary shelters and moving frequently according to the dictates of commissariat and climate. The population at first count, in 1914, was 250. Assuming that it had undergone a decline similar to that of other communities, and that it was bottoming out about this time, the number at contact could have been 500 or more.[4] This was no great density for a maritime economy, and certainly less than that of Mabuyag, from which Badu is said to have been settled.[5]

Less fertile and well drained than Murray, Badu still permitted the cultivation of sweet potato, bananas and yams, as well as taro. But the indications are that the people relied mainly upon wild yams and other tubers, wild plum and, in the wet season, mangrove pods, from which an edible paste called *biyu* could be prepared. (According to tradition it was this last food that attracted settlers from Mabuyag before colonization.)

Production entailed a sharper division of labour between the sexes than on Murray, and a greater degree of co-operation among nuclear families. As on the mainland, women gathered wild vegetables and fruits, as well as shell fish, and caught fish off

[3] For maps of Badu see Haddon (1904:8); Lawrie (1970:18).
[4] Harris has calculated that Badu may have had a pre-contact population of as much as 670 (1979:91). However, he assumes a population decline similar to that of Moa, which may not be justified.
[5] This tradition is supported by the representation of certain clans on both islands.

the rocks. Men spent much of their time hunting turtle and dugong in canoes that required a crew of at least three or four, and sometimes took many more. They also spent time at the *kwod*, the men's ceremonial ground which was off-limits to women (Haddon 1904:365–6). Here newly initiated boys fetched and carried for their elders, heard raiding parties planned and saw the trophies of war brought back (*ibid.*:213–15). It is clear from the historical record that Badu engaged in warfare far more frequently than Murray, and head hunting occupied a central place in its culture (*ibid.*:308–19).

Badu's social organization was continuous with, if not an extension of Mabuyag's (*ibid.*:162–71). The basic building blocks of social organization were patri-clans, each identified with a number of totemic species. While they did not trace their origins back to a founding ancestor, they did retain genealogies of some seven or eight generations in depths (Haddon 1904: tables 1–15), and membership was normally inherited from the father. Clans claimed joint rights to fetishes, sacred places and ritual offices, as also to stretches of foreshore, off-shore islands and tracts of land in the interior. However, certain garden places and wild yam patches were associated with individuals, or their immediate descendants (*ibid.*:284–92). Adjacent totemic clans were further grouped into three districts, called 'tribes' in the post-contact period, namely Badu, Argan and Wakaid. According to my informants they came together for war under the leadership of a chief, but the record is not entirely clear.

Although the clans were in effect exogamous, marriage prohibitions were defined in terms of kin categories, in such a way as to exclude anyone with whom a blood tie could be established. Such persons formed the 'sides' of bride and groom, much as on Murray.[6] Much as on Murray, also, the negotiation of the marriage was marked by expressions of antagonism, which were brought to an end by the presentation of gifts to the bride's family or an exchange of sisters in marriage. Thereafter affinal relations were maintained through the periodic exchanges of goods and services, culminating in the funerary rites, which must be conducted by a wife's brother or sister's husband of the deceased (Haddon 1904:148). The mother's brother also

---

[6] The Kala Lagaw Ya words for side – *dogam* – and kin – *buwai* – are obviously related to the Meriam *doge* and *boai*. The system of kinship terminology has been classified as Hawaiian, but it is in fact similar to the Meriam, with which it shares some terms.

assumed important responsibilities for his sister's son, acting as his guardian in initiation and his advocate in marriage.[7] As the people themselves conceived it, the relationship cut across lines of tension in the society, and even warring groups.

The clans were also grouped along with those of Mabuyag in a ritual division of labour that cut across territorial groupings (*ibid.*:172–3), the cult of the mythical headhunter, Kwoiyam, being by far the most important (*ibid.*:367–73). However, while the Baduans seem to have participated in the rites, the main fetishes were kept on Mabuyag. Indeed, Badu does not seem to have had any cults of its own, which may help to explain its relatively weak sense of historic community.

Although it was important in warfare, the cult of Kwoiyam did not give rise to the kind of hereditary government that held sway on Murray. Evidently there were hereditary headmen – called *kuwiku garka* – of some kind, but Haddon supposed that their executive power was weak, except perhaps in times of war (*ibid.*:265). In any case, while Badu's headman was appointed *mamoose* during the early period of colonial rule, the succession broke down around the turn of the century, leaving a vacuum that was soon filled by a succession of elected councillors.

Colonial reconstruction

Moa, Badu and Mabuyag were not on the early sailing routes, and they were not visited by any of the surveying vessels of the 1840s, possibly because of their murderous reputation. According to one of Haddon's informants, any stranger would 'stop all the time' in the sense of being killed and parts of him eaten (*ibid.*:278) – the ultimate form of domestication! One foreigner of undetermined origin, the 'Wild White Man' of Idriess's novel, succeeded in establishing himself there during the 1840s, but evidently urged the Baduans to kill anyone who came after, including some Europeans who were looking for turtle shell (Haddon 1904:278). According to tradition he was himself killed by an envious sorcerer, before European settlement. But in 1871, H.M. Chester was able to trade iron for pearl shell (Carroll 1969:46); in 1874 a Loyalty Island pastor spent several weeks on Badu without coming to any harm. His departure was not, as

[7] Rivers' discovery of these brother-in-law relations and the role of the mother's brother did much to fire his interest in anthropology (Haddon 1904:134–5; 144–50).

tradition suggests, because they were unwilling to abandon their heathen wickedness – the cult of Kwoiyam had lost much of its relevance with the end of warfare, and the Mabuyag custodians had consented to the destruction of the sacred objects – but simply because they could not afford to come together in one village (McFarlane 10.1874:14). Ten years later they sent word to the Mabuyag mission that they were ready to meet its conditions. This suggests not just an eagerness for the Gospel, but an increased dependence on wage labour. There were already two pearling stations on the island.

In the late 1890s the Reverend F.W. Walker began the enterprise that was to become Papuan Industries, near to the sheltered anchorage provided by the channel between Badu and Moa islands. Within a few months the people had followed him there, occupying the site of the present village. The ready access to store goods and the opportunity to earn the money with which to buy them must have been a powerful incentive to the Baduans, as Walker realized. However, their traditional commitment to maritime pursuits and the prolonged absences for hunting and raiding may have predisposed them to the work of pearling. Once they had their own boats, moreover, they could combine commercial production with the traditional pursuit of turtle and dugong.

By the 1900s Badu had become a fairly typical Torres Strait village community, living by a combination of cash and subsistence production, focussed on the church and ruled by a European government teacher and native authorities. The family assumed somewhat the same character as on Murray, although the sexual division of labour was more marked. With the young men working for their parents, the age of marriage was postponed to the mid-twenties and sexual conduct was strictly regulated. A new festive complex was developing around weddings and tombstone openings, and a new dancing style unobjectionable to the pastors had come in from neighbouring Mabuyag.

These changes, combined with the sharp decline in population, were accompanied by a re-ordering of the social structure, in particular the eclipse of the clans. Badu was incorporated within the colonial order through the three 'tribes'. Headed by a *mamoose* and later by a councillor, each operated its own boat and occupied a distinct section of the village. In addition to the indigenous inhabitants, eight Pacific Islanders, a Buginese and a

Malay also lived on Badu as employees of Papuan Industries. They built their houses a short distance from the main village, but their children enjoyed tribal membership through their Baduan mothers. A Samoan, known as Moses or Tipoti Nona, had earlier married a Baduan wife, but following her death had gone to Saibai and married again. When he returned to Badu, his children from the second marriage were distributed among the three tribes by a form of adoption. Later, with the dissolution of the tribes and the emergence of 'families' as the basic units, the descendants of these foreigners re-identified themselves by reference to their fathers.

Teaching Badu how to work

In 1901 the Government Resident of Thursday Island described the Baduans as 'nice but rather lazy' (Douglas 1899:39). The company boats provided work for married men who did not want to venture too far from home, and who might make only two or three trips in the year. As on Murray, skippers were elected for short terms, and took the same share as the crew. However, a letter of 1913 mentions that Tamwoy, son of a Niuean skipper, 'by incessant toil' had acquired a small cutter which he and his family worked independently (Harris 1913). Though the government regarded such half castes as coming under its control, it allowed a number of them to conduct small businesses on their own account, outside the company boat framework. Tanu Nona, who later married Tamwoy's daughter, was impressed by his father-in-law's achievement, but chose to transform the system from within.

Born in 1900, some twenty years later than Tamwoy, Tanu Nona showed his talents at an early age, explaining,

> I got my first boat from Mr Luffman [a master pearler] in 1918. When I was nineteen I got the *Coral Sea*. I was going up to New Guinea to work out from Samarai, but my mother wanted me to stop and I took over as skipper of the island cutter. I've been a skipper ever since. Later the Poid people [a former village on Moa] made me captain of their lugger, the *Manu*. The government set me to race [i.e. compete] with Douglas Pitt from Darnley. In six weeks I got ten ton of trochus; Douglas Pitt only got five. That's how Badu got the *Wakaid*, the biggest lugger in Torres Strait. For six years we kept the cup [awarded by the government] until they finished the competition.

The harsh regime that he had to maintain in order to win became a legend in later years, with those who had experienced the regime retailing it for the edification of younger and supposedly softer generations. In his own words:

> We stayed out sometimes for ten months on the coast, from Cape York to Gladstone. You must have a strong captain to make those boys work. If they no been get much shell I no let them into dinghy to eat dinner, midday. They got to eat their piece of damper standing on the reef. Some skippers work only half day, six in the morning till dinner time, then sail on to the next reef night time. Making the crew work is the main thing. Also knowing the tides. But you must make those boys finish the reef. Bad skippers leave some shell behind.

By general agreement, Tanu Nona's forceful personality was the key factor in the transformation. But he was able to work through established community structures. While the parents of his crewmen may have regretted not seeing them for months on end, they were delighted with the relatively large sums of money that came to them at lay-off time. Chance also provided him with a religious legitimation. Around 1930 the community decided that its decaying wooden church would be replaced by a large cement building. Tanu, already elected councillor, was now made churchwarden and director of the project. All able bodied men were to work on the boats, giving up the greater portion of their wages to buy cement. Those who stayed at home, women as well as men, were to mix the cement, going to the gardens only on Saturdays. Finding them loafing on the job, one day, Tanu is said to have tipped buckets of water over them and laid about him with an oar. But if this behaviour was unprecedented and to some outrageous, it was justified by the erection of a fine church and the clearance of the debt in a mere two years, a remarkable achievement given the depressed wages of the period.

Once instituted, the by-law requiring all able bodied men to go to sea remained in force after the church was built. Tanu also seized the opportunity to effect another longterm change. The lugger *Wakaid* was nominally owned by the tribe of that name, who also provided the crew. Tanu, though himself a member, began recruiting from Badu and Argan. 'I thought it silly that a good man couldn't work with others because he didn't belong to their tribe, and might have to work with other men who were no good. That was how *Wakaid* got all the best men.'

As is often the way with innovators and entrepreneurs, Tanu Nona's relationship to the community was ambiguous. Though Badu-bred he was not Badu-born, and his ties with Badu people, through his wife and through friendship, were qualified by his connections with other part-Samoan families in the Strait, and with certain free families on Thursday Island. Although his marriage gave him affinal ties with Baduans through his wife's mother, it also linked him to the part-Niuean, Tamwoy, and his countrymen. Like Tamwoy before him, he was developing a special relationship with the government, which was of course gratified to have such an energetic skipper. Indeed there were rumours that they gave him a secret retainer so that he would not go over to the master pearlers. When the 1936 strike broke out, he and all but one of his brothers remained at work; and in the reorganization that followed, the *Wakaid* became the boat of the Nona brothers, renamed after their sister.

The family company put brotherly bonds to new uses and subjected them to new strains. The Nonas were now united around a substantial economic interest and a source of pride *vis-à-vis* other families. At the same time, with six brothers already over twenty and two in adolescence, there were problems of authority and equity to be worked out. How long could they work together before rivalry reared its head? In the event, the company was able to expand, so that by 1940 the three oldest brothers had boats of their own, leaving only the younger ones to work under Tanu. The sequence was repeated after the war, when once again the Nonas had to begin with one lugger. Other family companies, both before and after the war, fared less well, only the Tamwoys surviving into the 1950s. The invariable verdict on the rest was a laconic 'too many bosses'. The dissolution of the tribal groupings into their component families had also occurred on Murray and other islands, but it assumed particular significance on Badu because family now provided the structure for the organization of pearling enterprises. Families not only differentiated themselves from one another, but put their reputations on the line. As some prospered while others failed, a hierarchy began to emerge.

Now we are first

Coming to Badu for the first time in 1959, the first sight to catch my eye was the church, built at such sacrifice a generation earlier, an imposing white building amid a grove of tall coconut palms. The village was less easily discerned, for the old tribal wards had now broken up into more or less isolated hamlets, scattered over a wide area. Along the beach were the remnants of the old village, pre-war houses built of mangrove wood and galvanized iron turned rusty by the sea air. Further back, newer houses of the same materials alternated with more substantial buildings and small fibrolite cottages built by the government. Still further back, on the ridge overlooking the rest, were five large, new houses, belonging to prosperous skippers of the Nona family.

The Badu fleet was in this year at its zenith. Thirteen boats worked out from the island, employing some 200 men, around half of whom had been recruited from neighbouring islands. With more than 90% of the able-bodied men between sixteen and sixty employed in this way, the life of the community was governed by the monthly movement of boats from home to the working grounds, thence to Thursday Island for unloading and repairs, and home again. For about half the time Badu was virtually bereft of males, save the two police sergeants who handled official business while the councillors were away. Three church-wardens, two of whom were in their eighties, acted as figure-heads in church affairs, but it was the women who were in charge at such times, taking care of important visitors and organizing feasts if a church holiday fell due. If there were no pressing calls on their time, they might organize fishing parties to make up for the lack of meat; or alternatively beg a passage on some boat to Thursday Island for a few days shopping and visiting.

When the boats came in there was a stir of activity, as women and children hurried down to the beach where dugong and turtle were being butchered. Later the paths were thronged with men, still in their heavy working shirts and trousers, heading home. Later still one might hear the sounds of revelry, as parties began drinking the alcohol that had been illicitly smuggled back from 'town'. If a feast were being held at ths time the younger men might dance, but there was some fear that the normal rivalry between teams might erupt in brawling. Otherwise, the single men were soon usefully employed by their skippers, while the married men stayed at home with their families. Whereas the Meriam lived most of their time out of doors, within sight of their neighbours, the Baduans stayed indoors and they felt less obligation to attend feasts or even church services. The skippers, for their part, seemed to seek out one another's company.

As for government, this too was carried on out of sight, in the houses of Tanu Nona, his eldest son and a brother, who made up the council, and of another brother who was the senior sergeant of police.

Skippers and boats

During the brief boom that followed the end of the Pacific War, Badu made a substantial commitment to pearling, and within two years its boats were accounting for more than 30% of the shell obtained by the government fleet. As economic conditions became less favourable, ventures succumbed, but Badu's boats fared far better than those of other islands. By 1959 it was running nine government boats, accounting for more than 50% of the total catch. In addition, it provided skippers for four master boats.

Of the nine government boats, all but one old cutter was under the management of Tanu Nona, three of them being under the command of his brothers, two of his sons, and two of his brothers' sons. Two other brothers had charge of master boats. Of the other men who held or had held boats, all were either kinsmen or protégés of the Nonas, owing their advancement to Tanu.

Tanu's harsh regime of the 1930s remained a mythical charter for the current generation of skippers, but it could be a direct model only for the two boats which still worked trochus. Gathering mother-of-pearl shell with helmet and corselet required tight discipline while the divers were down, but not long hours of gruelling work, or long absences from home. Safety regulations required that a diver not stay down for more than a brief period, while changes in light and tides ensured a relatively short working day. Moreover, the water was only clear enough for working for about half of each month. The control of labour nevertheless remained a critical factor. The skipper must round up his men – a perennial problem – and have them at the working grounds by the time the water cleared. Once there, he must get his divers down as soon as there was sufficient light, and replace them in due course with the minimum delay. They could scarcely be supervized under water, but most skippers were themselves divers and so had a fair idea of how much shell should be coming up. The supervision of the engineer and tenders, on whom the

Plate 7.   A Badu skipper aboard his lugger, Pilemon Nona

diver's life depended, was no less taxing. The cook was often the scapegoat, who had only to produce burned rice or a half-cooked damper to bring down on his head the pent-up tensions of a trying day. Apart from all this, the skipper had to know the best places to work at different times and seasons, ensure that the engine and compressor were in order, and check the consumption of food and fuel.

Each skipper was spurred by the prospect of monetary reward, and the fear of losing his boat to one of the many young divers who were only too ready to show their mettle. A rebuke from Tanu was itself something to be avoided. But there was also among skippers a rivalry which, with a dozen or more at work and others retired or resting, took on a greater intensity than on islands where there were only two or three. The monthly release of each boat's tonnage was a topic of lively discussion, and if a skipper seemed to be falling behind his movements were closely watched. If he proved to be slow in getting to sea people were likely to call him 'woman sick', or as we might say, tied to his wife's apron strings.

Skippers had various ways of maintaining labour discipline. Some were in the habit of using their fists on the younger workers, and with a court made of fellow skippers, they had no fear of censure. On the positive side, the men's earnings were geared to productivity, with the result that the best skippers tended to attract the most highly motivated workers. Ambitious divers would also seek out such skippers in the hope of securing a recommendation that would get them boats of their own. Outside the cash nexus, however, the distribution of turtle and dugong meat provided a critical means of labour control.

A boat returning home after unloading its shell would usually spend a few hours hunting along the way. With a small expenditure of fuel, charged to running costs, it could bring in 400–500 kg of meat, and at certain seasons much more. For a special occasion a boat might go out for a whole day and I saw as many as twenty turtle lying on the beach after one such expedition.

In the days of the company boats the catch had been divided equally among members of the tribe that owned the boat; now distribution was the prerogative of the skipper, and while it was usual for each crewman to get a share, there had been a subtle shift from right to privilege. Since this would be his family's only source of fresh meat, any sign of conflict with his skipper would range his family up against him rather than in his support. The same consideration discouraged men from working on boats based elsewhere, since they would be depriving their families of meat for the whole year. Finally a skipper could secure the loyalty of a favoured worker by providing him with meat for his wedding feast or a tombstone opening. Thus turtle and dugong hunting, though strictly speaking production for subsistence, had become wholly subordinated to pearling, subsidizing wages and facilitating labour discipline, at very little cost to the enterprise.

Material considerations aside, labour relations were intertwined with ordinary ties of a traditional kind. Thus at least half of any crew were kinsmen or in-laws of the skipper. On the one hand skippers used such connections to compete for good divers; indeed, with the local labour force fully employed, it was remarkable that skippers with wives from Mabuyag recruited most of their men there. It was remarkable also that a skipper liked to have some older kinsman, perhaps an uncle, as his second-in-command. On the other hand, parents might persuade a son to work for some relative. If it was a sister's husband he was said to be 'helping his sister', and the skipper was 'teaching' him. Representing the relationship in such terms, they felt able to request a passage to Thursday Island, or meat for a feast. One consequence of this was that parents and older siblings were likely to support the skipper in any conflict.

To judge from the camaraderie among crew members, and the lack of boys seeking a career in government service or the church, it would seem that the younger generation had come to accept their role in the pearling industry, even to take pride in it. They seemed scarcely aware of the long-term debilitating effects of deep-water diving, and drew no conclusions from the small but continuing number of fatalities. The bursts of heavy drinking that followed each period of work might perhaps be interpreted as the release of a tension that had no other outlet; but there was no direct challenge to the view that there was no danger 'as long as you're careful'. Rather there was a contempt for the skipper who did not himself put on the helmet, he was only a 'deck diver'.

Rich households and poor households

The average per capita cash income in 1959 was around $200, which was about twice that of Murray. With social service payments at about the same level, and rather fewer in government employment, the main difference was in the income derived from pearling. (The difference would have been greater had I included the food consumed on board while working.) This, of course, did not necessarily produce an equivalent difference in material wellbeing, since Baduans had to pay for many things that the Meriam got for free. On the other hand, they were getting per capita an average of at least two kilograms of fresh meat each month. Finally, one has to say that they had more of the things that the Meriam would have liked to have had, such as iron and timber houses, cooking stoves, alcohol, manufactured clothing, domestic furniture and refrigerators, dinghies and outboard motors.

Badu, unlike Murray, was one of those communities where average per capita figures are misleading, in that they even out substantial differences in wealth. Skippers earned two and three times as much as divers, who in turn got more than tenders and deck hands. The top skippers earned as much as three times the money of the marginal performers, while Tanu Nona, as manager and head of the company, received an additional payment which was a well kept secret. Nor did the differences end here, for the skippers took the lion's share of any meat, and maintained large gardens which their men worked during dirty water time. However, the patterns of consumption differed.

An ordinary family passed through a cycle not unlike that of Murray, although the husband would continue working rather than becoming a gardener. The cycle began with living from his wages and from the endowment coming to their small children, unless they were lucky enough to live with or take in a relative who was drawing a pension. It reached its high point when several unmarried sons were bringing home their wages, when a couple might hope to build a new house.

Several big skippers provided accommodation not just for their families or aged parents, but for as many as a dozen crew members. Most of these were from other islands who had no place to stay, but some Baduan crew members also found it preferable to be in a big household with others of their own age. An added attraction were the single girls who had been sent by their parents to help the woman of the house. They were a small drain on the household's resources, for the skipper could draw on the boat's supplies and had meat in plenty. In return, he and his wife had ample help about the house and in the gardens. There was also a certain prestige associated with such extended households, and a degree of rivalry between the retainers of each one, which lay behind much of the brawling. On such occasions, the regular police withdrew, leaving the skippers to put on police uniform.

With more money, meat and manpower, the skippers were able to stage feasts that were beyond the capacity of ordinary households. Even minor occasions such as a homecoming or the birthday of a favourite child were substantial affairs. But when it was a wedding or a tombstone opening, several luggers and households could be mobilized to get meat and transport visitors from other places. If it were a Nona affair, all eight boats could be involved, with the burden spread over as many households.

Strong leadership

Tanu Nona had effected his quiet revolution of the 1930s, not just through force of personality, but by being simultaneously skipper, churchwarden and chairman of council, and drawing power from all three institutional structures. By 1959 this concentration of power had become extended and entrenched. Tanu himself was still chairman of council, churchwarden and skipper, and also Western Islands Representative and manager of eight government boats. The other two councillors were also skippers, while the senior police sergeant was also store manager and parish secretary. The junior police sergeant was churchwarden. Outside the formal structure of offices, power was further unified through the kinship ties which linked all the incumbents except the junior sergeant. The councillors were Tanu's brother and son, while the senior sergeant–store manager was another brother. Even the Mothers' Union had been brought within this framework, for one officer was the wife of the senior sergeant while the other was married to another skipper and son of Tanu. Secure and unified, then, Badu's leadership could keep the community on a consistent course.

With a council composed of skippers it was predictable that local government would facilitate pearling, particularly in the control of labour. It still enforced the by-law requiring all able-bodied men to work, which had been introduced when the church was being built. Moreover, it used its control over the movement of its people to block emigration to the mainland. In any dispute between skipper and crew it could back the skipper, in the confidence that DNA officials on Thursday Island would give support in the event of an appeal. Indeed, it was generally believed that the two worked closely together.

Badu's leaders spoke of themselves as the 'backbone of the government'. Their boats kept the Island Industries Board fleet solvent and provided work for men throughout the Western Islands. Their councillors supported the DNA at conferences and in releases to the media, keeping the lid on political dissidence at home. In the same way, they ensured that everybody paid their church dues, and they had a short way with dissenters. The justification was that Islanders lacked the education for citizen rights or life on the mainland, and were generally better off where they were.

The regime had been established by degrees. Tanu had been a

councillor since 1929 and chairman for almost as long, but until the 1950s he had shared power with members of other families. During 'army time' he had been out of office for six months, and the councillors elected by Baduan troops had talked of sending him and his brothers back to Saibai. But presently the DNA had reinstated him, and in 1949 he had become Representative and chairman for life. Once in charge of elections, he assumed the right to reject nominations, and in due course council office became a family preserve.

Although this outline seems to be accurate as far as it goes, I found it extremely difficult to reconstruct the events. Even after interviewing two of the councillors elected by the soldiers and others involved with them, I found the details to be muddled and contradictory, as though they too were confused by what had happened. Others said that they had been so intoxicated with the idea of freedom, that they had neglected the daily administration of essential affairs; but they insisted that the DNA had been determined to reinstate Tanu Nona at all costs.

The proposal to drive the Nona brothers away from Badu had been justified by the fact that neither father nor mother belonged to the community. Without hereditary rights to land, they and other immigrant families were dependent on the generosity of the Baduans, and could be expelled by the owners taking back what they had lent. One of Tanu Nona's first actions on his reinstatement was to abolish all such traditional rights, placing all garden and residential land under the control of the council, to be allocated according to need.

Dissidents next attempted to revive the old tribal divisions, by establishing separate settlements on the other sides of the island. This too the council blocked, on the ground that the children would be unable to attend school and the sick would be unable to get treatment. During the years that followed, many of those involved in this movement, as well as the radical ex-servicemen, moved to Thursday Island, where by 1959 some 33% of Baduans lived. They maintained regular contact with their kinsfolk at home, but returned themselves rarely if at all. Their reasons for emigrating were, of course, multiple and various. They were a rather older population than the one on Badu, and some had gone to find less strenuous jobs ashore, or to practise skills acquired in the boatyards of Papuan Industries before the war. Others were invalids who wanted to be near to medical treatment. But a considerable number spoke of themselves as exiles, and represented the whole emigration in this light. Their island had been usurped and they no longer cared to live there.

Whatever the truth of these assertions, the absence of some 60% (54 of 89) of Baduan men between the ages of 40 and 59 (as well as almost half those between 30 and 39) depleted the cohorts from which political leadership traditionally came. This was also the generation that had experienced 'army time'; as it happened few of those who remained on Badu had seen military service. Among the younger generations there was less radicalism, and less antagonism towards the Nona family. Many of them had gone to school with the younger Nonas and, being linked to them by ties of kinship, treated them 'as their own'. Given the scarcity of jobs on Thursday Island for those without special skills, many of those who had grown up there worked on Badu boats.

The younger generation had also grown up with a more limited sense of civic responsibility. The parish was the concern of the Mothers' Union and the churchwardens, two of whom were over eighty. No one sought to become a lay reader or a Sunday school teacher. Similarly, no one nursed political ambitions, believing that the DNA would not accept anyone other than Tanu Nona and those he nominated. In any case, the ordinary Baduans no longer understood how the council was run. Not only were its dealings with the government conducted behind closed doors, but its domestic proceedings as well. The court sat, not in a public court house, but in the home of one of the councillors, leaving the people dependent on the 'village wireless' for an account of what happened. As likely as not, those convicted would serve their sentences in one of the councillors' households or on one of their boats. As on Murray, there was a general expectation that the council would be partial; but with no prospect of a change, the response was for families to try to ingratiate themselves with one of the councillors or police. Such ties, of course, were vital for anyone seeking government assistance.

Skipper class, crew class

Although I had been led to expect inequality even before I reached Badu, I was surprised when a friend said of his family, 'we're skipper class, not crew class.' Asking another friend, not of the 'skipper class' whether the community had such divisions, he replied after some thought, 'they do, but they don't know it'. He could say this because the changes had to a considerable extent been mediated by island custom, so that they were represented as something other than they were. The 'crew class' were not unaware of the increasing differences in power and material circumstances, but their responses to these differences were disoriented by the continued use of the old customary codes. As for the skippers, they were certainly moved by an ideology of their own, which combined notions of modernization and hard work with a belief that leadership qualities were hereditary. They may be said to have been manipulating custom to their advantage, and yet they were not free of it themselves.

Badu's 'class' structure belonged to colonial Torres Strait rather than to metropolitan Australia. Thus while Nona Brothers 'owned' the luggers they worked, their rights in them were ill defined. Tanu Nona took the major decision in consultation with the DNA, appointing the other skippers on a year to year basis. In the case of the established skippers, this was a formality; but there were others who had lost their boats after a year or two. Some said the government was the real owner, but since Tanu's managerial role had never come under challenge, the question had never been put to the test.[8]

If the control of the 'skipper class' over capital was less than that of most entrepreneurs, their control over labour was greater, being reinforced in different ways by council, parish and kinship. Everyone must work, and there were few acceptable alternatives to working on the Badu boats. A man could transfer from one skipper to another at the end of the year, but ties of kinship inhibited such movement and the advantages of being a client made it inadvisable. Collectively the people of Badu must support their skippers in order that the island should remain 'first', its church maintained and its feasts supplied with meat.

The allocation of economic surpluses also took on a distinctively colonial character. Capital accumulation, mainly through the

---

[8] The Aborigines' and Torres Strait Islanders' Affairs Act of 1965 provided for the possibility that assisted Islanders and Aborigines might manage their own property, subject to official approval (part IV.27). However, it seems that Tanu Nona continued to avail himself of the marketing and accounting services of the Island Industries Board and the Department of Aboriginal and Island Affairs, as it was now named.

acquisition of new boats and the purchase of engines and equipment, was arranged by the government. The skippers themselves saved little, dissipating their surplus cash by mounting customary feasts on a scale far beyond the capacity of ordinary folk. The Nonas, in particular, pooled their resources to bring hundreds of visitors from all parts of the Strait, including not only 'town half castes' but government officials and even one or two master pearlers. The bride prices they paid were the highest in the Strait.

The ideology of the skippers was likewise colonial in that the critical factor was said to be an infusion of 'foreign blood'. The man who described his family as 'skipper class', had gone on to claim that 'Torres Strait people are no good as skippers', thereby giving pride of place to his Tannese grandfather. Tanu Nona, no less proud of his Samoan father, told me, 'Torres Strait natives can work, but when they get a little bit good their head gets big, and they go down then.'

Such notions had their origins in the racial stratification of earlier years, and they had little currency in communities such as Murray; but they were maintained among the half castes of Thursday Island and the two church missions, among whom there was a marked tendency to intermarry. Badu's skippers tended to identify with this set. The Nonas had gone to some lengths to re-establish ties with their paternal kin in Samoa. As though to counter such pretensions, some native Baduans represented themselves as descendants of the Wild White Man.[9] One went so far as to suggest that the original population of Torres Strait was Polynesian rather than Melanesian.

The doctrine that capacities are inherited not only predicts that the children of able parents will succeed, but assumes that the parents of successful children gave some indication of the same qualities. Consistent with this, the Nonas gave due recognition to the Samoan father from whom they took their name. As it happened he had never owned a boat or been a skipper, but they recalled that he had been awarded a prize for getting the most shell on a boat where he was working. They gave him credit

---

[9] This claim was substantiated by identifying as the Wild White Man, a man named in one of the Badu genealogies published in the Cambridge Reports and credited with settling the Argan side of Badu. I cannot say whether there was any basis for this identification. The castaway is said to have had children, but their names do not appear on the genealogies.

for raising them strictly and encouraging them to excel. Tanu
Nona recalled his father's pride in his early successes: 'He always
wanted me to win. If I didn't win he was sorry.' They also gave
him credit for keeping the family united, appointing Tanu to be
its head and making the older sons responsible for their younger
siblings. They were now less close than they had been in the days
when they were making their way. According to village gossip
there were tensions and rifts, and two brothers had moved away
to Thursday Island. But they came together for family occasions
and severally saw a good deal of one another.

The Nona Brothers Company maintained a nominal existence, providing a small income for their widowed mother and
funds for family purposes such as tombstones and weddings.
Otherwise, income went only to those actively engaged in production, and Tanu was the only one involved in deciding who got
what. However, he continued to speak of it as a family business.
In an interview he gave me in 1959, he stated that three of the
boats belonged to him and would pass to his sons, but there must
be a boat for each of his brothers or their sons. Indeed, two
brothers already had their own boats, one in partnership with a
third, while two others – one dead, one retired – were represented
by a son. Another brother was accommodated in the following
year. Tanu was perhaps harking back to the rapid expansion of
earlier years, which had saved the brothers from quarrelling
among themselves; but with the next generation coming to
maturity there were now many more aspirants than there were
boats, or ever would be, given the stagnation in the industry. In
practice, Tanu let the market do the allocating, choosing young
men who looked like skipper material and dismissing them if
they did not come up to expectations. Already by 1960 one
branch of the family had dropped out of the race, while two
brothers were making their own way with master boats. It was
still possible for a young man to look forward to the day when he
would skipper his own boat; a decade later such expectations
would seem unrealistic.

The economic downturn of the 1960s deprived Badu's 'skipper
class' of the means of doing what classes are supposed to do, reproduce itself. However, there was no crisis such as Murray
experienced; rather a gradual and relatively smooth transition to
a less controlled and less unequal society.

The decline of the skippers

The year 1960 saw Badu at its high point, with fourteen boats at work. In 1961, with the market starting to contract, only eleven boats were at work, but the relative efficiency of Badu's enterprises enabled its industry to decline at a slower pace than the industry as a whole. The establishment of pearl culture stations, with a small demand for live shell, kept boats at work after the traditional market had vanished. However, the decline continued, to eight in 1967 and, after a suspension of pearl culture in the early 1970s, to two.

At its high point, Badu's need for manpower had been well in excess of the local supply, necessitating recruitment from other islands. By the end of the 1960s, with a reduction in the number of boats and a considerable natural increase in the working-age population, Badu could no longer achieve full employment. Consequently, the council could no longer deny its men the right to work on the mainland, particularly when there were employers ready to fly them to the Northern Territory and home again when their contract had expired.

The problem was that the council could not simply release the surplus workers, keeping back those needed for the surviving boats. And since the skippers could not match the wages paid by mainland employers, they stood to lose their best workers. During the lay-off time of 1968, they were to be seen buying drinks for their men, to 'sweet' them – so cynics said – into signing on for the next year. One notoriously rough skipper was rumoured to have given up because he could no longer get men to work for him. Some alternated spells of work on the mainland with years on the boats at home, but as they became used to high pay and urban living, they sent for their families and returned no more. A number, also, were exploring the possibility of fishing for cray on their own accounts. Thus skippers were increasingly forced to take on Papuans, who though eager for the money were not equal to the rigours of life at sea.

A smaller proportion of the community now worked for skippers, and those who did were less dependent on them than formerly. A man working on the mainland for a year could accumulate enough money to finance a wedding or a tombstone opening, without obligating himself to some skipper. Alternatively, he could buy an aluminium dinghy and outboard motor for hunting or trips to Thursday Island, so that the skippers no

Plate 8. Butchering a turtle on Badu

longer monopolized meat or transportation as they had once done.

By the end of the 1960s some of the younger skippers had themselves given up and gone south, while the ranks of their seniors were being thinned by sickness, old age and death. Few had managed to save much from their days of prosperity, so that they were soon dependent on pensions and the help of their children, like other Baduans. Finally, Tanu Nona's two luggers were the only ones still working, though now under the command of his sons. Of the family company nothing remained, leaving a degree of disillusionment among the members. Their numbers were thinning, and with many of their numerous children scattered on the mainland the family lost much of its old cohesion. As the circumstances and prospects of the younger generation ceased to mark them off from the mass, kinship reasserted itself; and while they might retain pride of family, they were to all intents Baduans.

Despite these changes, Tanu Nona remained a figure to be reckoned with until a few years before his death in 1980. At his peak in the 1950s he had controlled the industrial, governmental and ecclesiastical structures at the point where they connected Badu with the colonial order. Nor was he simply their agent, for just as his control over the community improved his standing with the authorities, so his standing with the authorities strengthened his control over the community, to the point where he seemed to be exempt from the restrictions to which other Islanders were subject. Becoming a power in his own right, his legitimation came as much from the achievements of his long career as from the institutions in which he held office, and Badu seemed at times as though it were his personal domain.

As pearling declined, Tanu Nona's economic role diminished, and with it the importance of his control over the community, which he left increasingly to sons and brothers. But his services as Western Islands Representative, for which he was honoured with an OBE in 1968, were becoming indispensable to a government whose practices were increasingly under criticism. His control over the Western Islands councillors during the Whitlam Labor government, was a critical factor in the contest between State and Commonwealth. By this time he was in his mid-seventies, and in 1976 infirmity finally necessitated his resignation. His last act was to secure the appointment of his son Joey, already chairman of Badu, to the Representative's position.

VII Welfare colonialism

In June 1973 the Australian government brought a delegation from Torres Strait to Canberra to confer with it regarding the proposed changes to the border with Papua New Guinea. The visit was historic, not only on account of its occasion, but because this was the Islanders' debut onto the national stage as Australia's other indigenous minority. It was also an early exercise in the Commonwealth's new strategy of dealing directly with Islanders and Aborigines, where it had formerly worked through the States. In the same year Torres Strait gained official representation in Canberra through the National Aboriginal Consultative Committee, while the newly formed Department of Aboriginal Affairs opened an office on Thursday Island and entered into formal relations with island councils. This did not cause the Department of Aboriginal and Islander Advancement, successor to the DNA, to cease operations, for Queensland regarded the Commonwealth's intervention as an infringement of State rights and a slight on its achievements in the region. Since that time the two governments have shared responsibility for Torres Strait in an uneasy condominium. Despite the rivalry and disagreements over policy, their practice has been almost indistinguishable, consisting primarily of programmes designed to improve the living standards of Islanders. And if the Commonwealth has set the pace in spending, Queensland has provided the representative structures through which funds have flowed. The combined effect of their activities can best be termed welfare colonialism.

Queensland had kept its colonial apparatus virtually intact up to the time of Commonwealth intervention. While it regarded Islanders working on the mainland as assimilated and left them alone, it kept those in the Strait firmly under its control. As a gesture to the more liberal climate of the time, it had divested itself of some of its legal powers over their persons and property; but its economic dominance had increased with the decline of the marine industry since it was now the principal employer and source of services. The reasons for this continuation are not immediately apparent. The collapse of the pearling industry removed one of the original reasons for the regime's existence, while the demand for Torres Strait labour on the mainland provided a good reason for winding it down. To disperse the island communities would relieve the Queensland Treasury of a substantial burden. But while the DAIA let Islanders emigrate in considerable numbers, it did not press them to do so. The possibility that a sudden influx would provoke a white backlash on the mainland may have been a deterrent, but it scarcely explains the expenditure of further funds to improve conditions in the dwindling communities of the Strait. Perhaps, as is sometimes said, certain senior officials retained an affection for the Islanders and their way of life – a Bleakleyan nostalgia. Perhaps the ruling conservative National/Liberal coalition government had decided that Torres Strait voters were sufficiently numerous to determine the outcome in the State seat of Cook. Perhaps the State government, already sensitive to Canberra's criticisms, feared that if it left a vacuum its rival would come in to fill it. At all events, once the Commonwealth had arrived with promises of generous assistance it had no option but to follow suit.

Though the Commonwealth's intervention may have been precipitated by its rivalry with Queensland, its strategy was consistent with its national policy of supporting indigenous communities without consideration of their longterm economic viability. Over the preceding twenty-five years it had supported many such communities in the Northern Territory and created others, albeit with the declared intention of securing their assimilation into Australian society at some future time. The first Report of the DAA, for the years 1972–4, made integration the new aim, 'based on recognition of the value of the minority culture and of the right of Aboriginals to retain their languages and customs and maintain their own distinct communities' (DAA 1975:5). The Commonwealth would underwrite these communities and would assist them to acquire secure tenure of the land on which they lived (*ibid*.:22).

Following Paine (1977) I have called this policy welfare colonialism, on the ground that it arises out of the intersection of two previously distinct modes of state intervention. To summarize the argument I set out in chapter I: following Stavenhagen

(1965) I see colonial relations as a product of underdevelopment, giving way to class relations with development and the freeing of labour. Following Marshall (1963), I see the capitalist democracies denying class through the doctrine of 'basic equality', as expressed in the civil, political and social rights of citizenship. The redistributive activities of the welfare state are carried out in recognition of the social rights of citizens, in particular to a guaranteed minimum living standard. While citizenship initially arises as an ideological response to class division, it can subsequently spread into colonial enclaves for which it is not intended. Under certain conditions, the extension of citizen rights to indigenous minorities becomes a moral and political issue for the society at large and even internationally. Welfare colonialism is as much a matter of politics and ideology as of economics.

Changes of such magnitude require not just legislation but active state intervention. In particular, minimum living standards can only be established in underdeveloped areas through costly programmes or direct subsidy. Ironically, the beneficiaries of such expenditure are likely to end up not as regular citizens, but as bearers of a special status that derives from the original colonial encounter and is maintained by reconstructed colonial agencies. The special entitlements associated with this status stand in a problematical relationship to those of normal citizens; indeed welfare colonialism contains both ideological and political contradictions.

Australia extended the first tokens of citizenship to its 'native peoples' under the unusual circumstances of the wartime emergency. The Cold War provided further reasons for improving their lot, because of the need to answer charges of maltreatment in international forums such as the United Nations, and to win the friendship of new Asian and African states that were sensitive on the matter of racism.[1] During the 1960s, news of civil

---

[1] Thus on 8 June 1950, the responsible Minister, Paul Hasluck, addressed the Federal House of Representatives in the following terms: 'The Commonwealth Parliament is the custodian of the national reputation in the world at large. Our record of native administration will not stand scrutiny at the standard of our own professions, publicly made in the forums of the world, of a high concern for human welfare. We should be condemned out of our own mouths if those professions were measured by the standard of native administration accepted in Australia today. When we enter into international discussions, and raise our voice, as we should raise it, in defence of human rights and the protection of human welfare, our very words are mocked by the thousands of degraded and depressed people who crouch on rubbish heaps throughout the whole of this continent' (Hasluck 1953:5–12; reprinted in Stone 1974:192).

rights campaigns in the southern United States and South Africa not only alerted liberal Australians to the domestic situation but structured their perception of it, so that they began to talk of Australia's 'Deep North' and of *apartheid* in Queensland. It was during these years that white Australians accompanied Aborigines on 'freedom rides' and attended annual meetings of the Federal Council for the Advancement of Aborigines and Torres Strait Islanders.[2]

The public also became concerned over reports of Aboriginal poverty, as the newspapers of the period attest. During the long post-war boom many had come to believe that a middle class standard of living was within everyone's reach. The discovery of Aboriginal shanty towns, located on rubbish tips and without water or sanitation, threatened this belief and started a clamour for something to be done. But providing a minimum living standard was harder than legislating for civil and political rights. While 'crash' programmes could bring housing and medical care to the worst trouble spots, they could not generate employment or bring industry to places that were inaccessible and without resources. Equal wage legislation sometimes resulted in the dismissal of Aboriginal workers, who then became dependent on the government (cf. Kolig 1981:52). High unemployment rates in the cities cast doubt on the value of relocation programmes, while the mining developments of the north relied mainly on white labour (Hinton 1968). The downturn in employment of the early 1970s cast further doubt on the economic viability of the assimilation policy.

The new direction in Commonwealth policy from 1970 is to be understood against the background of this impasse. Government would continue to provide material assistance in the welfare mode, but progress towards integration would no longer be the touchstone. As in the field of social welfare (cf. Raysmith and Einfeld 1975) the goal was now community development, with the community itself as the final arbiter of its needs. In the words of the first DAA Report:

[2]   A multitude of organizations, mostly small and controlled by Europeans, concerned themselves with Aboriginal rights during this period. The achievement of FCAATSI from the early 1960s was to provide a national focus for their efforts at its annual Easter conferences in Canberra. Although initially dominated by Europeans, it provided a forum and eventually a political springboard for the emerging Aboriginal leadership. There is as yet no history of this period, but see Bandler 1983; Duncan 1974.

> Elements in the traditional Aboriginal culture and system of
> values may 'impede' programs aimed at changing Aboriginals,
> but if the aim is rather to help Aboriginals achieve their
> own goals as individuals and communities, such elements
> cease to be seen as obstacles and can be seen rather as fac-
> tors for influencing the choices. (1975:7)

The application of such a policy to the great variety of situations
to be found throughout the continent has produced a range of
programmes, from the funding of special services in medical
care, education and legal aid, to the comprehensive underwriting of entire communities in the outback. The outcome likewise
varies, but while overall Aborigines are now more closely
integrated with the rest of the society, the dominant mode of
this integration is governmental. Whether they are seeking
employment or economic aid, claiming land, defending Aboriginal
rights or practising traditional arts, they work through the
state.

A further effect is to reinforce the special status of Aborigines
in Australian society. This is no longer an alternative to
citizenship; rather, citizenship has been redefined along pluralistic
lines to accommodate not just Aborigines but the large population of immigrants from non-Anglophone countries, through
the doctrine of multiculturalism (see Martin 1983). The difference is that while 'ethnics' are defined in terms of their country
of origin, Aborigines are defined in terms of their original
occupation of Australia and their subsequent conquest. Indeed
the injuries that they suffered as a result of colonization are
made the basis for an entitlement to special status and consideration. The very category 'Aboriginal' has its origin in the
colonizing process, while the communities that are to be
developed under the new dispensation were either created or
reconstituted in the process of reducing 'troublesome natives'.
The agencies implementing the new policy are for the most part
linear descendants of the old Protectors, and while they have
divested themselves of the legal apparatus of control, they continue to exert an extraordinary influence through the strategic
allocation and supervision of funds.

It is one of the paradoxes of welfare colonialism that, while it
increases economic dependence, it also fosters political autonomy.
The citizenship now accorded to its subjects requires their consent to, and participation in, the process. In Australia the doctrines of self-determination and self-management have brought

into existence representative structures outside the framework of normal government. As a result, Aborigines are politically active to a greater degree and at higher levels than they were twenty years ago. The political processes in which they are involved are structurally complex. When the state undertakes to redistribute part of its resources according to principles of 'social justice', it brings into existence a political arena in which concerned groups compete for public sympathy and the advocacy of politicians. At another level, bureaucrats compete with one another to gain funds for their respective departments and clienteles. Which factors in the equation are decisive vary according to the composition of the constituency and its standing in the society. Correspondingly, claimants adopt different strategies according to their numbers, their political leverage, their access to the seats of power and their control of information. In so far as welfare politics engages the public and the media, it generates its own discourse, in which particular cases of need are strategically linked to sacrosanct doctrines such as 'social justice' and the 'national interest'. Anyone wishing to compete in such an arena must be in control of these tropes, and the smaller, less powerful claimants may be largely dependent upon them.

Government itself has been the principal supporter of the Aboriginal cause in this arena. Its personnel, particularly those who are themselves Aboriginal, have been advocates, not just in the bureaucratic process but in the public domain. At the same time it has fostered a political elite in a variety of semi-governmental bodies. Given the lack of resources, Aboriginal leaders have found it hard to be effective without government assistance, although receiving it limits their freedom of action. As Sally Weaver has shown (1983:4–5), the National Aboriginal Consultative Committee was intended as a means of stabilizing Aboriginal pressure group activity and integrating it with the processes of government. When it proved too independent for such a role it was replaced by a weaker National Aboriginal Conference, and an Aboriginal Development Commission which is virtually an arm of government. Only a few leaders manage to survive outside this framework, mainly on support from sympathetic bodies such as the churches. As one might expect, political strategies range from the discrete approach through official channels and action through the courts, to skilful use of the media and dramatic demonstrations designed to embarrass government in the eyes of national or international public opinion.

The Torres Strait Islanders, less numerous than the Aborigines, less known to the public at large, and less pathetic in their deprivations, have been the incidental beneficiaries of these developments rather than the primary targets. Yet they have been brought within the same framework of government operations and received substantial assistance. As a result, Islanders in Torres Strait have increased their dependence on the cash economy and especially on the government sector. However, their mode of integration has been distinctive. Having representatives seasoned through years of dealing with the Queensland government, they have been quick to respond to the approaches of the Commonwealth and to take advantage of the rivalry between the two. Thus situated, they have had little occasion to make common cause with Aborigines or to appeal to the public.

The experience of Islanders on the mainland has been different. Drawn from their homes by the economic developments of the 1960s, they quickly found a niche for themselves in the labour market. At this time their involvement with government was no more than, and of the same kind as, that of other Australians of similar socio-economic status; and it required no collective organization. With the economic downturn of the 1970s the going became harder, so that they now had to turn to the proliferating government programmes for help. These, however, have lumped them together with Aborigines, an arrangement that conflicts with their previous experience and sense of identity. To respond to this situation has been difficult, for in leaving the Strait they ruptured the nexus between identity, community and representation. They are neither part of the constituency to which the official Torres Strait spokesmen are answerable, nor do they have official representatives of their own. The outcome has been some political action outside the recognized framework and an upsurge of non-political expressions of Islander identity.

Where the Islanders are

That the Torres Strait Islanders have increased rapidly over the last twenty-five years, and have emigrated in large numbers to the mainland, is incontestable. The number of surviving children on any genealogy is evidence of the population

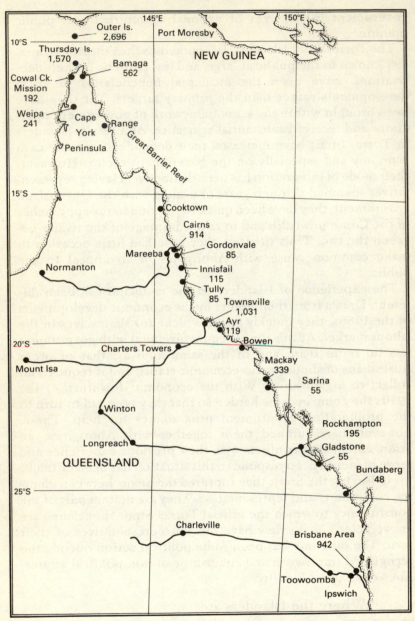

Map 2. Distribution of Torres Strait Islanders in Queensland according to 1981 census and Department of Aboriginal Affairs surveys for outers islands. (Only populations over 40 included)

increase, while a Saturday morning stroll down the main street of Townsville provides evidence of emigration, as do the many unoccupied houses on the home islands. But quantifying these impressions is difficult. As I noted earlier, Queensland's post-war population estimates are notional, and they ceased in 1961. Commonwealth censuses, while intended to be accurate, have encountered various problems of data collection, particularly regarding ethnic identification.[3] The 1976 total of 16,533 represented an improbable advance on the 1971 figure of 9,663, and proved to be slightly above the 1981 total of 15,232.[4] Elaborate statistical processing of such data is probably unwarranted (but see Caldwell 1974).

It must be said that the data are not uniformly unreliable. The chances of misidentification and concealment are less in the Strait, where the collectors know the people, and their figures can be compared with those collected by the DAIA and DAA for their own purposes. These suggest that the Islander population of the Strait, including the island reserves, Thursday Island township and the Bamaga government settlement, has remained around 4,500 from 1961 to 1981. The natural net increase, which has certainly been substantial (cf. Caldwell 1974), has no doubt been offset by emigration to the mainland. Within the region there has been a drift to Thursday Island, leaving the reserves with two-thirds of the population they had in 1961. Individual communities vary, with Saibai and Boigu only slightly below the earlier figure, but Badu reduced to 56% and Murray to 37%. Only one small community, Naghir, has gone out of existence, but more than half of the remainder have fewer than 120 people.

Despite the high rate of emigration, the Torres Strait population no longer displays the distortions characteristic of rump

[3] L. R. Smith, who has subjected the census data to careful scrutiny, has linked the problem of identification to puzzling fluctuations in the numbers of Torres Strait Islanders (1980:125–7; 195), and of Aborigines (*ibid.: passim*). The Australian Bureau of Statistics (17.8.82) has admitted further problems arising from changes in the mode of determining identity in the 1981 census. A possibility that does not seem to have been considered is that immigrants from the Pacific Islands may either have seized upon the term 'Islander', disregarding 'Torres Strait', or may have taken this identification as a means of concealing their illegal status.

[4] 2,000 'Torres Strait Islanders', born in Europe and mainly located in Victoria, who mysteriously appeared in the 1976 census and disappeared from that of 1981, seem to have been the figment of some malfunction in data collection or processing.

communities, with the very old and the very young predominating, and females outnumbering males. These tendencies manifested themselves in the early days of emigration, but eased as families joined the breadwinner on the mainland, parents followed children and girls went south in search of husbands.

Census data for the large emigrant communities in Townsville and Cairns present a similar profile. As I have suggested, there are reasons for doubting their accuracy, but I shall summarize their main findings since they are all that we have. The majority of Islanders, including those in the Strait, still live in Queensland but whereas they amounted to 97% in 1966, they fell to 78% in 1971 and 70% in 1981. There is no doubt that there are sizeable numbers in Western Australia and the Northern Territory, but the large populations 'discovered' in major urban centres of NSW and Victoria are problematical. According to Islanders I have questioned, Townsville and Cairns, the original points of entry, remain the principal centres. However the 1981 figures of 1,031 and 914 respectively, though almost double the 1971 figures, are well below what is generally believed. The DAIA recently estimated the Townsville population with generous latitude at between 4,500 and 8,000 (DAIA 1979:23).

Data on mobility are even more meagre, though it is clear that there is a continuing emigration from the Strait. It seems that while there is a steady traffic of visitors back to the home islands, few return to stay. On the mainland the days when parties of men flew to remote parts of the north on work contracts are ended, but the sense of adventure that induced Islanders in the 1960s to pioneer new territory has not evaporated, and where one has established himself others will follow. The north Queensland coast, with its core of long established families and its various associations, nevertheless remains the recognized centre of the Islander emigration, and as such sets up a counter polarity to the Strait.

The remittance economy of Torres Strait

With the removal of legal and administrative restrictions and the development of public transportation to the islands, Torres Strait and the mainland have become a single field, and residence in one or the other must be regarded as an act of choice. Movement from one to the other nevertheless represents a shift to a very different social, economic and political milieu. In Torres

Strait welfare colonialism is the prevailing mode. There is some commercial fishing, but even the Baduans, who have benefited most from it, receive considerable government aid. And despite official attempts to foster local industry, the other islands can best be described as remittance economies. As for Thursday Island, its primary function is to channel government funded goods and services to the outer islands and Cape York.

The increase in State and, even more, Federal funding has no doubt left Islanders materially better off than they were a generation ago. They are also, as a result of this intervention and intermittent involvement in the mainland labour market, more dependent on cash. The subsistence economy, meanwhile, has contracted and what remains has become monetarized. Gardening is the principal casualty. As a Baduan put it, 'the store is our garden now.' Even on Murray, only a few make gardens and they sell part of what they grow. Hunting is still a major source of protein (Nietschmann 1981; Marsh *et al.* 1984), but the chase now involves the use of aluminium dinghies and high powered outboard motors, with some of the produce being sold to other Islanders.[5]

The pearling industry is virtually defunct. During the 1960s, though the disappearance of the traditional markets for pearl shell was partially offset by the need of local Japanese–Australian pearl culture stations for 'live shell', the number employed declined from 951 in 1960–1 to 373 in 1970–1, the last year in which figures were published (QYB). This date coincides with a curtailment in pearl culture operations, following a disease affecting the oysters. By the end of this period a sizeable portion of the work force was recruited in Papua, Islanders being no longer willing to work for wages that scarcely exceeded the dole, or put up with the discomforts of lugger life. One skipper of the damper and dough-boys generation complained that they now expected frozen foods such as chicken and ice cream. Papuans on the other hand were unused to ship board life and succumbed to sickness. Beset with rising costs, the old skippers have either retired or found other outlets. Dinghy operators in the Eastern

---

[5] There is some reason to suppose that the Torres Strait dugong population has fallen to such a low level that its survival is in question. Reasons for this decline are by no means certain, but it is possible that the increased efficiency of motor boat fishermen, combined with a small but growing traffic in the meat, on both sides of the border, may be important factors (Marsh *et al.* 1984). The turtle population appears to be holding, however.

Islands collect some trochus and also trepang, but only two or three luggers all based in the Western Islands have worked gold-lip in recent years.

Since the demise of pearling, the Island Industries Board has virtually ceased to foster local industry. Major initiatives have come from the Commonwealth government, but they have all been unsuccessful. In 1972 it started turtle farming on a number of islands, evidently intending to combine ecological objectives with job creation. At its height in the mid-1970s the project employed around 170 men and women; however, it proved neither ecologically nor economically sound, and caused considerable political embarrassment before its dissolution in 1980.[6]

By the end of the 1970s a European concern was running a highly profitable prawning and fishing enterprise from Yorke Island. However, it was employing few Islanders and contributing little to the regional economy. In 1982 the Commonwealth Aboriginal Development Commission set up the Keriba Lagau Development Company, with the intention of enabling Islanders to find a foothold in the industry. Unfortunately, the earnings of the boat it had equipped for the purpose did not cover running costs, so that in 1984 it went into receivership, without having made any appreciable impact on the island economies (*Sydney Morning Herald* 25.8.84).

Cray fishing has also proved a viable industry, but it requires less in the way of capital than prawning and has provided work for some 500 Islanders, as well as opportunities for Islander enterprise. Starting in a small way at the end of the 1960s, it has grown over the last decade with the opening up of foreign markets. In 1984 and 1985 its annual gross earnings exceeded $3 million.[7]

---

[6] The turtle farming project was the earliest of the Commonwealth government's interventions in the Strait. Pre-dating the Whitlam administration in its conception, its concern with conservation made it more acceptable than other forms. Along with crocodile and emu farming projects elsewhere in the north, it was run by Applied Ecology Pty Ltd with government backing. The turtle farming project alone cost the government as much as $6 million, according to one estimate, as well as considerable political controversy (*SMH* 24.5.79).

[7] I am indebted to Peter Channels, of the Department of Primary Industry, for passing on to me material he has been collecting on the Torres Strait cray industry. When fishing began in earnest during 1969–70, the catch was 16,959 kg of 'lobster tails' (Australian Fisheries 1970 29(3)). Although there are no further official figures until 1978, catches seem to have increased steadily,

Crays are widely distributed throughout the Strait for about half the year and they can be caught by skin diving from a dinghy. Thus while the use of a large freezer vessel brings economies of scale, there is room for the small operator with $2,000–$3,000 to buy a motor dinghy, providing that he can get his produce to a freezer before it spoils. The Eastern Islanders are disadvantaged in this respect and also because they run a greater risk of shark attack in the deeper waters. Dinghy operators on Badu and Moa, on the other hand, have been able to run their catch into Thursday Island. In 1983 33% of the catch came from this section (Channels pers. com.). There were also fourteen freezer boats at work, three owned by former pearling skippers on Badu, the rest mostly by Europeans. They were largely manned by Islanders. The recent introduction of larger 'mother ships' suggests a trend towards greater capitalization which could jeopardize the small Islander operator. However, two former Badu skippers received government assistance in fitting out freezer boats, and in 1984, even as Keriba Lagau was going into receivership, the ADC formed the cray fishermen of Badu, Moa and Mabuyag into the Bammoa Torres Strait Islanders Corporation. Providing them with a mother ship and a barge, it transported their crays to Cairns and brought back fuel and retail goods. But after just fifteen months and a turnover of $1.3 million, the corporation was forced to sell some of its assets, precipitating a withdrawal by the four Islander directors. They immediately formed a private company, selling their catch to a large dealer in Perth.

While the Commonwealth has failed to intervene in the fishing industry directly, it provides a de facto subsidy through the unemployment benefits and short term employment that it funds during the off-season. It also funds other kinds of employment in the region, though the Queensland government remains by far the biggest employer, including the police, municipal authority, hospital and schools. The former DAIA (now called Department of Community Services) and IIB alone employ around 300, the great majority of these being Islanders. The government is virtually the only employer at its large settlement at Bamaga, on Cape York, and it pays the wages of most of

reaching 119.3 tonnes in that year, and 193.7 tonnes in 1982. In the following year production fell to 121.7 tonnes, recovering to 130 tonnes in 1984 and a record 207 tonnes in 1985. The price per kg. in the last three years has averaged $15.

those working on the island reserves. Since the ending of the turtle farming project, the Commonwealth maintains a relatively small number of permanent employees, mostly Europeans, with a much larger number of Islanders on short term projects in the communities.

When one adds the wages bill for these employees to Commonwealth social service payments it becomes apparent that the bulk of the region's cash income derives from the state. M.L. Treadgold, in a social accounting analysis conducted in 1972, observed that 'in recent years a rapidly expanding inflow of Australian and Queensland funds has become the major force in the generation of economic activity' (1974:1–2).[8] At this time the Commonwealth government's involvement was limited. The Department of Social Security had not yet begun to provide pensions for supporting parents, or follow the liberal policy on unemployment benefits that it was to follow from the mid-1970s.

The Commonwealth's turtle farming programme was already in operation when Helen Duncan conducted her survey of four reserve communities in 1973. From this and other sources, principally social service transfers, it provided 70% of an annual per capita income of $555 on Murray, the State provided 27%, and the balance came from the Anglican Church, allotments from workers elsewhere and local enterprise (Duncan 1974:52).[9] Badu derived 49% of its annual per capita income of $512 from the Commonwealth and 24% from the State, with 26% coming from workers' allotments, earnings on pearl culture stations and

---

[8]   In a breakdown of gross market product at factor cost over the period 1969 to 1972, Treadgold showed that while primary production and manufacturing declined, public administration, community services and public utilities increased by 34%, accounting in the last year for 31% of the total (*ibid.*:6). From another perspective, he reported that total final consumption and fixed capital expenditure of all public authorities amounted to about 41% of gross regional expenditure in the same period, as compared with the national figure of 22% (*ibid.*:19–20). Public authority cash benefits in this period amounted to almost one-third of total wages, salaries and supplements paid in the region, being equivalent to $241 per head of population, compared with a corresponding figure of $164 for the whole of Australia (*ibid.*:18).

[9]   While these figures provide some sense of rough magnitudes, they must be understood in terms of the modes of data collection followed (Duncan 1974:42–54). The figures for Murray were also inflated by very high, once only, Commonwealth repatriation payments to ex-servicemen, and probably reduced by the omission of remittances from workers on the mainland.

local enterprise (*ibid.*).[10] A similar survey conducted ten years later would have to allow for the termination of turtle farming, and the further decline of pearling in the Western Islands, more than offset by cray fishing. The overall dependence on the state would be greater rather than less, however. Indeed this mode of analysis understates the dependence in that it ignores aid coming in the form of housing, equipment, school buildings, educational services, medicines and transportation. The allocation of such funds and resources is the stuff of everyday politics in Torres Strait, but complicated by the rivalry between State and Commonwealth and between the major political parties.

The new politics

Welfare colonialism entails a political process since its ideology requires consultation with, and the consent of, its subjects. Queensland already had such an apparatus in Torres Strait, but the Commonwealth's intervention in 1973 decisively altered the balance of power in which the process functioned. The region's politics had been taking on increasing complexity as Queensland came under criticism in the south, but DAIA had taken some of the pressure by maintaining a monopoly over official access to the Islanders, while confining their political activities to the channels that it controlled. In 1973 the Commonwealth broke this monopoly. The Islanders now have considerable room for manoeuvre. With the two governments competing to provide assistance, their bargaining power is inevitably increased. And with their approval required to give legitimacy to government practice, their voices have become a valuable resource. Taking advantage of these opportunities, however, has placed new demands on Islander representatives.

Before 1941 the formation of Torres Strait policy had been a simple matter, except for occasional conflict between the Protectors and the master pearlers over wages and employment. As for the Islanders, they were safely confined to their communities and preoccupied with regulating one another's conduct. Un-

---

[10] Badu's lower score is mainly due to the omission from the count of boat crews, who were deemed not to be residents of the island (Duncan 1974:43). Badu seems also to have included a smaller percentage of ex-servicemen and so received less in the way of repatriation payments.

accountably they had achieved a momentary unity during the 1936 strike, and whether they intended it or not, had managed to attract attention and even some sympathy on the mainland. They could not sustain their protest for long, but long enough to persuade the Protectors of the need for some consultative process. The triennial councillors' conferences of the post-war years provided the formal channels through which Islanders could communicate with the relevant Minister and the government, but officials guided the deliberations and the outcome. The only resolutions to reach the public were those the authorities deemed suitable. The Islanders had no access to the media on their own account. In any case, Torres Strait was scarcely news in those years.

The Commonwealth made no attempt to intervene. During the 1930s it had regarded Queensland as a leader in the field of 'native affairs', and during the post-war years it left the State to implement the policy of assimilation to which they both subscribed. Not until the end of the 1950s did Canberra register some unease over reports of racial discrimination and civil rights violations, but the constitution limited its powers to a few matters such as the Federal franchise. I have already described (pp.73–4) the contest to control the Islanders' opinion on this matter, and the eventual outcome, which indirectly forced Queensland to give them the State franchise.

Although Torres Strait's Federal Member of the House of Representatives in Canberra raised local matters in the Parliament from time to time, as did at least one of the Federal Senators for Queensland and the State Member of the Legislative Assembly in Brisbane, there was no major political consequence of this enfranchisement for some years. It was left for private groups to keep up the pressure. The southern press increasingly criticized Queensland's treatment of Aborigines, but took little notice of Torres Strait. A few Islanders made their way to the annual meetings of the Aborigines – later the Aborigines and Torres Strait Islanders – Advancement League, but their particular circumstances and grievances were little understood. When the Queensland Parliament brought in new legislation in 1965, it was responding to bureaucratic convenience rather than external criticism.

The Aborigines' and Torres Strait Islanders' Affairs Act of 1965 renamed the DNA the Department of Aboriginal and Islander Affairs. Otherwise its principal innovations were to remove the restrictions on Islanders consuming alcohol off the reserves, and to provide for the possibility that they might be granted exemption from the normal controls over property. In fact these changes simply regularized existing practice of ten years and more on the mainland. Over the persons and property of Islanders living on the reserves, the government retained all its former powers. In practice these were applied with a light hand, perhaps due to Islander resentment, but also in recognition that with the decline of pearling the powers were losing their reason for existence. Although DAIA clerks continued to challenge large withdrawals of money, the pass book system increasingly functioned as a banking service.

The Referendum of 1967 is generally understood to have given the Commonwealth the power to take national responsibility for Aborigines and Islanders, but the Conservative coalition governments that ruled until the end of 1972 confined themselves to discreet approaches as far as Queensland was concerned. A meeting between Prime Minister William McMahon and Premier Johannes Bjelke-Petersen in April 1971 resulted in a communiqué that set out a number of matters to be attended to in new legislation (Nettheim 1981:6–7). These mainly related to the controls over the persons and property of Aborigines and Islanders. As Nettheim shows (*ibid.*), Queensland seemed reluctant to abandon these powers all at once.

Meanwhile the Whitlam Labor administration took office in Canberra, declaring its determination to intervene directly in Queensland. In the adversary relationship that quickly developed, it is difficult to separate the dispute over Aboriginal control from that over states' rights and the opposing political philosophies of the two governments. However, the relationship scarcely improved with the return of the Liberal–Country Party coalition to power in 1976, since intervention continued.

Within a few weeks of Labor's election in 1972 the Islanders found themselves in the firing line in a dispute over proposed changes to the border between Australia and Papua New Guinea. The history of the border and the several negotiations over its revision need not concern us here (Fisk *et al.* 1974; Griffin 1976). Suffice it to say that, as independence approached, Papuan politicians began talking of moving the border from its location within a kilometre of the coast, to the tenth parallel, a measure that would detach eight island communities from Australia. Gough Whitlam had expressed sympathy for the proposal in 1970 (*SMH* 4.5.72), so that his declaration, on election, that Papua New Guinea would soon have its independence set off fears that the border might be changed before the Islanders could voice their objections.

In February 1973 the Queensland Premier toured the islands, giving his blessing to a Border Action Committee mainly composed of councillors. When the Federal Minister for Aboriginal Affairs, Gordon Bryant, made a tour in April he denied that any change was planned (*Australian* 20.4.73), but the damage had been done and he suffered a series of rebuffs that were duly reported to the press. The rebuffs had a distinctively Islander character. Yorke Island took offence when a ministerial aide thoughtlessly readjusted a flag pole, Darnley used its Easter preparations as an excuse for ignoring the visitors, while Murray declared itself too busy with its Sabbath observances to send a dinghy to bring the Minister ashore. Eastern Island Representative and Border Committee chairman, George Mye, deflated Bryant's pretensions to rescuing Islanders from Queensland with the declaration that they were not in need of rescue (*Australian* 25.4.73). The large delegation that Mye led to Canberra in the following June delivered yet another rebuff to the Minister when he attempted to bring the Thursday Island committee of FCAATSI into the conference room (*Australian* 13.6.73). But the delegation listened respectfully to other government personnel, and to the Prime Minister's assurances that the border would not be changed without regard for their interests. As to offers of various kinds of aid, it remained noncommittal.

The press was too delighted with the Minister's discomfiture to find more in these events than that a party of Islanders had been frightened by the Queensland Premier. Certainly they had been alarmed by the prospect of a divided Torres Strait, and I had heard them at a preliminary meeting agree to withhold their criticisms of Queensland in face of such a threat. I did not immediately perceive the other message that they were delivering, which was that the Commonwealth must recognize the councils as the only legitimate representatives of the Islanders. But while they succeeded in establishing this point, and never wavered in their opposition to border changes, they presently succumbed to the competing pressures from the two governments.

Among the first was George Mye who, as a result of visits to

Canberra had secured Commonwealth funds for an Eastern Islands cooperative. This drew a sharp attack from the Premier, who alleged waste and the misuse of public money (*Courier-Mail* 8.10.75). The Brisbane reporter Bob Johnson, who chanced to be visiting Darnley Island a few days later, relayed Mye's rebuttal and described the Islanders as 'the meat in the sandwich' (*CM* 18.10.75; 20.10.75). Mye followed this up with an attack on the personal conduct of the Director of the DAIA which was tabled in Federal Parliament by the Minister for Aboriginal Affairs (CPD-HR, 21.10.75:2297–9), and reported in the press (*CM* 22.10.75). The Premier in turn denied these charges, alleging that Mye was a Labor supporter (*CM* 22.10.75), to be rebutted by a former National Party candidate for the seat of Cook, insisting that Mye was not a Labor supporter (*CM* 24.20.75).

The exchange was eventually displaced from the newspapers by the constitutional crisis in Canberra when the Senate blocked supply. Twelve months later, however, the DAIA and the Eastern Islands were still in a state of open hostility. Knowing that the DAIA could monitor messages transmitted over the radio communication system, which it controlled, Mye distributed walkie-talkies to his supporters on neighbouring islands and used a ship-at-sea hook-up on the co-operative's boat to talk to Canberra. (The installation of public telephones was an eventual outcome of this period.)

The next exchange involved Liberal Prime Minister, Malcolm Fraser. The visits of various representatives to the mainland to confer with officials and make statements to the press had left the people at home uneasy lest commitments be made without their knowledge. In October 1976 fourteen councillors cabled him expressing such fears, and requesting him to come up to the Strait in company with the Premier. The Prime Minister accepted their invitation, but came without the Premier and concluded a two day tour with an evening spent with Eastern Islands Representative, George Mye, on Darnley Island. The meeting was extensively reported in the press and Mye took the opportunity to inform the public that he did not need the Premier to speak on his behalf, also alleging that the IIB was withholding supplies from the stores in the hope of sabotaging the feast for the Prime Minister (Steketee 1976).

Other leaders also came to terms with the Commonwealth. The visit to Canberra in 1973 had worked its magic, and at least one Island conservative spoke glowingly of Prime Minister

Whitlam who had personally served him a drink. Others found it impossible to deny their communities the benefits the Commonwealth was offering. At the outset the DAIA had claimed the right to administer any funds allocated to the Strait. The Commonwealth acceded in some instances, but insisted on dealing with the Islanders directly in most. Learning from Minister Bryant's mistakes, it took care to work through existing representatives, who found themselves serving two masters. Queensland still exerted a powerful personal as well as political hold over the older generation of leaders, but its standing in the Strait was shortly to suffer with the emergence of the land rights issue.

Queensland continued its campaign over the border with Papua New Guinea (see for example *SMH* 15.6.78; 6.7.78); but the Torres Strait leaders, concluding that it was a lost cause, were starting to use the alienation of their traditional rights as a basis for demands on the Commonwealth. Long before the treaty with Papua New Guinea was ratified in 1985, another more immediate threat to their security had arisen, this time from Brisbane. Always believing that they were the legal owners of their ancestral islands, they had felt no great sympathy for the demands of dispossessed Aborigines. However, in 1980 some ex-servicemen were dismayed to discover that they were not entitled to housing loans, because the land on which they lived belonged to the Crown (*CM* 27.6.80). In the following year Queensland announced its intention to revise its Aboriginal and Islander legislation, including that relating to land tenure. The responsible Minister expressed a preference for perpetual leasehold, although the Premier was later reported to favour fifty year leases. The announcement caused widespread dismay in the Strait, prompting the three Islanders' Representatives to bypass the DAIA and seek direct access to the Premier. Having secured his undertaking that no precipitate action would be taken, they hurried back to test the feeling in the Strait. Consultations during the month of August revealed 1,047 in favour of inalienable freehold, 44 preferring ordinary freehold, ten perpetual leasehold and one ordinary leasehold. The Report of the Torres Strait Advisory Council, Submitted to the Honourable the Premier of Queensland (n.d.) communicated these findings together with a series of recommendations:

1.   That Torres Strait Islanders be given INALIENABLE FREEHOLD TITLE to all land presently designated Reserve Land under the

   Queensland Act 1962–78 and the Torres Strait Islanders Act.

2. That a LAND TRUST be established for the purpose of transferring title of Reserve Lands from the Queensland Government. Membership of such Land Trust to consist of 3 Elected Group Representatives and all Elected Torres Strait Community Chairmen.

3. That a STATUTORY BODY be established for the purpose of gradually assuming the present role and function of the Department of Aboriginal and Islanders' Advancement and its statutory bodies. Membership of the body to consist of elected Island representatives.

The July 1982 conference of island councillors reaffirmed its preference for inalienable freehold by a vote of 35 to one.

 Early in 1982 the Premier responded with a new proposal for a deed of grant in trust, a little used legal device through which the Queensland government grants to a group rights to use the land in question. These deeds of grant are of indefinite duration, though subject to revocation at any time. Islander representatives were firm in rejecting the proposal. In 1982 the State chairman of the NAC, Steve Mam, a Brisbane-based Islander, remarked that Queensland officials were 'acting like used car salesmen, trying to sell legislation Aborigines and Islanders did not want' (*SMH* 25.5.82). Later that year, Eddie Mabo, a Townsville based Meriam, along with several others resident on Murray, began legal proceedings in the High Court to establish their traditional ownership of land on Murray Island (*SMH* 12.4.85; 30.4.85). These proceedings, which are financed by the Commonwealth government, are still in train.

 Land is one of the matters on which the Queensland Government has legislated in the face of Aboriginal and Islander opposition. During the 1970s it went to some lengths to secure at least a semblance of consent. The 1971 legislation had constituted the three Islands Representatives as an Islander Advisory Council, with a parallel body for Aborigines (Nettheim 1981:19). However in 1976, when planning further changes in the Acts, it resorted instead to a nominated Aboriginal and Islander Commission, the Torres Strait member being the Representative for the Central Islands, who was known for his loyalty to the DAIA (*ibid.*:20). Despite submissions from the Federally funded Aborigines and Torres Strait Islanders Legal Service and the Foundation for Aboriginal and Islanders

Research Action, based on a survey of the views of some 1,800 Aborigines and Islanders (*ibid.*:21), the Commission submitted a report that resoundingly endorsed Queensland practice, while rejecting Commonwealth policies on land rights and separate development (*ibid.*:21–8; Ryan 1985). Despite this satisfactory outcome, the Queensland Government did not reconvene the Commission in preparing the further round of legislation for 1984, but entered into extended discussions with the Torres Strait councillors, now called an Advisory Council, and with a consultative committee elected by them during 1982.

The minutes of the TSAC conference held in July of that year are worth examination for the light they throw on the changing character of consultation. An elected Islander chairman presided over the three days of meetings, and there was no official intervention until the second day. However, on a vote of the members, the local representatives of the DAIA and the DAA, together with lawyers of the Aboriginal and TSI Legal Service and the local Members of Parliament, were admitted as observers. (On the second day the representatives of the Legal Service were asked to withdraw at the request of the Director of DAIA.) Having reaffirmed its wish for inalienable freehold of the island reserves, the conference proceeded to a discussion of the new legislation. The general tenor of this is apparent in the resolution that was passed at the outset:

> That this conference convey to the Honourable the Premier and the Queensland Government through the Minister our sincere thanks for the way the Government has controlled us under the old Torres Strait Islanders Act and Regulations and now we feel we need a change and our leaders to have greater control and management of our affairs.

The conference then went into detailed discussions of the means of implementing this policy, before accepting the Director's request to elect a five man consultative committee to discuss further details with the DAIA.

The committee met DAIA representatives in the following October to discuss its recommendations, the general thrust of which was as follows: the new legislation would establish by statute a Torres Strait Commission, comprised of the chairman of each of the community councils. The deeds of grant in trust would be held by the latter in the case of inhabited islands, and by the commission in the case of uninhabited islands. The DAIA would continue for a further period of three years, during which time it would hand over its powers and functions to the councils, the Commission or some other appropriate body. To coordinate this changeover, a planning committee, comprising six commissioners, representatives of six government departments, and a chairman appointed by the Governor in Council, would be formed. In addition, the Queensland Government was requested to approach the Commonwealth Government to produce 'mirror legislation'.

The courtesies offered in the preamble to these negotiations were in part Torres Strait protocol, in part a palliative to those who were still bound in ties of loyalty to particular officials; but the fact remained that the DAIA was being given notice to quit. Certainly the Islanders were asking Queensland to give them more than it proved ready to do in the final legislation. Meanwhile, as on the mainland, it suspended consultation and kept its plans a close secret until the new bill was presented to Parliament in 1984. Torres Strait, however, was given an unexpected opportunity to express its feelings in the State elections of 1983.

The Islanders had for some time recognized that parliamentary elections provided them with an opportunity for political expression on matters of concern to themselves. The candidates, for their part, were aware that they constituted a sizeable component in the Federal constituency of Leichhardt and about one third in the State constituency of Cook. Only the right wing Democratic Labor Party had ever run an Islander candidate, but the ALP and the National Party regularly appealed to the Islander vote through the pages of the Thursday Island *Torres News* and in visits around the islands. Over most of the period approximately 60% of Islanders had given first preference to the ALP, even in the election in which an Islander was running for another party. Those with whom I discussed the matter gave explanations such as 'only the ALP helps coloured people', or bluntly stated that a vote for the ALP was a vote against DAIA. (It was remarkable that pro-DAIA communities, such as Yam and Badu, favoured the National Party.) The trend was sharply reversed during the border scare of the mid-1970s, but was reasserting itself by the end of the decade with the emergence of the land issue.

The State election of 1983 had more than usual local

significance in that the National Party candidate was the Director of Aboriginal and Islander Advancement, P.J. Killoran. With thirty years of service behind him, and personally known to every adult Islander from his years in the Thursday Island office, he personified the DAIA and was reputed, both in the press and among the Islanders, to be at the very heart of Queensland's resistance to the Islanders' aspirations (*SMH* 20.11.82).[11] The consultative committee had referred pointedly to his imminent retirement, proposing that he become first chairman of the three year planning committee. His candidacy posed a very different possibility of his becoming the Minister responsible for Aboriginal and Islander affairs. The election might thus be seen as a vote of confidence in the man and his department; if so it was a crushing rebuff, for he won a majority in only three island communities, while the overall result from the polling booths in which Islanders predominated was below 30%.

It cannot be said whether these events affected the content of the Community Services (Torres Strait) Act, which was passed along with its Aboriginal counterpart in April 1984; however, it falls some way short of the proposals the Islanders had made in 1982. The re-naming, yet again, of the DAIA as the Department of Community Services suggests a rejection of the old native-settler distinction in favour of a term that could apply to all Queenslanders. In practice the DCS is solely concerned with Islanders and Aborigines. It seems likely that the officers of the old DAIA will continue to exercise their powers in the labyrinths of government. Yet the new structure is less monolithic, establishing more links with other departments than existed formerly. (In keeping with this trend, the island schools are to come under the Department of Education, a change long sought by Islanders.) The island council is also strengthened, through incorporation, and enabled to handle money with greater freedom than before, although with the requirement to submit

[11] Director Killoran has been interviewed by the press only once (*Aboriginal Quarterly* 7–9:1968). However, trenchant criticisms of Commonwealth intervention, Aboriginal land rights, and over-hasty change, have appeared over his name in the annual reports of the DAIA over the last decade. He may be said to be adhering to the ultimate goal set out in the 1968 interview: 'each of the reserves and [Aboriginal] towns will merge, no longer as special areas but as normal towns within a normal society in Queensland functioning on similar levels as all other towns'. The matter at issue at that time was the pace of change and the need for official control in the interim. In recent years the criticism has been that Queensland is trying to dissolve and disperse Aboriginal communities, rather than preserve them.

monthly statements to the Minister for the first three years.

The superior body, named the Island Co-ordinating Council and composed of island chairmen, has fewer powers over the councils than formerly. However, the four representatives that it will elect to the IIB will have a majority of one over the local representatives of the DCS together with the two appointees of the Governor in Council. The ICC is incorporated and empowered to receive funds and acquire property for use 'towards the progress, development and well-being of the communities resident in Torres Strait by such means as, in its opinion, are best calculated to achieve the purpose' (IV, 51 [1]). In as much as government can deal directly with the communities, the ICC would seem to be on trial, an impression that is confirmed by clause (2) of the above section, which provides that after four years the Council will submit to the Minister a report concerning the operations of the Act and recommendations for changes in it. Meanwhile the ICC has been meeting at monthly intervals, and has provided a milieu for local level cooperation between state and federal agencies.

These developments have been part of a significant restructuring of relations between Brisbane and the Torres Strait leadership. With the appointment of Robert Katter Jnr in 1983, the DAIA acquired a Minister who, unlike his predecessors, was determined to take an active part in its affairs. This may have created friction between himself and the long-serving Director, P.J. Killoran, as the press alleged (*CM* 14.6.84), but it enabled him to establish personal contacts with Torres Strait leaders. Subsequently, although some of the latter were present when the new Act was passed, they did not join the Aboriginal protest against it. They did oppose the appointment of the old Director as head of the DCS, but this request was disregarded.

Islander leaders asserted that the new legislation would substantially increase their autonomy. I heard George Mye compare it with the days of the DNA, when 'all belly scar long crawl'. He might also have seen it as a step towards the regional autonomy that Gerald Peel had proposed in his 1946 draft programme. However, the Commonwealth Government had yet to make matching concessions.

An opportunity for re-negotiation presented itself when the Federal Minister for Aboriginal Affairs, Clyde Holding, dissolved the NAC in mid-1985. In a message to the Minister, dated 30 May 1985, the three senior Torres Strait Representatives declared that 'we will not be satisfied with mere passive integration of our own leadership structure with some externally conceived and dictated organization, but we propose to deal independently with all levels and areas of government and politics through our own structures'. In a subsequent telex, dated 27 June 1985, a larger meeting stated as their terms of reference the establishment of 'a separate and complete representational, consultative and advisory structure for the Torres Strait and Northern Peninsula region', which would be separate and distinct from whatever structures succeeded the NAC. When, by August, the Minister had still not met their request for 'direct and personal consultation', they issued a similar invitation to the Prime Minister, who first accepted but then cancelled his visit at the last minute. Reporting this over the Torres Strait Media Association radio, on 12 September 1985, the Deputy Chairman of the ICC, Getano Lui Jnr, explained in Torres Strait Broken that they were demanding

> total control of land and total control of sea, irrespective of whether the state government is coming up with the Deeds of Grant in Trust; irrespective of whether the Commonwealth Government is coming up with its land rights legislation. What we want is a separate identity or separate status for Torres Strait Islanders – not to be lumped with Aboriginal people because while we share the same problems with themfeller, *yumi* [i.e. you and I or we] a unique race of people. I think that's one thing *yumi* must understand, that *yumi* should not be seen or should not be classified as being part of Aboriginal affairs, in the sense that when *oli* [they] fund *yumi*, *yumi* become just piecemeal funding for the Commonwealth Government, where they just give *yumi* money just to keep *yumi* mouth shut. And I think it's time now for *yumi* altogether Torres Strait Islanders to stand up and be counted, if you really feel for your islands, and feel for the destiny of your children, and everything like that, I think *yumi* really have to tell the government and initiate developments to take place in this area. I think the days are over for *yumi* to sit back and just get handouts.

Torres Strait leaders subsequently met the Prime Minister in Canberra, but were passed on to the Minister, Clyde Holding, who proposed that they take over the running of the area DAA. Six months later, however, negotiations had not progressed beyond the exploratory stage.

Plate 9. George Mye and Torres Strait ex-service representatives, Etti Pau and Sele Thaiday, with Minister for Aboriginal Affairs, Clyde Holding (courtesy David Bartho, Sydney Morning Herald*)*

Early in 1986 the Commonwealth abandoned its commitment to a national Aboriginal land rights policy, but the Torres Strait representatives, with the lone abstention of Murray Island, had already accepted Queensland's Aborigines and Torres Strait Islanders (Land Holding) Act. The Premier and his wife, Senator

Flo Bjelke-Petersen, received a ceremonial welcome on Darnley Island and were formally declared *baba* and *ama* (father and mother) of the island people (*SMH* 13.12.85).

Before long rumours were circulating among Islanders and others to the effect that the Torres Strait vote had been pledged to the National Party and that Mye or Lui would be its candidate. There can be little doubt that it was the unstated occasion for a leading member of the Queensland Labor Party to make a personal attack on George Mye (*CM* 13.3.86). In the 1986 Queensland election Getano Lui Jnr stood as the National Party candidate, but he failed to take the seat from its Labor incumbent and won a majority of Islander votes only in his home community, Yam, and in George Mye's Darnley.

While the developments of the last twenty years have brought Torres Strait into ever increasing economic dependence on Australia, its leaders have striven not just for local autonomy but to modify the forces pressing upon them from without. There are limits to their capacity to achieve either, but the ideology of welfare colonialism gives legitimacy to their attempts, and the condominium of Queensland and the Commonwealth has given them more leverage than they would have had, dealing with a single government. That they have been able to make such effective use of their opportunities has been largely due to the experience they gained under the O'Leary system of local government.

The political field in which the Torres Strait leaders move is, of course, controlled by European politicians and bureaucrats, and if the Aboriginal influence has been limited, it has nevertheless been greater than that of Islanders. Torres Strait's leaders have been able to get results by forming their own strategies out of the resources at their disposal and the opportunities open to them. Aborigines, particularly in the south, have often followed a confrontationist approach with resort to mass demonstrations – often highly dramatic – and skilful use of the media. Islanders have preferred a decorous approach, in which small parties of accredited spokesmen have worked through official channels or, discreetly, through personal connections. George Mye, who has featured in several television documentaries,[12] is the only one

---

[12] George Mye made his first screen appearance as early as 1967, in Cecil Holmes' documentary *The Islanders* (Commonwealth Film Unit). His attempts to use the opportunity as a platform were largely frustrated by censorship.

likely to be known to southern audiences. The close press coverage of recent years has been due to reporter rather than Islander initiative.

The Islander strategy is in part a product of the leaders' political education in the local government councils and councillors' conferences of earlier years, combined with experience in some branch of the government service. This has left them versed in the working of one bureaucracy, in its political and personal as well as formal aspects. However, they were largely unprepared for the politics of the last ten years, which has brought them face to face with an ever increasing diversity of government agencies and politicians, even including Premiers and Prime Ministers. Somehow these men, only one of whom has had secondary education, have gained a working knowledge of the legal and financial issues arising in negotiations, and learned to use white advisers without being controlled by them. They have mastered the tropes appropriate to these arenas and developed a feel for the alliances and schisms within the political–bureaucratic nexus. Not surprisingly, some of the older leaders have periodically relapsed into their old dependence on the safe and the familiar, but the long term trend has been towards a redistribution of alignments.

Earlier I quoted the former councillor who in 1960 remarked 'you have to be a smart man to be a councillor these days; not like before'. How much more is this the case today! As for the higher levels of leadership, it is confined to a few, and that few is entrenched. At the centre have been the three Islands Representatives, the senior of whom, George Mye MBE, has occupied the position since 1956. The Western Islands position was occupied from its inception by Tanu Nona OBE until his retirement in favour of his son, Joey Nona, in 1975. The Central Islands position was occupied by Jimmy Mosby of Yorke Island until his retirement in 1970. The office then passed to Getano Lui MBE of Yam Island, a former store manager who was later to serve on the State's Aboriginal and Islander Commission. In 1980 he gave way to his son, Getano Lui Junior, though continuing to fill the role of an elder statesman. George Mye's formal seniority is reinforced by his early experience in Canberra as leader of the border action delegation, and his continuous membership of the NAC, which has entitled him to a seat on its executive. He has been the moving force behind the push for local autonomy. Getano Lui Jnr has also been a Commissioner of the Federal

Aboriginal Development Commission along with Crossfield Ahmat, a former skipper and also chairman of Badu until his death in 1984. Both were contenders for George Mye's seat on the NAC in 1977. An earlier challenger was Ben Nona, brother of Tanu, a former chairman of Badu, DLP parliamentary candidate in 1972, and NAC representative for Thursday Island and the Cape York settlements from 1980. On his death in 1983 he was succeeded by his son. His predecessor on the NAC, from 1973, and once an independent candidate for the State seat, was Ted Loban. Of Islander and Malay parentage, he had lived most of his life on Thursday Island, without direct experience of life 'under the Act', and derived most of his support from his home town. He had, however, been associated with FCAATSI from the late 1960s and had appeared in the unofficial delegation that was ejected from the Canberra meeting in 1973. His involvement with the island communities was mainly through a Commonwealth funded cooperative that served those immediately adjacent to Thursday Island.

These figures differed from one another in personality, local affiliation, experience and loyalty to one or other of the competing governments. Several among them identified with the Liberal–National coalition or the ALP, although we have seen that Mye avoided commitment. However, it is remarkable that all were agreed on the kind of aid that Torres Strait needed, and the people's entitlement to it. The old debate between radicals and conservatives was a thing of the past. Everyone worked within the moral economy of welfare colonialism, the only dispute was over patrons.

This profile suggests a political elite that has monopolized not only the expertise but also the strategic connections in a few hands. Sons have succeeded fathers in three of the five instances of succession. Others, whatever their political aspirations, realize that they 'don't know that business'. The higher levels of politics have become detached from the experience of ordinary Islanders. Thus the reports of imminent autonomy, which filtered through to the communities in late 1985, left many uncertain and uneasy. But while such people are free to vote for whomever they wish, they have no realistic option other than to put their trust in those 'who know how to talk to white people'. Nor do they have the cultural means for articulating opposition, which is thus couched only in terms of personality.

The voters' participation nevertheless remains important in

terms of the politics of welfare colonialism. Identified with traditional community and region, the leadership not only looks like 'the real thing' as far as the general public is concerned, but is well placed to deal with pretenders and upstarts. Recalling Weaver's description of the Commonwealth's requirements of the NACC, it can be said that the community-based system of representation in Torres Strait stabilizes pressure group activity and facilitates integration with the processes of government (Weaver 1983:4–5). At the same time, this legitimacy, combined with the inter-government rivalry, saves it from co-optation.

Whether intended or not, the effect of this has been to disenfranchise Islanders living on the mainland. Ignored for the most part by the Torres Strait leadership, and without representative institutions of their own, they lack the official means of expressing themselves as Islanders. While the Queensland Government considers them as virtually assimilated, the Commonwealth groups them with Aborigines in the administration of its various aid programmes.

The emigration

Islanders came to the mainland as willing but unskilled and poorly educated manual workers, with few contacts and the problem of overcoming employer resistance to non-European labour. Given these difficulties, it can be said that the emigration has been successful, although they remain after thirty years concentrated in the lower brackets of the socio-economic scale.

Coastal north Queensland, where the first immigrants landed and where there are now sizeable settled communities, is given over to the cultivation of sugar, rice and bananas, and the handling of the cattle, minerals and tobacco produced in the interior. Townsville, a city of just under 100,000, is the main centre, with a small university and a military establishment. Cairns, with a little under 40,000 inhabitants, has a tourist industry, while Mackay, a town of about the same size, is engaged in meat processing. The region is linked to the rest of the State by a railway that runs the whole 1,678 km between Cairns and Brisbane, and penetrates inland as far as Mt Isa and Winton.

It was the railway system, which in its northern division alone has 3,042 km of line, which enabled the immigrants to establish an economic bridgehead. The first arrivals had found employ-

ment as cane cutters, but when mechanization put an end to this
they found work as fettlers, maintaining the line. During the
years of full employment this work was unattractive to Europeans because it required heavy exertion in extreme heat and
often took them to temporary camps at remote sidings in the
interior. Islanders, many of whom were single, or who had left
their families back in the Strait, were eager for jobs that would
bring them several times what they had earned in the Strait, and
they performed well, particularly in all-black teams with one of
their own as ganger.

Just as Torres Strait divers had striven to show themselves as
good as the Japanese after the war, so now Islander fettlers set
out to show that they were as good as Europeans. Although the
union set a limit on the number of sleepers to be laid, the gangers
acted like boat skippers, pushing their men to do more. When
reminded that they got no more pay for this, they explained that
they were doing it 'for name'.

Their enthusiasm recommended them to recruiters looking
for men to work on contract in Western Australia. As one of
them recalled, years later,

> Them Yankee got contract for complete that line in five
> years, but we done it in six months. We stupid enough to
> do that, I mean we don't know nothing about it. But for us,
> we play, just because the machine there to help us. And we
> enjoy with the jackhammer – like a dance. Oh we enjoy
> every bit of it, we never even got tired of it.

Northern development began to ease in the 1970s and machines
increasingly replaced Torres Strait muscle power. Fortunately,
Queensland Railways still had places for Islander fettlers. In
time, a number secured permanent positions and graduated to
lighter grades of work in the towns.

The railways continue to provide some openings for the new
immigrants and the mainland-born, but early hopes that a city
education would open up avenues to white collar jobs have not
been realized. Even the government agencies dealing with
Aborigines and Islanders employ few Islanders compared to the
number of Aboriginal staff. A number have enrolled for special
courses at James Cook University in Townsville and several have
graduated as teachers, but the great majority remain in poorly
paid, unskilled work or, with the recession of recent years, are
unemployed. There has been talk of utilizing Islander skills in

local fisheries, but only one scheme attracted government funds and that proved abortive.

As workers and as unemployed, Islanders have encountered the state in the same way as other Australians. It is mainly in the matter of housing that they have received special attention. Like any other immigrant group that arrives without capital and lacks the earning capacity to accumulate a deposit, they have been forced into rental accommodation. And given some prejudice among owners of rental property, there have been instances of exploitation (cf. Fisk *et al.* 1974). But already by 1974, twenty out of a sample of fifty households occupied accommodation provided by the DAIA. Since that time the Commonwealth has provided Queensland with additional funds for this purpose, the houses being now administered by an Aboriginal and Islander Housing Association. This, together with the Legal and Medical Services, channels the greater part of government aid to the two groups.

In keeping with the lower level of state intervention, the apparatus for consultation and self-management is less elaborate than in the Strait. Queensland has not thought it necessary to set up representative structures to parallel those in the Strait, dealing with its clients for the most part on an individual basis. The Commonwealth has gone further, but deals with Aborigines and Islanders as a single group, creating a situation in which the former have emerged as dominant. Some Islanders complain that the Aboriginal representatives ignore their needs and favour their own people, but they have failed to mount an effective challenge. In elections for the NAC position in the Townsville constituency, a multiplicity of Islander candidates gave the advantage to an Aboriginal from Palm Island. (Paradoxically, the NAC representative for the predominantly Aboriginal constituency of Brisbane was Steve Mam, who comes from St Paul's mission on Moa.) Islanders also lost control of the Townsville housing associations and have failed to win office in the medical service (Cromwell pers. com.). The only projects of their own to win government support have been the abortive fishing project and the small and now defunct Black Community School.

Islanders state that they lack the political skills and linguistic competence to succeed in welfare politics; but they also admit an inability to mobilize in force because of 'jealousy' among island communities and families. Eastern Islanders predominate in all the voluntary associations, with a much lower participation by other communities; but their energies are dissipated among five churches and two ex-servicemens' organizations. The same problem attended the formation in 1976 of the Torres United Party (TUP), which nevertheless proposed nothing less than the establishment of 'The Free Nation of Torres Strait'. In a printed statement it described itself as,

> an organization formed by Islanders to represent the traditional island communities of Torres Strait, and Torres Strait Islanders forced to live on mainland Australia in search of employment. The present TUP leader, Carlemo Wacando, acting as a symbolic Torres Strait islander, is currently challenging the legality of the Border Treaty between Australia and Papua-New Guinea, in the High Court of Australia, and he is also seeking an order from the Court that the Australian Government never properly annexed the islands and seabed of Torres Strait, so that the land and oil and gas and minerals and fish and sea will remain the traditional free property of the Torres Strait Islander people. The Torres United Party is strongly opposed to the interference of white Australian political parties in the life and affairs of Torres Strait, because those parties (the Australian Labor Party, the Liberal Party and the National Country Party) have proved that they do not understand the traditional and sacred cultures and life styles of the islanders. The TUP is convinced that the Torres Strait people will keep their traditional borders, only if the present appeal to the United Nations for sovereign independence, is granted to the islands of Torres Strait, when free, secret ballot elections will allow the islanders to choose their own national leaders each three years.

The 'free nation' would be financed from the leasing of oil and gas prospecting rights, postage stamps, fisheries and 'electricity from underwater turbines' which would 'harness the world's most powerful ocean exchange.' According to a newsletter dated 9 April 1980 and issued over the signature of Wacando, turbines from the Papuan coast to Cape York would make Torres Strait 'the power house of the next century'. The same source names a Sydney-based finance company, Essington Pty Ltd, as the party's 'principal financers', and states that 'Top scientists from Florida Current are now prepared to take up the feasibility study, which thousand of millions dollars [sic] will be spent to investigate all our resources in Torres Strait.' A European, who had had a long association with Islanders in various capacities, played a part in forming TUP and in setting up the link with the Sydney company.

It is reasonable to assume that the financial interests involved had their own agenda. So, however, did the Islanders. TUP drew on the continuing hostility towards the Queensland Government and resentment against some of the island councils over the refusal of re-entry rights. Wacando himself complained to the press that he had been denied the right to visit his native Darnley because he was a critic of Queensland and a minister of the Universal World Church (Crisp 1978). TUP also drew on the disillusionment with the Commonwealth Government and the major parties over the border issue. Just as an earlier generation of leaders had proposed the Commonwealth as an alternative to the State, so now their successors proposed the United Nations and big business as the underwriters for a sovereignty that had been lost for more than a hundred years.

TUP, however, remained dependent on the Australian legal system and in 1981 the Full High Court in Canberra found that Darnley Island, in respect of which the challenge was being made, had been part of Queensland since 1879, and part of the Commonwealth since federation (*SMH* 13.11.81). The appeal to the United Nations languished, along with numerous other such appeals, and TUP disintegrated. It was shortly to be succeeded by the Mabo case (see page 191), albeit on a more modest scale.

I was unable to discover how many became paid-up members of TUP during its four-year life. At its height it aroused wide-spread interest on the mainland and some discreet support in the Strait, but that support, like its director and secretary, came almost wholly from the Eastern Islands. While its name suggested all-islander unity, its acronym TUP referred to a small fish found only around Murray and Darnley. More to the point, had the court challenge been successful, it would only have affected islands outside the sixty-mile limit, those inside this radius coming under different provisions (*Australian Financial Review* 7.5.81). This detail was ignored not only in the party's statements, but in those of its European advocates in the south. According to G.G. Masterman QC, who presented Wacando's case in the High Court: 'We are dealing with people, we are dealing with an alien race, a race who sees themselves, rightly or wrongly, in bondage to Australia' (*AFR* 7.5.81). This assertion of

Torres Strait Islander identity was not achieved through the arousal of a mass consciousness or the working out of a consensus, but through the agitation of a small group, interacting with the Australian government and Australian sympathisers.

Being an Islander in the 1980s

Over the last twenty-five years Islanders have both intensified and diversified their relations with other Australians. This is particularly true of those on the mainland, but also of those in the Strait. Many of the latter have spent time in the south for one purpose or another, while other Australians visit the islands with far more frequency than before. Thursday Island has increasingly become a meeting ground as the old social and legal barriers have fallen. Island leaders, for their part, are no longer locked into intense, personal relations with a few officials, but deal with a changing round of bureaucrats and politicians. Island clergy now undergo training outside the Strait and occasionally attend conferences overseas.

The change in the patterns of interaction, and in the cultural contexts in which it occurs, poses anew the question of who the Islanders are and what their place is in Australian society. Fifty years ago such issues were a matter of common sense, scarcely requiring consideration. Today they demand resolution at the levels of thought and action.

The identity that Islanders have brought to the new encounters is a product of colonial rule. Their standing in the wider society is to be negotiated in terms of what they have done as Christians, workers and loyal subjects of the Crown. For the dwindling ex-service cohort, volunteering for military service during the Second World War remains the crucial act in the process they describe as 'fighting our way out to the Commonwealth'. In the words of a Meriam veteran, 'Mr Marou was the main one. He fight for boys to go into the army. Freedom come from that.' As another put it, 'Before time gate he shut. After volunteer gate he open. Now Torres Strait from Thursday Island to Western Australia.'

The ex-servicemen's self-evaluation is not just a matter of nostalgia. The Commonwealth has given substantial confirmation of it over the years, with the long-awaited repatriation benefits in the mid-1960s and, after forty years, by making up the difference between their wartime pay and that of regular troops. With accumulated interest, the latter sum has amounted to tens of thousands of dollars for each claim. On the mainland TSLI veterans have found that, although the Legion is defunct, the RSL now recognizes them and will on occasion provide advice and help.

Some of the younger generation have served in the regular armed forces or undergone periods of military training, which their elders regard as following in their footsteps. But this is an option for only a few. Religion is within the means of all, but it has proved a dead end as far as identification is concerned. The white Pentecostalists whom Islanders found so welcoming in the early years of migration became less so as their numbers increased, and ended by suggesting that they form their own congregation. Much the same has happened with the Anglicans, while the great majority of church goers belong to all-black congregations of one denomination or another. Church membership may assist Islanders to a life of social and material respectability in abstract terms, but it neither increases nor improves their actual relations with other Australians.

Membership of the regular work force, which is the experience of most able-bodied males on the mainland (though of few females), is also for them a significant way of taking part in Australian society. It is a daily reminder that they have emerged from colonial conditions to enjoy all the rights of other Australian workers. In particular, those having permanent positions in the railways point to the paid holidays, long-service leave and pensions, and the safety regulations and compensation provisions, which were so conspicuously lacking when they worked on the luggers. However, since they mostly work in all-black gangs, their contacts with white workers are limited, and as they are beginning to realize, a railway worker occupies a lowly position in Australian society.

In the early days of the migration, the numbers had been too small to support much in the way of island custom. Perhaps, also, such things seemed inappropriate in the white people's domain, and we have seen that Pentecostalists, returning home, condemned not merely dancing but wearing *lavalavas* and going barefoot as 'uncivilized'. In the Strait, however, Islander status was beginning to shed its penalties and attract rewards, to the point where some Thursday Island half castes were re-identifying. With the advent of welfare colonialism, being an Islander became compatible with citizenship; indeed it was a way of being a citizen. Correspondingly the benefits that went with it were regarded as entitlements rather than rewards for service, as in the older generation's understanding.

With their misgivings about their custom allayed, Islanders were able to put it to new uses. When Prime Minister Malcolm Fraser visited Darnley Island in connection with the border dispute, he was entertained to an island feast and re-enactment of the mythical charter for their claim to a cay that was under threat. This was still in the Islanders' domain, but in 1983 the delegation that went to Canberra to settle the ex-servicemen's backpay wore *lavalavas* in the white people's domain (*SMH* 19.10.83). Soon after, George Mye wore a *lavalava* when being presented to the Queen, something that would have been unthinkable a few years earlier. The statement of Getano Lui Jnr, likewise informed the Australian authorities as well as Islanders that they were 'a unique race of people'.

On the mainland Islander identity has been uncertain. Government agencies have found it administratively convenient to lump Islanders together with Aborigines, and officials urge them to make common cause. But they came from the Strait believing themselves to be superior, and had emphasized their distinctness as a means of avoiding the negative stereotypes to which Aborigines were subject. Of late schoolchildren have begun to refer to themselves and Aborigines collectively as Murries (Fuary pers. com.), and some leaders admit that 'we supposed to be one', but this has not been reflected in political practice. Finding themselves unable to compete, some Islanders have redirected their energies into cultural activities, particularly dancing, which is something urban Aborigines lack. (Palm Island Aborigines perform only Torres Strait island dance.)

Island dancing, like that of Australia's various ethnic communities, has found a ready acceptance with other Australians. Not only is it welcomed at multi-cultural and civic festivals, but schools are ready to pay for troupes to give demonstrations. Some Islanders are earning regular incomes in this way, and there are scholarships for talented performers to study with the Aboriginal and Islander Dance Theatre in Sydney. material considerations aside, island dance is now the principal way in which urban Islanders present themselves to their fellow citizens. However, it runs counter to the puritanism of the smaller Islander churches, giving rise to some ambivalence. One family defected from the World Church over the issue, declaring 'If we lose dance who are we?' Some who refuse to dance on religious grounds, nevertheless recognize it as part of the culture in which they take pride.

Robert Underwood, in a study of Guamanians who have migrated to California, suggests that much of their concern over Chamorro culture is due to a 'generalized need for a unique identity within the confines of Californian society. A visibly public statement about ethnic identity may be of greater importance to many Chamorro migrants than a personal desire to maintain their culture and traditions' (1985:179). Migrants elsewhere have suffered similar pressure. Indeed, since the late 1960s Australia, like the United States, has fostered ethnicity to the point where it has become a principal means of competing for public assistance. The problem, as Janet Dolgin has remarked, is that 'the symbolic forms through which ethnicity can be made known and defined are commutable between ethnic/racial groups' (1977:54). Indigenous people are also involved, and it is clear that the importance of land rights in the Aboriginal mobilization is at least partly because it is not liable to appropriation by migrant groups.

Islanders on the mainland have found themselves under similar pressures with the fading of their hopes of independence from government. Thus the homes that many have not seen for many years become once again important, if not as places to return to, then as points of reference. To be an Islander one must have an island!

It is in the light of such changes that I view the tombstone opening described at the beginning of this book and also the TUP episode. TUP went beyond a mere restatement of ancestral ties to propose a return to the Strait, not as it was but as it might become, developed as some dreamers had seen it in the 1950s, but still nurturing their 'sacred cultures and lifestyles', and a free nation. The bid for sovereignty translated the longstanding desire for local autonomy into the language of decolonization, thereby making Torres Strait part of the Third World. In earlier years Islanders had identified with South Sea people rather than with the Aborigines, and they had watched with interest as Samoa, Tonga and Fiji achieved nationhood. The independence of Papua New Guinea, which they had considered 'less civilized' than Torres Strait, came as a shocking reminder of their own

stagnation. TUP proposed an economic and political transformation, and in as much as the initiative had come from the
mainland, it implied that the 'true Islanders' were there rather
than in Torres Strait. One man made the point in more general
terms: 'Townsville keep all that custom bilong *yumi*'.

While TUP found its support mostly among Eastern Islanders,
it had articulated a programme that was meaningful for the
whole of Torres Strait and which could be presented to the world
as the aspiration of all Islanders. Once reported in the media and
taken up by European advocates,[13] its construction of Islander
identity assumed a life of its own that became in some degree
coercive on the people for whom it was devised. Such tension is
integral to the process by which ethnic groups are formed.
Dance, which is the usual way of presenting Islander identity, is
also vulnerable to appropriation, on the one hand from pro-
fessionalization, on the other from the insatiable appetite of
tourism and the media for the exotic. Even when managed by
the people themselves, presentations that are primarily intended for outside consumption tend inevitably to the obvious
and the picturesque. In the case of island dance these tendencies
are not as yet pronounced, although the commercial troupes use
the traditional feather headdress, called *dari*, for modern dances,
in a way that would be unacceptable at home.

Sider has suggested that when 'cultural nationalism' is no
longer based in concrete social organization, it becomes abstract
and so vulnerable (1976:168). Ceasing to reflect individual
experience, it readily degenerates into the 'alienated folkloric
consciousness' of which Muratorio has written (1980:51).
However, people may feel alienated from the public representations of their identity and yet recognize what Weaver calls a
private ethnicity, which is 'practised by groups or networks of
aboriginal minority members in their daily lives', being 'defined
and rationalized by the aboriginal groups, not the nation state'
(1983:186). To understand, then, what it means to be an Islander
in the 1980s, we must look more closely at the relations
Islanders maintain with one another, in the Strait, on the
mainland, and between the two.

[13] The Islanders' case was presented in two radio programmes in the Australian
Broadcasting Corporation's Broadband series in August and October 1980.

VIII   The society of Islanders

This study began with an account of a tombstone opening. The frequency of such celebrations, with their feasting, dancing and speech making, on the mainland as well as in the Strait, suggests that island custom retains at least something of its old vitality in the 1980s. But, as the preceding chapter has made clear, Islanders now live under conditions that are different from, and more diverse than those they knew around 1960. The decline of pearling, the easing of government restrictions, greater educational opportunities and improved communications have changed the face of Torres Strait, while almost half the Islander population now live in towns on the mainland. Can one then still think of them as constituting a society? And if so, to what extent does this society mediate their various experiences of the world?

Under the old colonial dispensation, Islander society was culturally homogeneous but socially segmented. Almost all Islanders until 1941, and the majority until the emigration of the 1960s, experienced the society of their fellows in the setting of a single island community. They could communicate with the people of other islands, in pidgin if not in the two Torres Strait languages, exchange hospitality within the framework of the festive complex, and share the rivalry of the dancing ground. But such encounters were occasional and charged with a degree of suspicion. Notionally all Torres Strait was integrated through a continuous web of kinship, but the links between communities were relatively few, becoming sparser as the distance between them increased.[1] Relations within a community, being complex, sustained and conducted in a context of shared experience and

---

[1]   The relocation of Pacific Islanders and their families from the Eastern Islands to St Paul's mission on Moa provided an exception to this rule. Moreover, as noted earlier, people with ancestors from the same Pacific island recognize a quasi-kinship relationship which is unaffected by distance.

tradition, took priority over intermittent contacts with outsiders. Even after the move to Thursday Island, the communities
maintained a degree of distance, while keeping up with events at
home through the succession of visitors who came seeking
their hospitality.

The same patterns re-emerged on the mainland as new arrivals
came seeking the help of kin and congregated in the same towns.
But while emigrants could keep abreast of events at home from
the latest arrivals, their families suffered from the lack of a
reverse traffic. Some emigrants had left after trouble and were
glad to put the island behind them. Others, intoxicated with
their new freedom and moving about a good deal, lost touch for
months and years on end. Parents received neither letters nor
money; wives were left to fret over rumours that their men had
found other partners. Some who did return with the intention of
spending Christmas at home got no further than Thursday
Island, for lack of a council permit or a place on the IIB
cargo boat.

Fisk, Duncan and Kehl, in their 1973 survey of Islanders in
Townsville, reported a low level of communication with
kinsfolk in the Strait (1974:42–4). But their assumption that
letters were the only means of communication available, ignoring cassettes which were widely used at the time, led them to
exaggerate the separation. Where they erred, however, was in
supposing that it was irreversible. With commercial light planes,
government helicopters and private motor dinghies, movement
is now easy and there is a steady two-way traffic between the
islands and the mainland. The regular air service between Cairns
and Yorke Island makes it possible for Murray Island bell fruit to
be in Sydney the same day that it is picked, while the installation
of public telephones throughout the Strait puts kin in touch
with one another the length and breadth of the continent. Even
without the telephone, news travels up and down the eastern
seaboard with surprising rapidity.

The heavy use to which these facilities are put is not simply a
matter of reviving sentiment, but of the social and economic
stresses to which islands and mainland are subject. The
emigrants, their dreams disappointed, keep the lines open
against the possibility of a return. The stay-at-homes, uneasy at
the economic and social stagnation, wonder whether they will
not shortly have to throw themselves upon the hospitality of
their countrymen in the south. These pressures are transcoded

into the sentiments of kinship and kin-focused activities such as the tombstone opening, which declare Islander society to be indivisible.

Such declarations notwithstanding, islands and mainland provide very different structural and cultural conditions for the practice of island custom. Islander society runs along a continuum from the remotest of Torres Strait communities through the Thursday Island township and the big emigrant concentrations of Townsville and Cairns, to smaller aggregations in Mt Isa, Brisbane, Darwin, Perth and a score of other places. In the Strait Islanders are the majority, in occupation of their own territory, and in command – if not in control – of their daily lives. Elsewhere they are more or less of a minority, living on someone else's land. Without political representation or mediating agency, one comes to terms with employer, official or landlord on one's own account.

Islanders are acutely aware of these differences. Indeed, now that movement has become easy, they may be said to have chosen where to live, as well as forming judgements about those who make different choices. I became aware of this, listening to a middle-aged couple argue over where to live when the husband retired from the railways. The wife declared that she did not want to return to their island because 'black people too much watching one another, not like white people.' Her preference was relative, for had she wanted to escape their scrutiny altogether she would not have lived in Townsville where the Islander population was large and closely knit, nor would she have attended an Island church, which reproduced some of the features of community life. But other considerations informed her choice. Back home, public opinion sanctioned a female drudgery, unrelieved by electricity or household appliance, that left her unresponsive to her husband's dream of self-sufficiency: 'turtle, fish, bush tucker, everything there!' Again, his plan to run for council and 'straighten out the island' stood in bleak contrast to the virtual exclusion of women from public office.[2]

Had the husband returned, his ambitions would probably have been disappointed, for the reduced communities of the Strait harbour a certain resentment against those who went away,

---

[2] Only two women have held council office, one on Murray in the early 1970s and the other on Boigu in the early 1980s. Several, however, are acquiring practical experience as council clerks which may qualify them for office in the future.

particularly when they return years later, telling the people at home how to run their lives. Their wives dress too well, their children lack respect. Offended by the brashness of their city cousins, island dwellers exclaim indignantly, 'this no south!'

Islanders, then, experience the society of their fellows at varying intensity and in the process of responding to a variety of structural conditions. In the pages that follow I shall attempt to convey a sense of this diversity, contrasting not only island with mainland, but Murray with Badu, each of which now, as in the past, is caught up in its own dialectic with the world outside.

Badu

Badu, with a population of 300, is only a little over half the size it was in 1960. This is largely attributable to the decline in pearling which eventually overtook even the Nona fleet. By the mid-1970s Badu seemed to be becoming a remittance economy like the rest, but with the development of the cray fishing industry the old dynamism reasserted itself. The organization of cray fishing, however, is different from that of pearling, leaving much more scope for the small independent operator. Recently the old economic leadership has reasserted itself, but in the meantime there has been a re-ordering of the lines of dependence that characterized the old 'skipper class–crew class' formation. In turn, these changes have combined with the diversification of relations with government to bring a greater degree of pluralism to the community.

As pearling declined through the 1960s other opportunities opened up. Some men took up fixed-term contracts on the mainland, some emigrated for good. At home there was work on a nearby pearl culture station. By the mid-1970s, two leading skippers were working ashore, supervising the Commonwealth's turtle farming project. Badu, however, was well situated to take advantage of the development of cray fishing, being only two or three hours away from the main fishing grounds and from the buyers on Thursday Island. Production began with two pearling skippers, Joey Nona and Crossfield Ahmat, who re-equipped the luggers they had been using for pearling – the former in association with the IIB, the latter in association with a Thursday Island company. Initially they provided their divers with motor dinghies, but in the years that followed an increasing number bought dinghies for themselves and went into business on their own account. These boats, made of aluminium and equipped with 30–40 horse power engines, cost between $3,000 and $4,000. Such an investment would have been beyond the means of most Baduans in the 1950s; now it was possible following a stint of contract work on the mainland, through the savings of a thrifty pensioner, or on hire purchase through a Thursday Island retailer. Organization was of the simplest: the low running costs left the owner free to work at his own pace, switching to hunting or visiting as he felt inclined. He reduced running costs by taking one or two others with him, but since the skills were widely distributed there was no difficulty about changing crew from trip to trip. Fishermen could run their catch in to one of the private buyers on Thursday Island, getting paid immediately and in full. Under these conditions, misunderstandings were less likely to arise than formerly. In the absence of any official funding or management or a need for 'strong leadership' at the local level, the kinship system provided the organizing structure.

This trend towards a peasant-like organization of production was arrested in 1983 when the ADC set up the Bammoa cooperative, with three lugger owners as directors. When Bammoa broke up at the end of 1985, these three established their own company, Badu Enterprises, with a contract to sell to a private buyer. Although independent dinghy operators remain free to sell their cray to the IIB or private dealers on Thursday Island, the majority find it convenient to utilize the freezer that the company inherited from Bammoa on Badu. Since two of the three councillors are directors of Badu Enterprises, it seems probable that once again economic and political objectives will be closely coordinated.

Overall, Badu is more affluent than it was in the 1950s. Apart from new houses, provided by the government at a modest rental, and the motor dinghies, a number of households have their own generators, supplying electric light, washing machines and videos. There is considerable economic inequality, but the sources of wealth are more diverse and no longer monopolized by one group. The unemployment benefits and pensions, including since 1975 the supporting parent's benefit, have largely eliminated the extremes of poverty that used to exist. Able-bodied men can also accumulate substantial sums by taking up a work contract on the mainland or, with some luck, by working hard in the cray fishing. As a result, the lines of dependence are distributed evenly through the community rather than being focused on a few individuals. The 'democratization' of boat ownership has had similar consequences. People can now go out for turtle or dugong on their own account, sharing the catch out among kith and kin. (The introduction of refrigerators has not ended this practice.) Anyone planning a feast can call upon the help of kin with dinghies, rather than having to cultivate a skipper. It is the same with transportation to Thursday Island, once a favour that had to be begged.

There have been comparable changes in politics. The intervention of the Commonwealth in what used to be a State jurisdiction has disrupted the simple nexus between council and government, subjecting councillors to conflicting demands and making their duties more onerous. Where once they were concerned only with the maintenance of law and order and the management of labour for the luggers, they now have responsibility for the considerable government funds that are allocated to the community. Here is a matter in which both the authorities and the inhabitants of Badu have a vital interest. These developments, combined with the reordering of economic dependence, came to a political head in 1976 when age and infirmity finally forced Tanu Nona to retire from office.

While Tanu Nona's importance to the DAIA as an economic leader declined through the 1960s, his political importance as a defender of its policies increased with the changing political climate. Leaving the chairmanship of the Badu council, first to his brother Ben and later to his son Joey, he continued as Western Islands Representative to keep the councillors of his group loyal to Queensland. Retiring at the age of 76, his last act was to secure the succession for Joey. However, his formidable personal authority could not be passed on with the office, so that the transition gave room for the expression of changes within the community, which he had hitherto held in check.

In the 1979 council election Crossfield Ahmat, the most popular skipper in the days of pearling, topped the poll and secured the position of chairman. He quickly established contacts with the Commonwealth government, becoming a commissioner of the ADC and the first head of the Bammoa cooperative. Joey Nona, who took second place, continued his collaboration with the DAIA as Western Islands Representative. The third member, elected on a handful of votes, lacked important external links but belonged to a large Badu family.

*Plate 10.   Tanu Nona's tombstone and the tombstone of Phillip
Nona waiting to be opened*

'That balance he come right', the verdict of one woman on the
new council, conveyed a number of messages about the Badu
community and its place in the wider scheme of things. Firstly,
Badu was assured of effective representation with both governments. Secondly, while Joey Nona stood for continuity, Ahmat
stood for the changes of the last decade. Thirdly, while certain
members of the Nona family were highly respected in the community, they had ceased to occupy a dominant position as a bloc;
indeed Ahmat enjoyed the support of several of the surviving
brothers. He did not, however, represent another family or faction. Like Tanu in the 1930s, he could represent himself as chairman 'for everyone'. Although originally a protégé of the Nonas
and related to them by marriage, he came from Mabuyag and had
no close kin on Badu apart from his own children.

Crossfield Ahmat and Joey Nona were re-elected in 1982, the
third place going to one of the two surviving Nona brothers.
Crossfield died before the 1985 elections, but his place at the top
of the poll was taken by his son, Jack Ahmat, who yielded the
chairmanship to Joey out of deference to his seniority and
experience. The third place went to a grandson of one of Tanu's

brothers. In fact all three are descendants of Tipoti Nona, two or three generations back, but they represent branches of the family that have become somewhat distinct through their inter-marriage with other families.

Baduans have as strong an awareness of the outside world as anyone in Torres Strait, but as the woman's remarks suggest, they also have a sense of their own community. They see their current economic prosperity in the light of their earlier successes in pearling, and locate it in inter-community and inter-family rivalries. They recognize the need for effective managers and political representatives, but have at the same time achieved some kind of balance between families. Kinship indeed remains the main idiom of Badu society, though its form is changing and the areas of life that it structures are contracting.

In the early years of this century the totemic clans gave way to the broader grouping of 'tribes', which in turn gave way to 'families', that is groups of siblings or first cousins, focused on a proximate ancestor. Some, though by no means all, families formed boat-owning companies and functioned informally as political blocs, and most mobilized intermittently to celebrate a tombstone opening or a wedding. By the 1950s only one family retained economic and political functions while the rest existed only as ceremonial groups. Today there are neither political nor economic families. Siblings and, less certainly, first cousins may be united by a sense of family honour, particularly when they are descended from a respected figure, but the means for expressing that sense are wholly ceremonial. And while the tombstone opening remains the island custom *par excellence*, the island wedding is now a rarity, not only on Badu but throughout the Strait.

In pagan times island society intervened in a relationship between a couple at the point where it threatened to become permanent and public, deeming marriage too important a matter to leave to personal preference. Taking a woman without the preliminary negotiations and the prescribed exchanges was considered 'stealing', and the father of a child conceived under such circumstances had no rights in it. The two families claimed the right to veto a marriage that would disturb existing relations – for example, if the couple were already close kin – or that would establish relations they considered undesirable. A proposal of marriage called into question their relative statuses, as well as the personal qualities of the man and woman. With colonization the Church incorporated the wedding within its ceremonial domain and, in combination with the council, did its utmost to prevent sexual relations outside marriage.

Over the last twenty years the island communities have ceased to regulate such matters with any consistency. Most couples get married eventually, though it may be in a registry office rather than a church; but only rarely do they go to the lengths of a full island wedding. The change is striking to anyone who can remember the zeal with which 'immorality' was pursued a generation ago, the virtual impossibility of cohabitation without the blessing of the Church, and the social importance of a wedding. The older generation is a little uneasy about the situation, and occasionally applies informal pressure to have particular relationships formalized, but old people have no desire to return to colonial restrictions. When a diocesan official proposed a return to the 'boy and girl law', a parish leader replied that Islanders lived 'free way now, like mainland'. Others shrug away the problem, saying 'you can't stop nature', but disregarding the fact that in early years the island authorities did 'stop nature'. That Islanders should appear uncertain over the matter is scarcely surprising, for it is the outcome of a complex of factors, social, cultural and economic.

Writing of Saibai, John Singe attributes the rarity of marriage to parental obstruction (1979:279). I too in my earlier field work found several instances in which parents either blocked marriages or delayed them inordinately (Beckett n.d.a.:1971). The diocese, alarmed at the increasing number of births out of wedlock, alleged that parents of daughters were holding out for a higher bride price, but the Island laity indignantly rejected this assault on their custom. In fact parents of both boys and girls had material reasons for delaying marriage, but the issues that arose when a particular marriage was proposed were various and genuine in themselves. Notwithstanding these obstacles, just about everyone married sooner or later.

Fitzpatrick-Nietschmann, who worked on Mabuyag during the mid-1970s, describes the contemporary situation in the following terms: 'Throughout the Western Torres Strait today Islanders are not getting married. This is a result of inflation in bride price, heavy financial burden of the wedding ceremony and receipt of social benefits' (1980a:1). The last of these factors is best understood in the context of the increasing independence of women from men and young from old.

Since colonization there has been little paid work for island women in the Strait, least of all on the reserves. The child endowment paid to mothers from 1941 was for most the first cash income they had ever received, and even this was earmarked for the children. In the mid-1970s, however, Badu offered well paid work on the turtle farm, and there is still money to be earned cleaning cray fish for the freezer. Moreover, from 1975 mothers without husbands became eligible for the supporting parent's benefit. This provides all Australian mothers not only with support in the case of desertion, but an alternative to an unsatisfactory marriage. By mainland standards it is too small to provide an attractive alternative in the long run, and while it may have contributed to a higher incidence of divorce it does not seem to have reduced the incidence of marriage, which is in fact also increasing. But as Collman has shown in his study of urban Aborigines in Central Australia (1979), such payments can have an impact on family structure when employment is scarce and irregular for men, and unobtainable for women. Not only is the benefit substantial by Torres Strait standards, it may be more reliable than the notional support of a husband who is away on the mainland, working irregularly or drinking heavily. A number of women evidently consider it an alternative, at least for a time.

Others consent to marry, but only in the registry office, or in what is called a 'quiet wedding' in church. Since the man's parents have not paid a bride price, they have no authority over her. Fitzpatrick-Nietschmann reports that Mabuyag women are well aware of the difference and prefer it (1980a:9). Maureen Fuary likewise reports Yam Island women as saying that not to be married is not to have a 'boss over you' (pers. com.). Women had enjoyed some autonomy in pearling communities while the men were away at sea[3] but this represents a significant modification of traditional male dominance.

Single men also enjoy a greater economic independence. The government no longer forces them to yield up an allotment to their parents, as they did in the days of pearling; nor does pay come in a lump sum at the end of the year when it is liable to be impounded for family purposes. Paid directly and in full at regular intervals, today's young men tend to spend as they go. If

[3] Despite the general disregard of tradition on Badu, as late as 1960 the women celebrated a boy's first turtle spearing in an all-female ceremony in which they dressed up as men.

they manage to save, a motor dinghy is likely to present a more attractive prospect than a wedding. Parents have an excuse for not providing the money, since they receive little or nothing from their sons.

Fitzpatrick-Nietschmann has laid particular emphasis on what she calls the 'high cost of marriage'. Noting that total expenditure can run into thousands of dollars, she states that 'marriage has become an economic impossibility for the majority of Islanders' (1980a:6). Her estimate, however, is based on the big weddings mounted by a few leading families in the Strait. The majority never could aspire to such grandeur and, in communities such as Badu where there was considerable economic differentiation, the obligation to hold a wedding only revealed their poverty and dependence. Such families have good reason to welcome the demise of the island wedding, while the young people are spared the long delay that preceded any wedding, big or small.

The decline of the island wedding has not meant a decline in the prestige economy or the festive complex. Rather there has been a strategic withdrawal from the risky shallows of marriage negotiation to the calmer waters of mortuary celebration. To judge by the number of new tombstones in the Badu cemetery, more dead are commemorated sooner, and the festivities are more lavish than ever. (Most tombstone openings cost no more than $4,000, but it is estimated that one recent event cost more than $30,000.) If a marriage can be prevented, death cannot, leaving the bereaved with an obligation that cannot be gainsaid. At the same time there is less urgency than with a wedding, and it is no disgrace to delay the opening for five years or more. On the other hand, family honour and, no doubt, filial piety, act as a spur. Tanu Nona's tombstone was unveiled less than four years after his death, although the preparations for over a thousand guests were more than usually burdensome. [4]

The tombstone opening is the centrepiece of island custom, transforming the universal currency that is money into local tokens of family prestige and continuity. It unites a family not just for the ceremony itself but for the months of preparation, and commonly involves those who live on the mainland as well as those in the Strait. Although there will be some change in the participants from one occasion to the next, a group of siblings

[4] This event, attended by senior politicians and officials, received extended reporting in the *Torres News*, 16.12.1980.

may come together to commemorate grandparents, parents, and those among them who die first. Each time the family name will be celebrated, not just on the tombstone but in the festive history of the community.

Although families occasionally make good an omission, commemorating someone who died as long as forty years ago, the majority of tombstones are for the recently dead, with the greatest priority given to parents. Thus while the principle of family continuity is asserted, it is by reference to proximate rather than remote ancestors, whose names may be forgotten if they have not been commemorated in the cemetery.

The same emphasis helps to solve the problems of social placement for children born out of wedlock. The traditional practice of adoption, which is still a common solution, amounts to a re-ordering of existing kin relations rather than the invention of fictive ties, since one of the adopting parents is invariably a blood relative (Beckett n.d.b.). Indeed, the usual arrangement nowadays is for the mother's parents to take the child. If she assumes her maternal role, it may address one of her brothers as father, thus establishing a link with the male line that is consistent with the assumption of the family name derived from the father.

The emphasis on nearest ancestors also facilitates the current tendency for families to assert their links with Badu rather than, as formerly, with countries outside the Strait. Although genetic and cultural continuity with the original inhabitants is weaker than in most communities, today's Baduans are no less determined to assert their identification with the island and their right to its land. Thus, while the tombstone opening is practised throughout the Strait, it has the particular function in Badu of integrating a somewhat heterogeneous population by bringing into relief the ties that they have in common.

Murray Island

With a population of around 200, Murray has dwindled to a little over one third of its size in 1959. Lack of opportunities for earning money is the reason usually cited for this decline and there seems little doubt that it is an important factor. The village nevertheless shows a higher level of involvement in the cash economy than was the case twenty years ago. There is a fine new Anglican church, and a new school house. All of the houses are made from European materials. There are motor dinghies drawn up here and there along the beach, and the cemetery is thronged with tombstones that have been imported from the mainland. The IIB store that used only to stock basic supplies such as flour, rice, sugar and a few tinned foods now stocks a wide range of goods including frozen meat. Meanwhile the interior of the island, where the older generation made their gardens, is overgrown, except for the large tract that has been cleared for a fair weather airstrip.

Very little of the money to pay for these things has come from local production. Except for the few men who occasionally take their dinghies to neighbouring reefs to collect trochus shell, and the few women who send baskets for sale to Thursday Island, no money is earned locally. Murray is the remittance economy *par excellence*. The new church was financed by a loan, the new school was built by the DAIA, and the new houses by one or other government, or from the money saved from a spell of work on the mainland. The tombstones have at least partly been paid for by people in the south and the motor dinghies often from the savings of thrifty pensioners. Households buy their store foods out of money earned in government projects, or from unemployment benefits and various forms of welfare payments. They also buy yams from the few older men who still plant them, and some pensioners are said to pay as much as $800 for a pig for some special occasion.

Murray is less favourably placed for commercial fishing than Badu. There is a higher risk of shark attack in the deeper waters, and it is too far for a dinghy owner to run his catch into the Thursday Island freezer. Unlike Badu also, there is no one with the experience and contacts to get help in acquiring a freezer boat. There is a freezer left over from the turtle farming project, but the cargo boat called infrequently and after breakdowns in which the catch was lost people gave up. The Keriba Lagau project brought few benefits to Murray during its short life.

The Meriam were scarcely surprised by the collapse. Since the failure of their pearling boats in the late 1950s they have been sceptical about such schemes, and several to whom I spoke before this one began were pessimistic about its prospects. Those who yearned for economic progress went to the mainland long ago; those who remain have settled for the kind of living that can be put together from government jobs, welfare cheques, fishing and perhaps a kitchen garden. Since only a few make gardens or swim for trochus it seems reasonable to conclude that the Meriam are not normally hard pressed for their daily needs. But this is not to suggest that they are indifferent to qualitative improvements, such as an electricity supply, that lie far beyond their capacity to achieve.

The council has played its part in the administering of government-funded programmes, but its participation in the processes of welfare colonialism has been mainly at the local level since the Eastern Islands Representative, George Mye, returned to his native Darnley Island in 1975. Murray is now dependent on his occasional visits for information on what is happening at higher levels. Its councillors are, as in the past, men of better-than-average education, who 'know how to talk to white people', but their experience has been in teaching rather than economics and government and there is no way that they can acquire the political know-how and connections that he has built up over almost thirty years. For this reason, if for no other, Mye's position as Representative has never been seriously challenged. For similar reasons, only two returned emigrants have been elected to council office, and these only to third place; whatever their urban experience, they know less of government than those who have spent the last twenty years in the Strait.

Of the twelve men who have held the four council positions since 1973, six have been teachers and two IIB employees. However, since the departure of George Mye none of them has proved indispensable. No one has been returned at all five elections, and the chairmanship has been held by no fewer than seven individuals – the position several times changing hands in mid-term.[5] The frequent turnover cannot be attributed to any major issue. The divisions of the post-war years have dissolved. Marou, who died in 1969, has undergone an apotheosis to become the father of Torres Strait freedom, while his old opponents seem to have forgotten that there were ever any differences between them. There is diffuse dissatisfaction about the lack of progress, but seemingly no way of articulating it politically, so that it remains tied to ephemeral concerns and directed against individuals. The ex-service cohort remains a presence; indeed, as though to deny the toll that death is taking on its numbers, it has

---

[5]   There have been no further instances since 1959 of councils being deposed by petition, but council chairmen can be deposed on the vote of their fellow councillors although the more common procedure is to persuade them to step down by informal pressure.

recently buried one of its leaders on the village meeting ground, and erected a monument to commemorate the first landing of Meriam soldiers, returning from the war. But while they sometimes give their blessing to a candidate, they have no policy. The freedoms that they fought for have been theirs for some years, and they are content simply to take the credit. The sectarian issue has also faded. The Pentecostalists have finally won toleration, in part by simply hanging on, in part because they seemed less threatening than some of the other new religions being imported from the south. When two councillors recently joined the Assembly, the event caused not a ripple. Even other churches enjoy toleration, though none has a resident pastor, and the Anglican Church occasionally hosts inter-denominational services. But while a variety of particular explanations can be found, the rapid turnover of councillors is more readily understood in terms of Meriam society, a combination of the old 'everybody *mamoose*' principle and family enmities that may go back to a dispute over land or a marriage.

The council still includes among its responsibilities the defence of the Meriam domain. With the increasing dependence on government and declining dependence on one another, the old intransigence has weakened. It revives occasionally, as when Murray refused point blank the request of agricultural inspectors to destroy their banana plants; but more often it keeps authority at arm's length simply by stonewalling.

The defensiveness is more in evidence in its application to returning emigrants. The exclusion of representatives from proscribed churches continued until the mid-1970s, and now it has ended there is still a reluctance to accept those who have lost touch with island ways. Children who have been brought up in a more permissive mode don't know how to respect their elders, and they get into mischief. Murray has accepted an Australian woman as the wife of a Meriam man, but some Australian men married to Meriam women were judged 'no good for the island'. Evidently the people feel a need to protect the culture, not just as folklore but as a way of life. While Murray no longer attempts to regulate sexual conduct, it still maintains a strict notion of public modesty and the community can be scandalized by a breach that would scarcely cause comment in suburban Australia.

Beneath these surface tensions lie problems of a more serious kind, relating to the rights of those who have emigrated. The council has always had the power to deny entry and, until recently, used it against representatives of other churches. But there has also been a suggestion that those who have gone to the mainland with the intention of settling, as distinct from those who went for training or to accumulate a sum of money, become what one councillor called 'ex-islanders', forfeiting their rights to residence and to ancestral land.

Land is important, apart from its economic uses, as evidence of one's hereditary membership of the community from time immemorial, and of one's ancestors' ability to defend it against predatory neighbours. There has been a contraction of cultivation in recent years, but the foreshore is still needed for residence and kitchen gardens, and the whole of one's inheritance is symbolically important, even if one does not know precisely where the boundaries run. Bearing this in mind, the prospect of all Meriam, who must now number well over one thousand, activating their rights is daunting, not only because of the fragmentation that would ensue, but because of the confusion and quarrelling that would arise.

Meriam in the south are prey to recurrent anxieties about their land; if the property of all immigrants has not been declared forfeit, then that of individuals has been usurped by their enemies. The customary arrangement in the case of prolonged absence is to appoint a 'caretaker', but this is risky if the arrangement is allowed to run on for too long. If the owner fails to return or send back an heir the land is liable to become the *de facto* property of the caretaker. Some owners have died before they could tell their children what land was theirs. Others have left wills but have had no opportunity to show their heirs where the boundaries lie. In the event of dispute it is the council's responsibility to resolve the matter through the questioning of knowledgeable elders, but it is often hard to determine the facts with any certainty and harder still to satisfy all parties. Presented with what is, in effect, a political liability, councils tend to let sleeping dogs lie. More than a few who returned during the Christmas break in the hope of getting a case settled, went south again without the case being heard.

Given the small number of emigrants returning to live on Murray and the limited use of garden land, the council might have gone on in this way, settling a few cases on an *ad hoc* basis and leaving the underlying issue undecided, had not the State government proposed to lay an airstrip. The island's hilly terrain left no room for choice over the siting; the council's task was to decide whether they wanted it and then to persuade resident land owners to agree. The chairman who presided over the discussions told me that he began by getting agreement in principle on the need for such a facility. This was not difficult since it promised an easier flow of passengers to and from the mainland, and quicker transit of the sick to hospital. Only then did he reveal that the strip would destroy prime garden land belonging to particular individuals. The initial response was anger and dismay, but gradually the owners present were persuaded by the argument, 'if you get sick are you going to lie down on that land and die?' Those with whom I spoke about the matter a few years later were sure that they had made the right decision, although one thought that perhaps the airline should pay compensation.

None of the owners on the mainland was consulted. To have done so would have been difficult and costly since they were widely scattered, but the expectation was that they would be obstructive. My own discussions with some of them confirmed this; gaining nothing from the airstrip, they felt themselves to be expropriated and disenfranchised.

While Murray was prepared to modify traditional rights in the case of emigrants, or for community purposes, it firmly rejected Queensland's attempt to reduce their tenure to a mere leasehold. It demanded inalienable freehold title in the poll of 1981, like the other communities, but then brought legal proceedings in the High Court to establish their traditional ownership. A remarkable feature of this action was that, while it included some leading Murray residents, the principal litigant was Eddie Mabo, who had lived in Townsville for many years. A subsequent meeting between Mabo's supporters and a Murray councillor went some way towards reuniting the Meriam diaspora. Murray's refusal to join with the other communities in accepting Queensland's 1985 Aborigines and Torres Strait Islanders (Land Holding) Act, can be seen as just the latest of many instances of resistance to outside interference. It is also consistent with their traditional representation of land as a religious and political, as well as economic good. At the same time, the surrender of individual holdings for public purposes, combined with the declining use of garden land, and the refusal of the court to hear disputes, has tended to impoverish the meaning of ownership.

Moreover, as owners cease to visit the land that links them with their ancestors and to practise the esoteric garden lore passed down to them, its value becomes increasingly abstract.

The older generation has a sense that its culture is not being transmitted. One old man, noticing that under the present organization of work young men spent little time with their elders, remarked, 'before on the boats the old men used to teach you. Nothing this time. Same in the gardens, they used to sit and yarn. That time we had a lot of contact with our older men.' Here as on Badu, island custom is increasingly concentrated in the festive complex, particularly the tombstone openings that bring scores of Meriam back from the mainland each Christmas.

The cemetery maintains the link between the Meriam and their dead, and between each family and its dead. Being consecrated ground and containing the physical remains of those who have died, the relationship is itself made sacred and the company sanctified. At such moments the differences between island and mainland are transcended, and the emigrants find confirmation of their continuing identification with the island.

Townsville

Islander society is not a problem for Islanders living in the Strait; although it changes constantly, they experience it as continuous since they are in daily contact with the same individuals over long periods. On the home islands they live, work and play in the company of their fellows, seeing few outsiders, and those they do see are transient. Thursday Island is a mixed community, but the majority of Islanders live in the government settlement at Tamwoy, some distance from the old town, which until recently had its own council.[6] Their numerical majority in the total population is reproduced in the principal public facilities such as hospitals, schools, hotels and churches, all of which are in some degree adapted to their needs.

The mainland, by contrast, is not Islander territory. Islanders are a small minority, even where they are most numerous, and the major public institutions take no account of their presence. The social organization of low rent and subsidized housing tends to disperse rather than concentrate them, while the daily business

---

[6] The Tamwoy council was abolished under the Community Service Act, but although the suburb is now formally under the Thursday Island council, the council continues informally.

of living falls to the individual and the household rather than to some broader collectivity. If Islanders are to constitute a society under these conditions they have to work at it, organizing occasions that will bring them together and renew the ties that bind. Islander society thus becomes problematic for the urban dweller, an option to be measured against others.

In the early days of migration one could scarcely speak of Islander society. Young men, often on their own, opened up new territory, finding work and a place to live, making friends and perhaps finding consorts among Aborigines, Pacific Islanders or other Australians, as the opportunity arose. But as the first arrivals established themselves they were sought out by new arrivals with demands for shelter and help in finding a job, giving the migration the familiar 'chain' pattern. As long as the emigration consisted of men without families it was highly mobile and integrated by the work group rather than place of residence; after the arrival of families, settled communities began to form in centres such as Townsville, Cairns and Mackay.

Fisk, Duncan and Kehl in their 1974 survey of fifty Townsville households document the chain migration and report that 68% had immediate family in the area (Fisk *et al.* 1974:44). But fewer than half the respondents (mainly women) gave indication of contact, and fewer still admitted to making any 'conscious effort' to keep up the connection (*ibid.*:44–5). Remembering the words of the woman quoted at the beginning of this chapter, we might conclude from this that they had opted for the majority Australian 'privatized', nuclear family household. However, more than half the households included one or more relatives or other persons who could provide the petty day-to-day help which comes from people outside the household in the Strait. It is also unclear whether the interviewers took into account encounters occurring incidentally to other activities, such as church attendance, or whether they enquired what happened in times of crisis. While there is considerable variation, my own impression is that Islanders keep themselves informed about the whereabouts and doings of their kinsfolk, even in other parts of the mainland.

Women, who made up the bulk of the survey's respondents, do tend to be housebound since there is little employment for them, and public transportation is either unavailable or expensive. Men, on the other hand, are mainly employed on the railways, often in the same gang, and they tend to congregate in the bars prepared to serve Islanders. Children, likewise, meet at school and since they are a minority tend to stick together.

Casual contacts are reinforced from time to time by festive gatherings such as tombstone openings and occasional weddings, which bring Islanders together from all over north Queensland. The four Islander churches also provide meeting places, and although by no means everyone attends regularly they can function as clearing houses for news which can then be diffused along the grapevine.

During the early years of migration the Church of England proved unable to accommodate its co-religionists from the Strait. The Assemblies of God, more welcoming to begin with, also found difficulty as the numbers increased; and they were further embarrassed with a number of Islander pastors who expected to find churches. Their attempt to solve the two problems by forming separate Assemblies only alienated the Islanders, who had been first attracted by the promise of social acceptance. In the long run, however, the bulk of churchgoers have ended up in one or other of the all-black congregations.

The Anglican diocese of Carpentaria viewed with dismay the straying of its flocks on the mainland, not least because the churches into which they strayed were gaining a foothold in the Strait. This led it to combine with the Australian Board of Missions to make special provision for Islanders within the diocese of north Queensland. In Townsville a small church has been set aside for their use under the care of an Islander priest. Services are virtually indistinguishable from those in the Strait, and a hall provides a venue for feasts and dancing as well as meetings.

The Anglicans' principal rival is the Universal World Church. Though it has a Los Angeles affiliation its membership in Australia is almost exclusively Islander and it has been extensively adapted to their needs and tastes. Although it is distinctive in its teaching that true believers need never die, it has brought together a number of strands in the Islanders' religious experience. It alternates vernacular hyumns with revival choruses, and testimonials from the body of the church with prayers and exhortations from the brightly robed leaders, standing around the candle-lit altar.

An Australian, Dr P.R. Nielsen, brought the Universal World Church from Los Angeles to Townsville in 1970. From the outset he concentrated his attention on the Islanders, who were soon flocking to his meetings, amid expressions of intense religious enthusiasm. His influence, which was by all accounts considerable, also extended to the personal affairs of his followers, particularly those who were newly arrived from the Strait and needed help with jobs and housing. As the church flourished, he appointed pastors to set up branches in neighbouring towns and on Thursday Island. But after several years he and his followers parted company. The particulars of the dispute need not concern us, for it seemed almost inevitable that the Islanders would sooner or later want to take control of an organization that depended wholly on their contributions. As one remarked, 'I got a white man over me at work. No need I get another boss when I go prayer.' Yet they have stopped short of complete autonomy, twice sending a delegation to Los Angeles to secure their affiliation with the mother church. This does not limit their freedom of action, since there is no superior body in Australia. At the same time, they can claim an overseas connection which, at least formally, parallels that of the Anglicans. Thus they display photographs of the large mother church and its gold furnishings in their own modest building.

The Townsville Universal World Church must be judged a success. It is now the mother church for a number of branches in Queensland and the Northern Territory. It holds regular Sunday services with attendances of around one hundred, smaller meetings during the week and occasional conventions that draw on the region. Its sixty members pay a tithe, and although the income is not enough to employ a full time pastor, it has brought them to within a few years of paying off the mortgage on the building.

Body Felt Salvation and the Cathedral of Love have broken away from the Townsville UWC, but claim affiliation to American churches which have broken away from the UWC in Los Angeles. The Revelation Church of Jesus Christ is organized around one family and follows the revivalist style of the Pentecostalists, but unlike the others it permits island dancing. While the first two are somewhat exclusive, none excludes attendance at customary gatherings such as tombstone openings.

Even the most eccentric of these churches can find a place in the continuum that constitutes the Christian religion in Australia; and if they are not highly regarded in the society at large they nevertheless enjoy sufficient respectabilty to qualify for bank loans. Thus established, they provide a shelter of legitimacy behind which Islanders can for a few hours forget the order that reduces them to units of production and consumption, to relive the claims and deferences they knew in the islands. Men can know again the power of leadership and the dignity of office. Men and women can submit themselves to the moral restraints of a closely knit community. Illnesses, which are objective 'facts' in the city's hospitals and clinics, are reunited with values and returned to a social context through the practice of faith healing and the shared belief in sorcery (cf. Taussig 1980).

To judge by attendances, only around 300 Islanders in Townsville feel a regular need for what the churches have to offer, though most have at least a nominal affiliation. Some of those whose attendance is confined to Christmas and Easter are active in other organizations which fulfil some of the same functions. The majority, however, seem content with the lower level of participation in Islander society that can be achieved within the household, through casual meetings, and by attendance at occasional birthday parties, funerals and tombstone openings.

Eastern Islanders, particularly Meriam, are the most organization-minded. They provide almost all the membership of the three fringe churches, and are well represented among the Anglicans. The Black Community School, the TUP and the fishing cooperative were all Eastern Island organizations, as are the several small dance and craft groups. Meriam explain this with their characteristic chauvinism. Their 'faith' and 'culture' are stronger than those of other islands! The paradox of Murray is that its people have been the most deeply engaged in the affairs of their community, and also the most eager to experience the freedoms of citizenship on the mainland. The realities of urban living have thus required of them a more profound adaptation and have inflicted a deeper disappointment. Their response, however, has been essentially the same as that of other Torres Strait migrants, although more pronounced. They have tried to reproduce a selective version of island custom, subject to the constraints of life on the mainland and to the commitments that some of them made during the early years of adaptation to it. Work routines that take men away during the week push voluntary activities into the weekend, and major festivities into the Christmas vacation. Finding accommodation for enthusiastic religious meetings and festivities, which should run until the small hours, has also been a problem. On the other hand, the passes available to railway workers make it easier for some people to come together. In the long run, Islanders have found ways to practise their custom without jeopardizing its integrity. In the absence of community structures, kinship provides the framework for organization, with the result that the tombstone opening has assumed even greater importance than in the Strait. As such it cannot unite the entire Islander community, but it has the capacity to override religious divisions.

Although some Islanders who die on the mainland are sent home to be buried, the majority are not. Expense is no doubt a consideration, but those who think of their settlement as permanent usually prefer to have their dead nearby. A tombstone opening on the mainland proclaims Townsville or Cairns as the new centre of Islander culture, even rivalling Torres Strait. Hence the claim quoted earlier: 'Townsville carry all that custom bilong *yumi*, no more island.' It is significant that these occasions draw increasing numbers of visitors from the Strait.

A tombstone opening on the mainland is not just an empty folkloric gesture or exercise in nostalgia. It is rooted in contemporary Islander social organization. Kinship, which is its ordering structure, also has a part in the formation and command structure of railway gangs, the recruitment of the smaller churches, and the informal exchange of hospitality and help. It is mobilized when visitors come south or mainlanders visit home. It is extended to include the increasing number of other Australians who are marrying Islanders.

The fact remains that kinship, and island custom generally, cannot organize life on the mainland to the extent that they do in the Strait. And what is practised cannot have for those who have grown up on the mainland the resonances that it has for their parents. The island churches cannot for them be semblances of something they have never known, and thus remain questionable examples of institutions which are themselves questionable in a secular urban environment. The knowledge and values imparted to Islanders in school or on the television screen have little to do with either fundamentalist Christianity or the ways of remote communities.

The now defunct Black Community School for children of primary age had the explicit aim of mitigating these influences through formal instruction in Torres Strait culture. On a more modest scale, several small associations attempt to perpetuate the culture through the medium of dance. But, as we noted earlier, dance is liable to appropriation through its very acceptability in the wider society. And if it escapes this peril, it must withstand the competition from football which, along with boxing, has provided other low status minorities with an avenue to fame and social acceptance. The popular music of Afro-America may offer a more effective mode of self-assertion for young urban dwellers if they come to care less that their parents came from Torres Strait than that, like Aborigines and Pacific Islanders, they are part of a black underclass for whom Australian citizenship is meaningless.

The predicament of Islanders on the mainland is that if their society can survive at all, it is only through the conscious perpetuation of island custom and the continual monitoring of its practice. The Strait does not have to worry about custom; the society of Islanders there remains axiomatic as long as they are in occupation of their ancestral islands and are living off resources which, whatever the legalities, are theirs by customary right. Welfare colonialism is predicated on this fact and reinforces it, so that Islanders at home experience Australian society as neither class nor underclass but as beneficiaries of a special relationship with the state which they enjoy as the original inhabitants of the islands.

The mainlanders withdrew from this nexus when they left the Strait, but they have a continuing claim on it through the bonds of kinship. The names to which children fall heir assign them to a particular island, not just as a place of origin but as a place to which they have the right to return, even though they may never have been there. In the final analysis, the society of Islanders is encoded in the genealogical ties that project the claims and deferences of family life beyond the domestic circle to include persons known and, as yet, unknown. Couched in these terms, it appears natural and so immune to criticism.

The tombstone opening plays an important part in reproducing these values. This is the time when faces become attached to names and photographs in family albums become living people, when the fine points of kin connection are spelled out, family lore recalled and family honour proclaimed. The occasion is sanctified by the prayers and hymns and solemnized by reference to the one who is dead; but the fear and bereavement to which the death gave rise have had time to ease, and at this point give way to happiness. The eating of island food and the performance of island songs and dances, the emotional reunions and the crush of people, all heighten the awareness of those who are experiencing the ceremony and reinforce its meanings.

The Torres Strait tombstone opening has another, more abstract meaning, as a celebration of Islanders enacting island custom by themselves, for themselves. It is thus a demonstration of the continuing capacity of Islander society, on the mainland as well as in the Strait, to call its members to customary order. Indeed it is this capacity, rather than the cultural content, that is finally definitive of island custom. Islander society cannot by itself account for the way in which its members participate in the wider society; it can regulate only a small part of their lives. It nevertheless provides key components in the construction of their identity, both for themselves and for others. It also gives them a base from which they can negotiate their minority status with the confidence which has been their distinguishing feature, throughout their history.

Bibliography

Allen, J. & Corris, P. 1977. *The Journals of John Sweatman*. St Lucia: Queensland University Press.

Anderson, R. 1979. *Vision of the Disinherited: The Making of American Pentecostalism*. New York/Oxford: Oxford University Press.

Austin, T. 1972. F.W. Walker and Papuan Industries Ltd. *Journal of the Papua and New Guinea Society* 6:1:38–62.

Bach, J. 1961. The Political Economy of Pearl Shelling. *Economic History Review* 14,1:105–14.

Bandler, F. 1983. *The Time Was Ripe*. Sydney: Alternative Publishing Co-operative Ltd.

Barrera, M. 1980. *Race and Class in the Southwest: A Theory of Racial Inequality*. Indiana: Notre Dame University Press.

Bastide, R. 1978. *The African Religions of Brazil: Towards a Sociology of the Interpretation of Civilization*. Baltimore: Johns Hopkins University Press.

Beaglehole, E. 1958. *Social Change in the South Pacific*. London: Routledge and Kegan Paul.

Beckett, J. no date(a) Marriage in Three Torres Strait Communities. Unpublished ms deposited in the library of the Australian Institute of Aboriginal Studies.

no date(b) Adoption in Three Torres Strait Communities. Unpublished ms deposited in the library of the Australian Institute of Aboriginal Studies.

1964. Politics in the Torres Strait Islands. Unpublished PhD thesis, Australian National University.

1971. Rivalry, Competition and Conflict Among Christian Melanesians. *Anthropology in Oceania: Essays presented to Ian Hogbin*, L.R. Hiatt and C. Jayawardena (eds.) Sydney: Angus and Robertson.

1975. A Death in the Family: Some Torres Strait Ghost Stories. *Australian Aboriginal Mythology*, L. Hiatt (ed.) Canberra: Australian Institute of Aboriginal Studies.

1977. The Torres Strait Islanders and the Pearling Industry: a Case of Internal Colonialism. *Aboriginal History* I:77–104. Also, slightly revised in M. Howard (ed.) 1982, *Aboriginal Power in Australian Society*. St Lucia: Queensland University Press.

1982. Modern Music of Torres Strait: Disc with accompanying booklet. Canberra: Australian Institute of Aboriginal Studies.

Beckett, J. & Mabo, K. n.d. Dancing in Torres Strait. Unpublished ms.

Bee, R. & Ginderich, R. 1977. Colonialism, Classes and Ethnic Identity: Native Americans and National Political Economy. *Studies in Comparative International Development 12*.

Bleakley, J. 1944. Submission to the Joint Parliamentary Committee on Social Security: Minutes of Evidence. Canberra: Commonwealth Government Printer.

1961. *The Aborigines of Australia*. Brisbane: Jacaranda Press.

Blunden, V. 12.4.85. Queensland Acts to Head Off High Court. *Sydney Morning Herald*.

Bruce, J. n.d. Letter to A.C. Haddon. Haddon Papers, item 1004.

Brunton, R. 1975. Why do the Trobriands Have Chiefs? *Man* (NS) X:544–558.

Buckley, K. & Klugman, K. 1982. *The History of Burns Philp: The Australian Company in the South Pacific*. Sydney: Burns Philp and Co. Ltd.

1983. *The Australian Presence in the Pacific: Burns Philp 1914–1946*. Sydney: George Allen and Unwin.

Caldwell, J. with H. Duncan & M. Tait. 1974. The Demographic Report. *The Torres Strait Islanders*, vol IV. Canberra: Research School of Pacific Studies, Department of Economics, Australian National University.

Carroll, J.M. (ed.) 1969. Journey into Torres Strait. *Queensland Heritage* 2:35–42.

Chalmers, J. 1897. Report to the directors of the London Missionary Society. London Missionary Society Reports and Correspondence.

Chester, H. 20.10.1870. Letter to the Colonial Secretary: Account of a Visit to Warrior Island in September and October 1870, with a Description of the Pearl Fishery on the Warrior Reef. Queensland State Archives (COL/A151, Letter No. 3425 of 1870).

20.4.1884. Letter to the Colonial Secretary. Queensland State Archives (COL/A151).

Collman, J. 1979. Women, Children and the Significance of the Domestic Group to Urban Aborigines in Central Australia. *Ethnology* 18:379–98.

Comaroff, J. 1984. The Closed Society and its Critics: Historical Transformations in African Ethnography. *American Ethnologist* XI:571–83.

Crisp, L. 16–17.12.1978. Angry Islanders Claim Sell-out over Torres Strait Border, *Weekend Australian*.

Cromwell, L. 1982. Toward an Anthropology of Idiom. Unpublished PhD thesis, Australian National University.

Daniels, A. 1983. How a Favourite Uncle Interfered. *Sydney Morning Herald* 28.9.83.

Davies, A. n.d. The Cult of Bomai–Malu. Typescript, item (n)(a)(v). Notes and Papers on the Murray Islands, Torres Strait. Davies Papers.

Davis, S. 9.1.36. Letter to the Governor of Queensland. Governor's Correspondence, A 12228, Queensland National Archives.

Devanny, J. 28.2.1948. I Discovered Disgraceful Jim Crowism on Thursday Island. *Tribune.*

3.3.1948. Labor Must End Thursday Island's Jim Crow Scandal. *Tribune.*

6.3.1948. Colour Bar Hits Health on Thursday Island. *Tribune.*

10.3.1948. Thursday Island's Islanders Need a New Deal. *Tribune.*

Dickey, B. 1980. *No Charity There: A Short History of Social Welfare in Australia.* Melbourne: Nelson.

Diocese of Carpentaria 1960 (a) Bishop's Charge to Synod.

1960 (b) Aborigines – What of the Future?

Dolgin, J. 1977. *Jewish Identity and the JDL.* Princeton University Press.

Douglas, J. 1899–1900. The Islands and Inhabitants of Torres Strait. *Queensland Geographical Journal 15.*

1900. *Past and Present of Thursday Island and Torres Strait.* Brisbane: Outridge Printing.

Duncan, H. 1974. Socio-Economic Conditions in the Torres Strait: A Survey of Four Reserve Islands. *The Torres Strait Islanders*, vol. 1. Canberra: Research School of Pacific Studies, Department of Economics, Australian National University.

Elkin, A. 1944. Submission to the Joint Parliamentary Committee on Social Security: Minutes of Evidence. Canberra: Commonwealth Government Printer.

Evans, G. 1971. Thursday Island 1878–1914: A Plural Society. BA Hons. thesis, Department of Anthropology, University of Queensland.

Evans, R. 1975. 'The Nigger Shall Disappear . . .': Aborigines and Europeans in Colonial Queensland. *Exclusion, Exploitation and Extermination: Race Relations in Colonial Queensland.* R. Evans, K. Saunders, Kathryn Cronin (eds.) Sydney: Australia and New Zealand Book Company.

Feil, D. 1984. *Ways of Exchange: The Enga Tee of Papua New Guinea.* St Lucia: Queensland University Press.

Feit, H. 1982. The Future of Hunters within Nation-States: Anthropology and the James Bay Cree. *Politics and History in Band Societies*, E. Leacock and R. Lee (eds.) Cambridge University Press: 373–412.

Fisk, E., H. Duncan & A. Kehl. 1974. The Islander Population in the Cairns and Townsville Area. *The Torres Strait Islanders*, vol. III. Canberra: Research School of Pacific Studies, Department of

Economics, Australian National University.

Fitzgerald, R. 1984. *From 1915 to the Early 1980s: A History of Queensland.* St Lucia: Queensland University Press.

Fitzpatrick-Nietschmann, J. 1980a. The High Cost of Marriage in Torres Strait. Unpublished paper presented at a symposium on Torres Strait in the 1970s, Australian Anthropological Society Meetings.

1980b. Another way of Dying: the Social and Cultural context of death in a Melanesian community, Torres Strait. Unpublished PhD thesis, University of Michigan.

Flinders, M. 1966 (1814) *A Voyage to Terra Australis . . . in the years 1801, 1802 and 1803 in H.M.S. the Investigator.* Adelaide: Adelaide Libraries Board.

Foster-Carter, A. 1978. The Modes of Production Controversy. *New Left Review* 107:44–77.

Gartrell, B. 1986. 'Colonialism' and the Fourth World: Notes on Variations in Colonial Situations. *Culture* 6:3–17.

Gathercole, P. 1976. Cambridge and the Torres Straits, 1888–1920. *Cambridge Anthropology* III:22–9.

Genovese, E. 1974. *Roll, Jordan, Roll: the World the Slaves Made.* New York: Pantheon.

1975. Class, Culture, and Historical Process. *Dialectical Anthropology*, 1:71–9.

Godtschalk, C. 5.1.44. Report upon an investigation of alleged promises of increase in pay for certain members of D Company who were detailed for special duty with RAAF at Merauke. TSLI Battalion Records. Australian War Memorial Library, 628/4/5.

Graburn, N. 1981. 1, 2, 3 . . . Anthropology and the Fourth World. *Culture* I:66–70.

Gregory, C. 1982. *Gifts and Commodities.* London, New York etc.: Academic Press.

Griffin, J. 1976. *The Torres Strait Border Issue: Consolidation, Conflict or Compromise.* Townsville: Townsville College of Advanced Education.

Haddon, A. 1888. Journal. Unpublished ms. Haddon Archive no. 1029. Cambridge University Press.

1901. *Headhunters, Black, White and Brown.* London: Methuen.

Haddon, A. (ed.) 1901–3. Physiology and Psychology. *Reports of the Cambridge Anthropological Expedition to Torres Strait,* vol. II.

1904. Sociology, Magic and Religion of the Western Islanders. *Reports,* vol. V.

1907. The Languages of Torres Strait. *Reports,* vol. III.

1908. Sociology, Magic and Religion of the Eastern Islanders. *Reports,* vol. VI.

1912. Arts and Crafts. *Reports,* vol. IV.

1935. General Ethnography. *Reports,* vol. I.

Hall, R. 1980. Aborigines and the Army: The Second World War Experience. *Defence Force Journal*, vol. 24.

Hanlon, E. 1939. Speech introducing the Torres Strait Islanders Act. *Queensland Official Record of the Debates of the Legislative Assembly*, 8 August–23 November, 1939, vol. clxxiv, pp. 463–4.

Harris, D. 1977. Subsistence Strategies Across Torres Strait. *Sunda and Sahul: Prehistoric Studies in Southeast Asia, Melanesia and Australia*, J. Allen, J. Golson and R. Jones (eds.) London: Academic Press 422–461.

   1979. Foragers and Farmers in the Western Torres Strait Islands: an Historical Analysis of Economic, Demographic, and Spatial Differentiation. P.C. Burnham and R.F. Ellen (eds.) *Social and Ecological Systems*. London: Academic Press.

Harris, O. 18.8.1913. Letter to the Home Secretary of Queensland. London Missionary Society Reports and Correspondence.

Hartwig, M. 1978. The Theory of Internal Colonialism – the Australian Case. *Essays in the Political Economy of Australian Capitalism*, E. Wheelwright and K. Buckley (eds.) Sydney: ANZ Book Co.

Hasluck, P. 1953. *Native Welfare in Australia: Speeches and Addresses by the Hon. Paul Hasluck, MP*. Perth.

Hechter, M. 1974. *Internal Colonialism: the Celtic Fringe in British National Development 1536–1966*. London: Routledge and Kegan Paul.

Hilder, B. 1980. *The Voyage of Torres: the Discovery of the Southern Coastline of New Guinea and Torres Strait by Captain Luis Baez de Torres in 1606*. St Lucia: Queensland University Press.

Hinton, P. 1968. Aboriginal Employment and Industrial Relations at Weipa, North Queensland. *Oceania* XXXVIII:281–301.

Hunt, A. 4.3.1889. Letter to directors of the London Missionary Society. London Missionary Society Reports and Correspondence.

   24.10.1889 Letter to directors of the London Missionary Society. London Missionary Society Reports and Correspondence.

Hunt, E. 1977. *The Transformation of the Humming Bird: Cultural Roots of a Zinacantecan Mythical Poem*. Ithaca and London: Cornell University Press.

Idriess, I. 1938. *Drums of Mer*. Sydney: Angus and Robertson.

   1950. *The Wild White Man of Badu*. Sydney: Angus and Robertson.

Johannes, R. & MacFarlane, J. 1984. Traditional Sea Rights in the Torres Strait Islands, with Emphasis on Murray Island. *Senri Ethnological Studies* 17:253–266.

Jukes, J. 1847. *Narrative of the Surveying Voyage of H.M.S. Fly, commanded by Captain F.P. Blackwood, R.N. (during the years 1842–1846)*. London: Boone.

Keesing, R. & Tonkinson, R. (eds.) 1982. Reinventing Traditional Culture: The Politics of Kastom in Island Melanesia. Special Issue, *Mankind* 13.

King, P. 1837. *Voyage to Torres Strait in Search of the Survivors of the Ship 'Charles Eaton', Which was Wrecked upon the Barrier Reefs, in the Month of August 1834 in H.M. Schooner 'Isabella'*. Sydney: Statham.

Kolig, E. 1981. *The Silent Revolution: the Effects of Modernization on Australian Aboriginal Religion*. Philadelphia: Institute for the Study of Human Issues.

Langbridge, J. 1977. From Enculturation to Evangelization: an Account of Missionary Education in the Islands of Torres Strait to 1915. BA Hons. thesis, Department of Education, James Cook University.

Langham, I. 1981. *The Building of British Social Anthropology: W.H. Rivers and his Cambridge Disciples in the Development of Kinship Studies, 1898–1931*. Dordrecht: Reidel.

Lawes, W. 3.10.1889. Letter to the directors of the London Missionary Society. London Missionary Society Reports and Correspondence.

Lawrie, M. 1970. *Myths and Legends of Torres Strait*. St Lucia: Queensland University Press.

Lee, I. 1920. *Captain Bligh's Second Voyage to the South Seas*. London: Longmans Green.

Loos, N. 1982. *Invasion and Resistance: Aboriginal-European Relations on the North Queensland Frontier 1861–1897*. Canberra: Australian National University Press.

McCarthy, F. 1939. 'Trade' in Aboriginal Australia and 'Trade' Relationships with Torres Strait New Guinea and Malaya. *Oceania* 9:405–38; 10:80–104, 171–95.

McFarlane, S. 10.1874. Report to the directors of the London Missionary Society. London Missionary Society Reports and Correspondence.

11.1875–1.1876. Report to the directors of the London Missionary Society. London Missionary Society Reports and Correspondence.

8.9.1876. Report to the directors of the London Missionary Society. London Missionary Society Reports and Correspondence.

17.7.1882. Letter to the directors of the London Missionary Society. London Missionary Society Records and Correspondence.

12.1884. Report to the directors of the London Missionary Society. London Missionary Society Reports and Correspondence.

1888. *Among the Cannibals*. London.

MacFarlane, W. 16.7.1959. Letter to the author. (Copy deposited in the Australian Institute of Aboriginal Studies.)

MacGillivray, J. 1852. *Narrative of the Voyage of H.M.S. Rattlesnake, Commanded by the Late Captain Owen Stanley R.N., F.R.S. etc. during the years 1846–1850. Including Discoveries and surveys in New Guinea, the Louisiade Archipelago etc. To which is added the account of Mr. E.B. Kennedy's expedition for the exploration of the Cape York Peninsula*. London: T. and W. Boone.

Markus, A. 1982. After the Outward Appearance: Scientists, Administrators and Politicians. *All that Dirt: Aborigines 1938.* Bill Gammage and Andrew Markus (eds.) Canberra: Research School of Social Sciences, Australian National University.

Marsh, H., B. Barker-Hudson, G. Heinsohn & F. Kinbag. 1984. *Status of the Dugong in the Torres Strait Area: Results of an Aerial Survey in the Perspective of Information on Dugong Life History and Current Catch Levels.* Report to National Parks and Wildlife Service.

Marshall, T. 1963. Citizenship and Social Class. *Sociology at the Crossroads and other Essays* 67–127 London: Heinemann.

Martin, J. 1983. The Development of Multiculturalism. Committee of Review of the Australian Institute of Multicultural Affairs: *Report to the Minister for Immigration and Ethnic Affairs.* Canberra: Australian Government Publishing Service.

Mintz, S. 1974. *Caribbean Transformations.* Chicago: Chicago University Press.

Monaghan, D. 30.4.85. Islanders Take White Australia to the High Court. *Sydney Morning Herald.*

Moore, D. 1979. *Islanders and Aborigines at Cape York: An ethnographic reconstruction based on the 1848–1850 'Rattlesnake' Journals of O.W. Brierly and information he obtained from Barbara Thompson.* Canberra: Australian Institute of Aboriginal Studies. New Jersey: Humanities Press.

Moresby, J. 1876. *Discoveries and Surveys in New Guinea and the D'Entrecasteaux Islands – a Cruise in Polynesia and Visits to the Pearl Shelling Stations in Torres Strait of H.M.S. 'Basilisk'.* London: Murray.

Muratorio, B. 1980. Protestantism and Capitalism in the Rural Highlands of Ecuador. *Journal of Peasant Studies* 8:37–60.

Murray, A. 9–12.1872. Voyage from Loyalty Islands to Cape York to take charge of the New Guinea Mission. Report to the directors of the London Missionary Society. London Missionary Society Reports and Correspondence.
4–5.1874. Report to the directors of the London Missionary Society.

Murray, A. & McFarlane, S. 1871. First Voyage to New Guinea from the Loyalty Islands. Report to the directors of the London Missionary Society. London Missionary Society Reports and Correspondence.

Nettheim, G. 1981. *Victims of the Law: Black Queenslanders Today.* Sydney: George Allen and Unwin.

Nietschmann, B. 1977. Torres Strait Islander Hunters and Environment. Mimeographed paper presented to the Department of Human Geography, Australian National University.

Nietschmann, B. & Nietschmann, J. 1981. Good Dugong, Bad Dugong; Bad Turtle, Good Turtle. *Natural History* 90,5:54–63.

Paine, R. (ed.) 1977. The White Arctic: Anthropological Essays on Tutelage and Ethnicity. *Newfoundland Social and Economic Papers,* No. 7. Toronto: Institute of Social and Economic Research, Memorial University of Newfoundland.

Paterson, A. 1983. *Song of the Pen: Complete Works 1901–1941*. Sydney: Lansdowne Press.

Peel, G. 1946. *Isles of the Torres Strait*. Sydney: Current Book Distributors.

Pennefather, C. 1879. Letter to the Police Magistrate, Thursday Island. Queensland State Archives, COL/A288/460.

Philipps, L. 1980. Plenty More Little Brown Man! Pearlshelling and White Australia in Queensland 1901–18. E. Wheelwright and K. Buckley (eds.) *Essays in Australian Capitalism 4*.

Pitt, D. 13.5.1882. Letter to the Queensland Minister for Lands. Queensland Lands Department.

Raysmith, H. & Einfeld, S. 1975. *Community Development: the Process and the People*. Canberra: Australian Government Social Welfare Commission.

Redfield, R. 1956. *The Little Community. Peasant Society and Culture*. Chicago: Chicago University Press.

Rex, J. 1982. Racism and the Structure of Colonial Societies, in R. Ross (ed.) *Racism and Colonialism: Essays on Ideology and Social Structure*. Leiden: University of Leiden Press.

Roe, J. (ed.) 1976. *Social Policy in Australia: Some Perspectives 1901–1975*. Sydney: Cassell Australia.

Rosaldo, R. 1980. *Ilongot Headhunting, 1883–1974: A Study in Society and History*. Stanford University Press.

Roughley, T. 1936. *Wonders of the Great Barrier Reef*. Sydney: Angus and Robertson.

Rowley, C. 1971. *The Remote Aborigines*. Canberra: Australian National University Press.

Ryan, L. 1985. Aborigines and Torres Strait Islanders, in *The Bjelke-Petersen Premiership 1968–1983: Issues in Public Policy*, Allan Patience (ed.) Sydney: Longman Cheshire.

Sahlins, M. 1972. *Stone Age Economics*. Chicago and New York: Aldine-Atherton Inc.

Scott, J. 1976. *The Moral Economy of the Peasant: Rebellion and Subsistence in Southeast Asia*. New Haven: Yale University Press.

Searcy, A. 1907. *In Australian Tropics*. London: George Robertson.

Sharp, N. 1980. *Torres Strait Islands, 1879–1979. Theme for an Overview*. Melbourne: Department of Sociology, Latrobe University.

—— 1982. Culture Clash in the Torres Strait Islands: the Maritime Strike of 1936. *Royal Historical Society of Queensland* XI:107–126.

Shnukal, A. 1983a. Blaikman Tok: Changing Attitudes towards Torres Strait Creole. *Australian Aboriginal Studies* 2:25–33.

—— 1983b. Torres Strait Creole: the growth of a new Torres Strait Language. *Aboriginal History* 7:173–185.

Sider, G. 1976a. Lumbee Indian Cultural Nationalism and Ethnogenesis, *Dialectical Anthropology* 1:161–72.

—— 1976b. Christmas Mumming and the New Year in Outport Newfoundland. *Past and Present* 71:102–25.

1980. The Ties that Bind: Culture and Agriculture, Property and Propriety in the Newfoundland Village Fishery. *Social History* 5:1–39.

Silverman, S. 1979. On the Uses of History in Anthropology: the Palio of Siena. *American Ethnologist* 6.

Singe, J. 1979. *The Torres Strait Islanders.* St Lucia: Queensland University Press.

Smith, L. 1980. *The Aboriginal Population of Australia.* Canberra: Australian National University Press.

Sommers, T. 1966. *Religion in Australia.* Adelaide: Rigby.

Stavenhagen, R. 1965. Classes, Colonialism and Acculturation. *Studies in Comparative International Development* 1:53–77.

Steketee, M. 27.11.1976. The Necessary Therapy: But the Seabed Line Issue Disturbs the Balmy Torres Nights. *Sydney Morning Herald.*

Stone, S. (ed.) 1974. *Aborigines in White Australia: A Documentary History of the Attitudes affecting Official Policy 1697–1973.* South Yarra: Heinemann Educational Books.

Strachan, J. 1888. *Explorations and Adventures in New Guinea.* London: Samson Low, Marston Searle and Rivington.

Swain, J. 30.12.1943. Report of a Sit Down Strike by A, B and C Companies. TSLI Battalion Records. Australian War Memorial Library, 628/4/5.

10.1.44. Report to Intelligence Office, Torres Strait Force. TSLI Battalion Records. Australian War Memorial Library, 628/4/5.

Taussig, M. 1980. Reification and the Consciousness of the Patient. *Social Science Medicine* 14B:3–13.

1980. *The Devil and Commodity Fetishism in South America.* Chapel Hill: University of North Carolina Press.

1984. Culture of Terror – Space of Death. Roger Casement's Putumayo Report and the Explanation of Torture. *Comparative Studies in Society and History* 26:467–97.

Tennant, K. 1959. *Speak You So Gently.* London: Gollancz.

Thompson, E. 1968. Time, Work Discipline and Industrial Capitalism. *Past and Present* 38:60–93.

1971. The Moral Economy of the English Crowd in the Eighteenth Century. *Past and Present* 50:76–128.

Treadgold, M. 1974. Economy of the Torres Strait Area: A social accounting study. *The Torre Strait Islanders*, vol. II. Canberra: Research School of Pacific Studies, Department of Economics, Australian National University.

Turner, V. 1969. *The Ritual Process: Structure and Anti-Structure.* Chicago: Aldine.

Underwood, R. 1985. Excursions in Inauthenticity: the Chamorros of Guam, in *Mobility and Identity in the Island Pacific.* Murray Chapman (ed.) *Pacific Viewpoint 26.*

Walker, D. (ed.) 1972. *Bridge and Barrier: the Natural and Cultural History of*

Torres Strait. Canberra: Department of Geography, Australian National University.

Walker, F. 13.7.1896. Letter to the directors of the London Missionary Society. London Missionary Society Reports and Correspondence.

Wallerstein, I. 1979. *The Capitalist World Economy: Essays*. Cambridge University Press.

Warren, K. 1978. *The Symbolism of Subordination: Indian Identity in a Guatemalan Town*. Austin and London: University of Texas Press.

Weaver, S. 1983. Australian Aboriginal Policy: Aboriginal Pressure Groups or Government Advisory Bodies? *Oceania* 54:1–22; 85–108.

——— 1985. Struggles of the Nation-State to Define Aboriginal Ethnicity: Canada and Australia. *Minorities and Mother Country Imagery*, G. Gold (ed.) St Johns, Newfoundland: Memorial University Press.

White, G. 1915. Torres Strait Mission, *Australian Board of Missions Review* VI:119–20.

——— 1917. *Round About the Torres Straits*. London: Central Board of Missions.

Wilkes, G. 1978. *A Dictionary of Australian Colloquialisms*. Sydney University Press.

Williams, R. 1977. *Marxism and Literature*. Oxford University Press.

Wolf, E. 1982. *Europe and the People Without History*. Berkeley: University of California Press.

Wolpe, H. 1975. The Theory of Internal Colonialism: the South African Case. *Beyond the Sociology of Development*. I. Oxaal, T. Barnett and D. Booth (eds.) London: Routledge and Kegan Paul.

Wurm, S. 1972. Torres Strait – a Linguistic Barrier. D. Walker (ed.) *Bridge and Barrier: the Natural and Cultural History of Torres Strait*. Canberra: Department of Geography, Australian National University.

Government Publications

COMMONWEALTH OF AUSTRALIA

Australian Bureau of Statistics 17.8.1982. Census of Population and Housing, Counts of Aboriginals and Torres Strait Islanders, Australian States and Territories 30 June 1971, 1976, 1981. *Information Paper* Catalogue Number 2164.0

——— Census 81 – Aboriginals and Torres Strait Islanders. *Information Paper* Catalogue Number 2153.0

Northern Australia Development Commission 1946. *Pearl Shell, Beche-de-mer and Trochus Industry of Northern Australia*. Mimeographed.

The Parliament of the Commonwealth of Australia, House of Representatives, 1961. *Report from the Select Committee on Voting Rights of Aborigines, together with Minutes of the Proceedings of the Committee*. Canberra: Government Printer.

STATE OF QUEENSLAND
Legislation relating to Torres Strait Islanders
   1897–1934. The Aboriginals Protection and Restriction of the Sale of
      Opium Acts.
   1939. The Torres Strait Islanders Act.
   1965. The Aborigines' and Torres Strait Islanders' Affairs Act.
   1971–9. The Torres Strait Islanders Act.
   1984. Community Services (Torres Strait) Act.
   1985. Aboriginal and Torres Strait Islanders (Land Holding) Act.

Parliamentary papers
Reports of the Government Resident of Thursday Island.
Reports of the Department of Harbours and Marine Fisheries.
Report of the Commission appointed to enquire into the general
   working of the laws regulating the Pearl-shell and Beche-de-Mer
   Fisheries in the Colony of 1897.
Report of the Royal Commission appointed to enquire into the
   workings of the Pearl-shell and Beche-de-Mer Industries of
   1908.
Reports of the Chief Protector of Aborigines, 1903–17.
Reports of the Aboriginals Department, 1918–1940.
Reports of the Sub-Department of Native Affairs, 1946–1965.
Reports of the Department of Aboriginal and Islander Affairs, 1965–
   1971.
Reports of the Department of Aboriginal and Islander Advancement,
   1972–1984.

Queensland Year Book.

Archival sources

Davies, A.O.C., Notes and Papers on the Murray Islands, Torres Strait.
   Australian Institute of Aboriginal Studies Library.
Haddon Archive. Manuscripts Department, Cambridge University
   Library.
Governor of Queensland. Correspondence. Queensland State Archives.
London Missionary Society. Reports and Correspondence. Papua
   Journals. New Guinea Boxes. Microfilm, Australian National
   Library.
Somerset Magistrate's Letter Book. 1872–7. Queensland State Archive.
Torres Strait Light Infantry Battalion. Records from Head Quarters,
   Thursday Island. Australian War Memorial Library.

Index